IMAGES
of America

ALLEGANY COUNTY

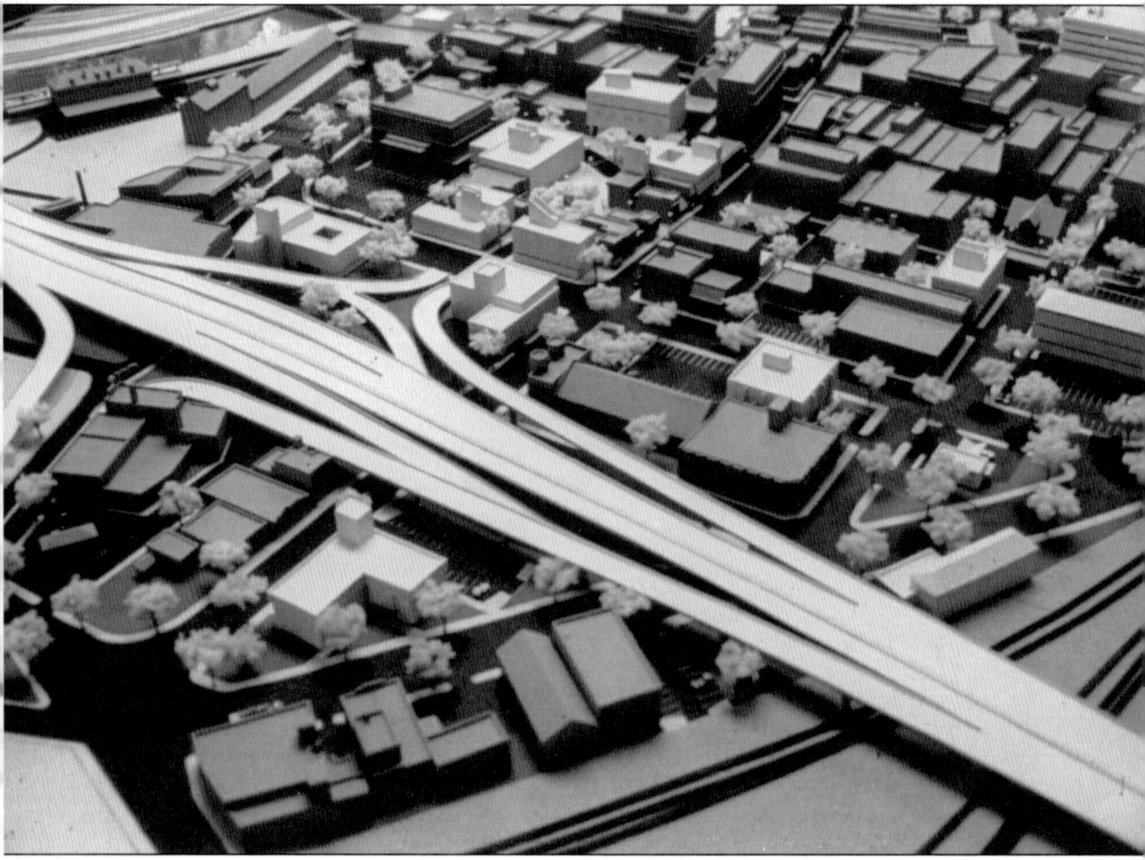

The city of Cumberland experienced major changes during the 1960s when urban renewal planners and Maryland Highway Administration officials completed construction projects. The crosstown bridge—as depicted in this architectural model from the 1960s—was a state project designed to carry U.S. Route 40 vehicle traffic through Cumberland. The model also depicts South George, Centre, Liberty, and Mechanic Streets as envisioned by planners in the 1960s. (Courtesy author's collection.)

On the Cover: This view was looking west on Baltimore Street in downtown Cumberland at Christmastime around 1957. Cumberland was the retail center of Allegany County until suburban shopping centers and regional malls began to erode its influence during the 1970s. In the 1950s, most of the businesses located on Baltimore Street were locally owned. (Courtesy *Cumberland Times-News.*)

IMAGES
of America

ALLEGANY COUNTY

Dan Whetzel

ARCADIA
PUBLISHING

ISBN 978-0-7385-8704-2

Published by Arcadia Publishing
Charleston, South Carolina

Printed in the United States of America

Library of Congress Control Number: 2010931674

For all general information, please contact Arcadia Publishing:
Telephone 843-853-2070
Fax 843-853-0044
E-mail sales@arcadiapublishing.com
For customer service and orders:
Toll-Free 1-888-313-2665

Visit us on the Internet at www.arcadiapublishing.com

This book is dedicated to my wife, Annie, and children, Joe and Carrie.

Contents

ACKNOWLEDGMENTS

Many residents have assisted in the researching and writing of *Allegany County*.

I am especially indebted to Albert Feldstein, Elizabeth Bray, Rich Richmond, Cora Carter, Jeff Kirk, Paula Morgan, Heidi Laupert, Jack Ayers, Edwin Eckhart, Jim Rada, Dutch Blank, Julie Fisher, the oral history program at Allegany High School, the Board of Education of Allegany County, Jan Alderton and the *Cumberland Times-News*, Dr. David Gillespie and Frostburg State University, Allegany College of Maryland, John Taube and the Allegany County Public Library system, and many residents who have shared memories and provided information and photographs over the years. While residents have generously shared their time and memories, any shortcomings in this publication are the responsibility of the author.

Unless otherwise noted, all images appear courtesy of the author.

INTRODUCTION

Western Maryland was originally part of Prince George's County, Maryland. During the 18th century, new western counties were created from the original Prince George's jurisdiction, including Allegany County, which was split from Washington County in 1789.

The earliest inhabitants of what was to become Allegany County were Native Americans. Archeological evidence suggests the earliest Native Americans associated with the Clovis culture arrived around 8,000 B.C.E. and the last group, the Algonquins, no later than 1,000 C.E. The Algonquins were divided into several branches or confederacies, among them the Piscataway, Powhatan, and Shawnee, who lived across a wide-ranging region from the eastern shore of the Chesapeake Bay through northern Virginia, Pennsylvania, and western Maryland. While different groups lived across that expanse, it was the Shawnees who made their home in western Maryland, particularly along the Potomac River.

Native American heritage is evident in local names, including the term "Allegany." The origin of the word is difficult to determine but seems to have derived from Native Americans and is associated with a description of streams and mountains. It has been suggested that *allegewi* meaning "land of endless mountains" and "fairest stream" is the origin of the county name.

The Shawnees apparently anticipated the westward movement of European settlers and abandoned the area prior to 1751. The earliest known map of western Maryland (dated 1751) noted "Abandoned Shawnee Lands" and early European trappers only found remnants of villages in the once populated area. Native Americans did return to western Maryland in 1755 during the French and Indian War (1754–1763) when the British and French struggled for control of colonial America. Native Americans allied with French forces and launched raids on European settlers who lived near Will's Creek and the Potomac River.

The French and Indian War resulted in the British building a fort in western Maryland that would establish and project military influence into the Ohio River Valley. European interest in the area was generated by Christopher Gist, an agent for the Ohio Company, who built a small stockade and trading post on a hill that stands in what is today Ridgeley, West Virginia. A more substantial fort was erected on the west bank of Will's Creek and completed by the time of British general Edward Braddock's arrival in 1755; he named it Fort Cumberland. Today Emmanuel Episcopal Church occupies the site of Fort Cumberland.

Construction of Fort Cumberland proved to be the genesis of a fledgling settlement. A nearby water gap to be known as the Cumberland Narrows facilitated transportation and economic development of the area—the National Highway, several railroads, a trolley company, and motorized vehicles have passed through the gap on their way westward over a span of more than 200 years. The Chesapeake and Ohio Canal's completion from Georgetown to Cumberland, in 1850, provided additional commercial enhancements because it increased shipping services for local entrepreneurs. Transportation advantages and the exploitation of natural resources caused Allegany County to prosper as an industrial and commercial center during the 19th century. The county's largest city, Cumberland, became known as the "Queen City."

Industrial prosperity accelerated from the late 19th century into the early 20th century with the opening of coal mines in the George's Creek region. Coal mining and railroading were complementary labor-intensive industries. European immigrants, primarily from Great Britain, Ireland, Italy, and later from eastern European countries, made Allegany County their home.

Industrialization continued in the second decade of the 20th century when the Celanese Corporation, a synthetic yarn manufacturer, the Kelly-Springfield Tire Company, glass companies, and other smaller businesses began operations that employed thousands of workers. Along with the growing economy came the development of commercial, social, cultural, and educational enterprises. Cumberland could boast that it was the second-largest city in the state of Maryland—in 1940, the city had more than 39,000 residents.

This book is intended to augment the work of previous historians who have documented much of Allegany County's early history. Therefore, the focus of *Allegany County* is on life in the 20th century.

Photographs provided memories and documentation of educational, recreational, transportation, and everyday experiences that depicted the life and times of residents in the previous century.

Hopefully, readers will enjoy the historical narrative and accompanying photographs.

One

School Days, Allegany County Public Schools

A public school system was established in Allegany County, Maryland, in 1865. Tax dollars were not plentiful and financing of the fledgling system was supplemented by gifts from individuals. Despite limited resources, small elementary school buildings were constructed throughout the county over the next two decades, under the authority of a board of school commissioners. Each school was identified in official ledgers by number and election district but commonly called by a proper name. Schoolhouses were located within walking distances of pupils, thereby creating a large number of facilities whose exact locations cannot be completely accounted for today.

Historian John Thomas Scharf published a survey of Allegany County in 1881 that identified 78 elementary schools for white children and three schools for African Americans; 19 of those buildings had more than one room of study. The average salary for schoolteachers was $36.50 per month, and the average length of annual employment was 11 months.

The largest schools were located in the Cumberland area, while many smaller buildings in rural areas typically offered only one or two rooms for instructional purposes. As bus services became available, small schools were closed, and the buildings were sold at public auctions. Students were subsequently transferred to larger schools, located farther from their homes.

The first public school for African Americans was built on Independence Street in the late 1860s or early 1870s. Mary Hoye, Washington Street resident and philanthropist, facilitated construction of the school by deeding property. While the Hoye property was not where the school was eventually constructed, her gift expedited plans to build a school for African Americans.

Over the next two decades, the Mary Hoye building deteriorated. Construction of a new African American school started in the spring of 1898 along North Mechanic Street near Bedford Street. The new school offered grades one through eight until 1918, when administrators initiated a two-year high school program. In 1919, the program evolved into a four-year curriculum, thereby establishing the first comprehensive African American high school in Allegany County.

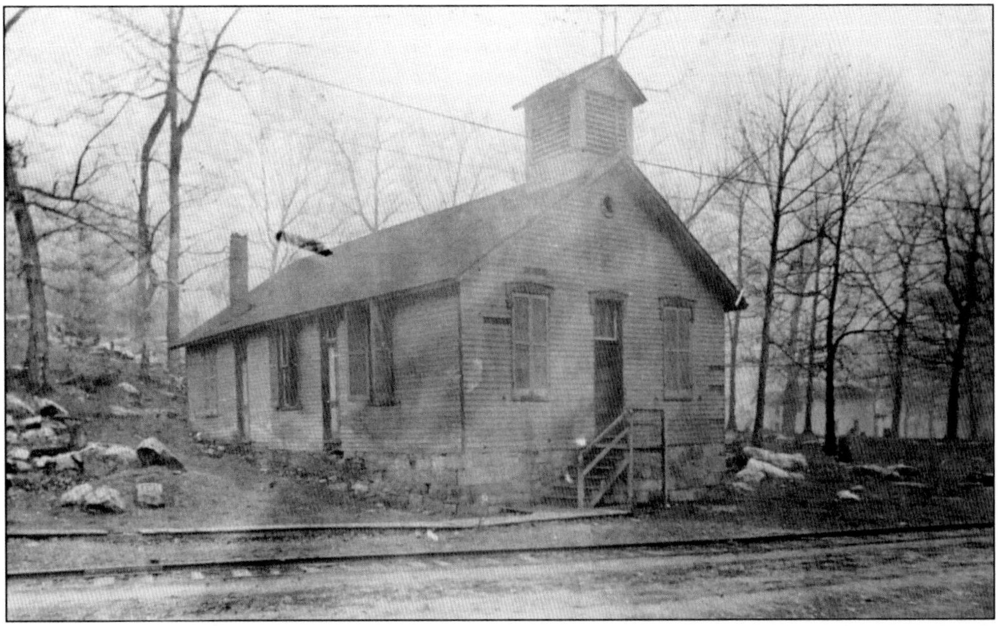

The Franklin Mines School, located about 1 mile north of Westernport along George's Creek Boulevard, provided educational services until around the time of World War II. The building was subsequently purchased in 1944 by "Miss Arthur," a textile worker at the synthetic yarn manufacturer, Celanese Corporation. Arthur converted the schoolhouse into a Colonial-style double dwelling house in 1945. Trolley tracks leading to Westernport are visible in the foreground. (Courtesy Allegany County Public Schools.)

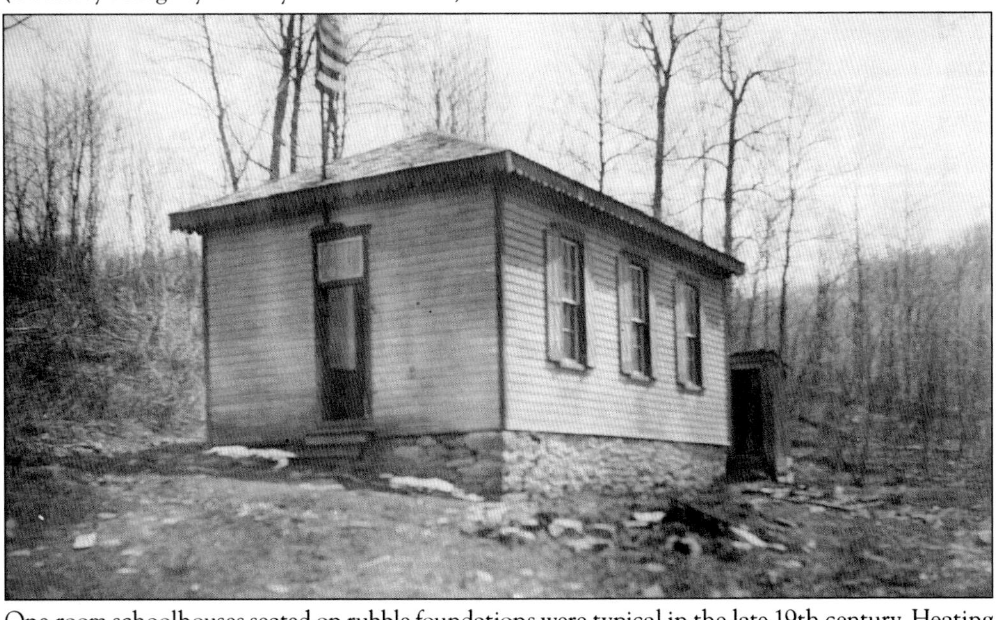

One-room schoolhouses seated on rubble foundations were typical in the late 19th century. Heating was provided by a potbellied stove and restrooms were built outdoors. Meese School, shown in this photograph, was a typical late-19th-century rural school located near Barton. Meese School opened for classes prior to 1881 and remained open into the 1920s. Mary J. Cavanaugh was one of the first teachers. (Courtesy Allegany County Public Schools.)

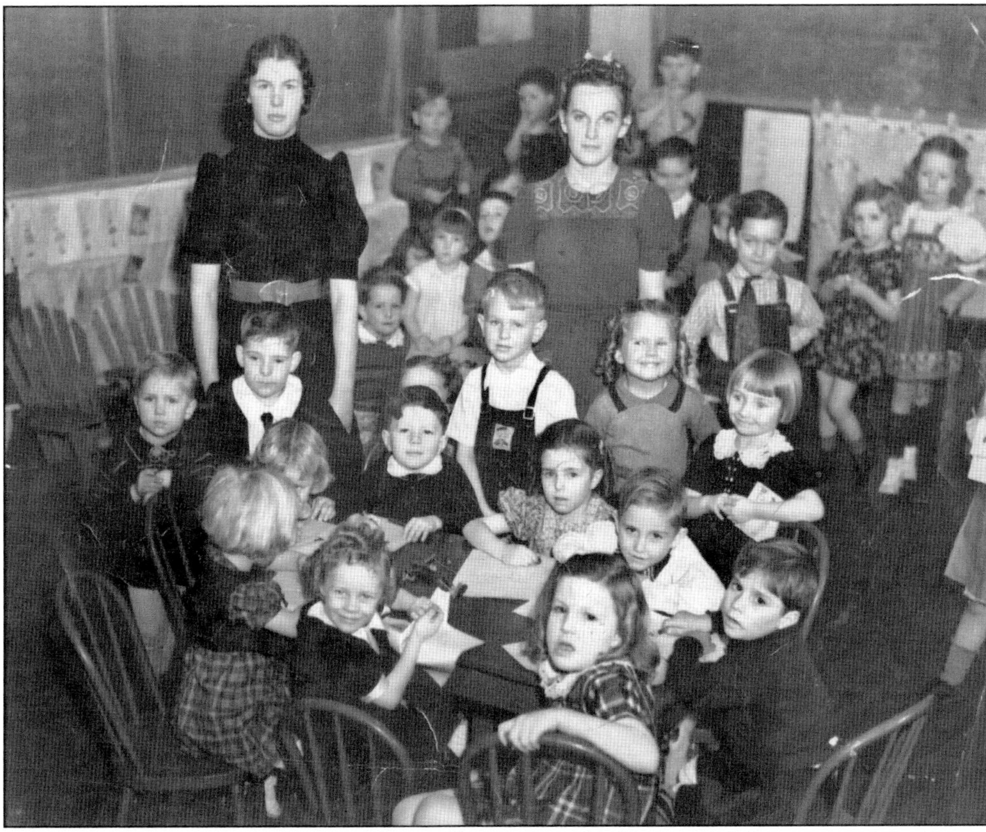

Barton School's first-grade class was directed by "Mid" Kirk of Barton (adult in center). The Barton School was located on Latrobe Street and included grades one through 12. Barton High School closed when Central School of Lonaconing and Barton were consolidated in 1953. The teacher on the left was Maude Kirk, mother of Mid Kirk. (Courtesy Jeff Kirk.)

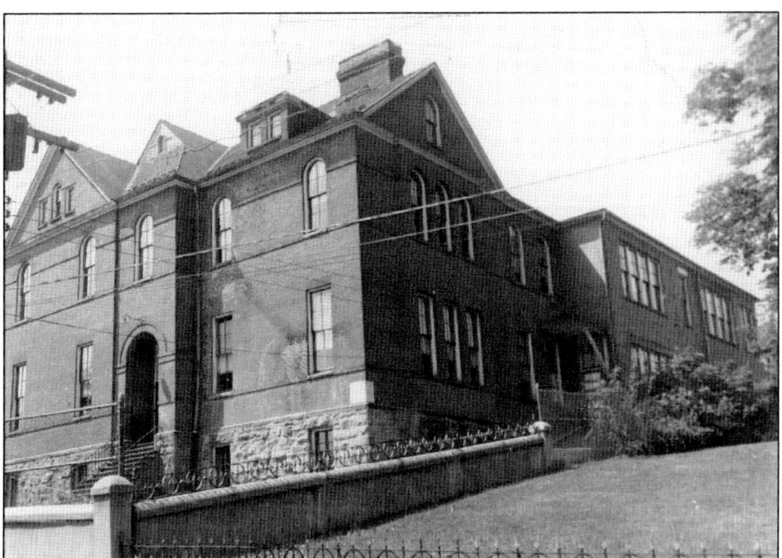

This image shows Barton School as it appeared in the 1950s. (Courtesy Allegany County Public Schools.)

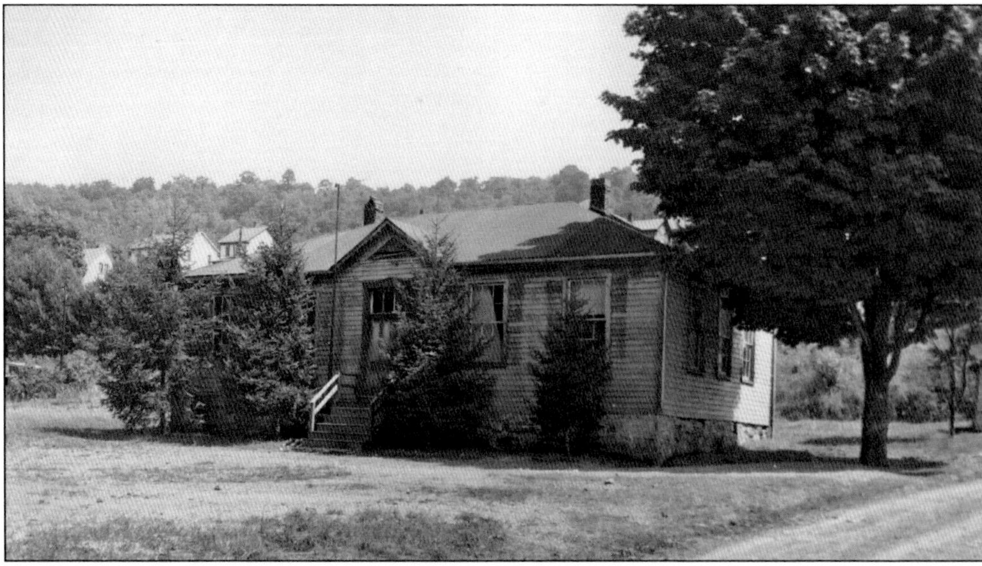

Rockville School, located near Lonaconing, is believed to have been built around 1880. By September 1912, the school reported an enrollment of 88 students. A newspaper reported in 1922 that Rockville School required fencing around the property because of its location near the Cumberland and Pennsylvania Railroad tracks and because "cows keep the school yard filthy." (Courtesy Allegany County Public Schools.)

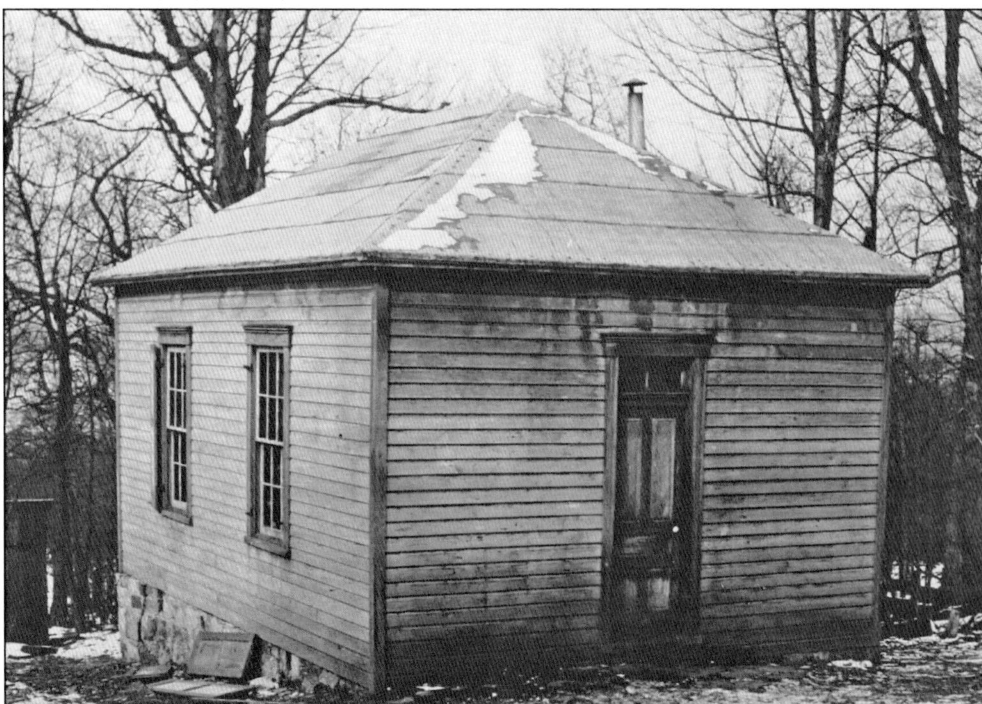

Dye School, located about 2 miles from Lonaconing, was built around 1881 and closed in 1939. The school was apparently named for a trustee, John Dye. After closure, the building remained vacant until it was sold for $75 in September 1945. (Courtesy Allegany County Public Schools.)

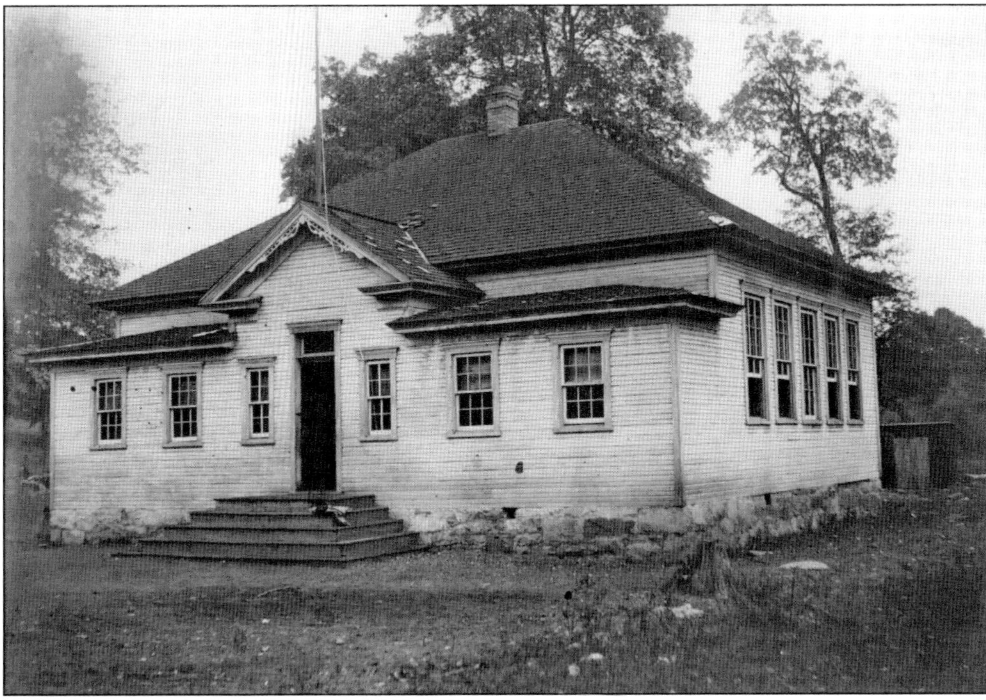

Lord School and the surrounding community were named for Charles Lord, president of the local coal company, though residents later changed the name to Klondike. The school was likely built after the town's establishment in 1897. Klondike School closed prior to World War II and was offered for sale at public auction in 1941. (Courtesy Allegany County Public Schools.)

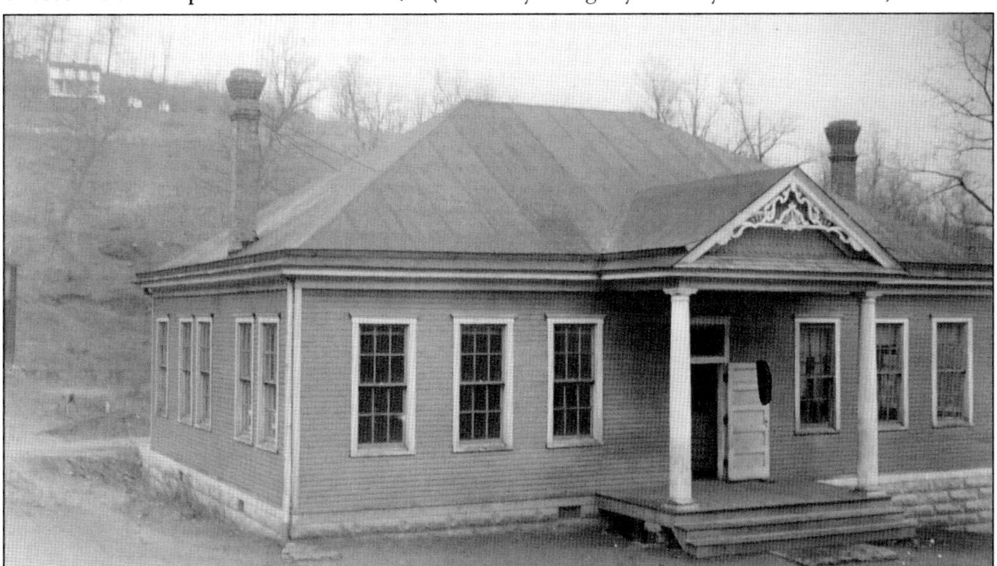

Borden School's name was derived from the Borden Mining Company. A schoolhouse was erected around 1880 along the eastern side of Maryland Route 36, what is present-day Maryland Route 936. The Board of Education of Allegany County closed Borden School before World War II and accepted sealed bids for its sale in 1941. The school was later converted into a dwelling. (Courtesy Allegany County Public Schools.)

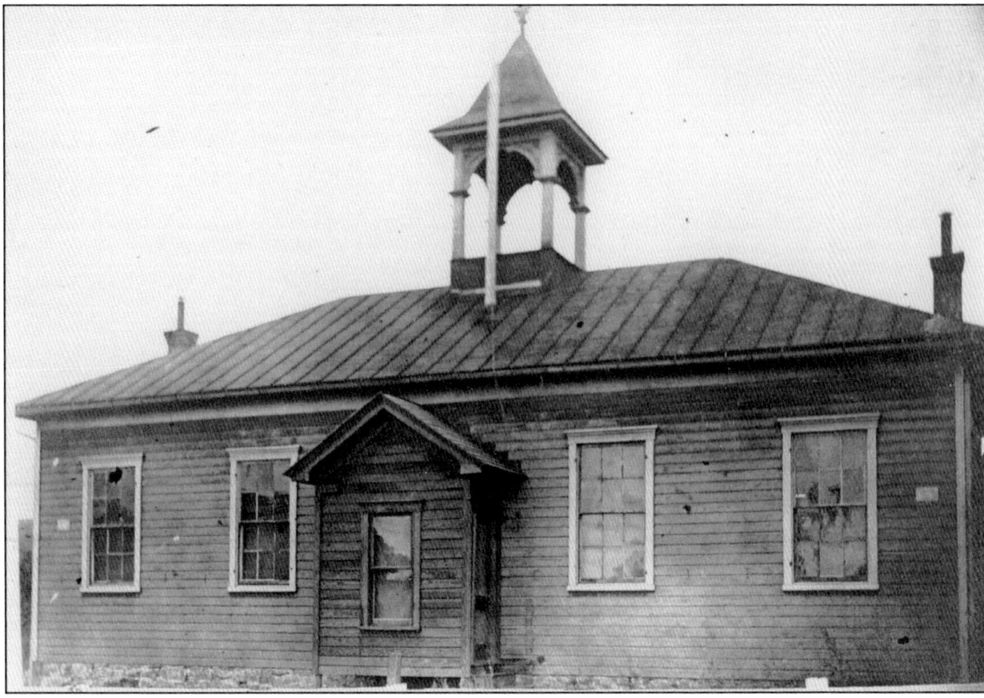

The Board of Education of Allegany County built Lincoln School for the purpose of providing African American children with educational programs and services. The school was located on the present-day campus of Frostburg State University. Lincoln School was moved several times and eventually replaced with a new brick facility located on Park Lane, currently the location of Frostburg State University's Campus Police Department. (Courtesy Allegany County Public Schools.)

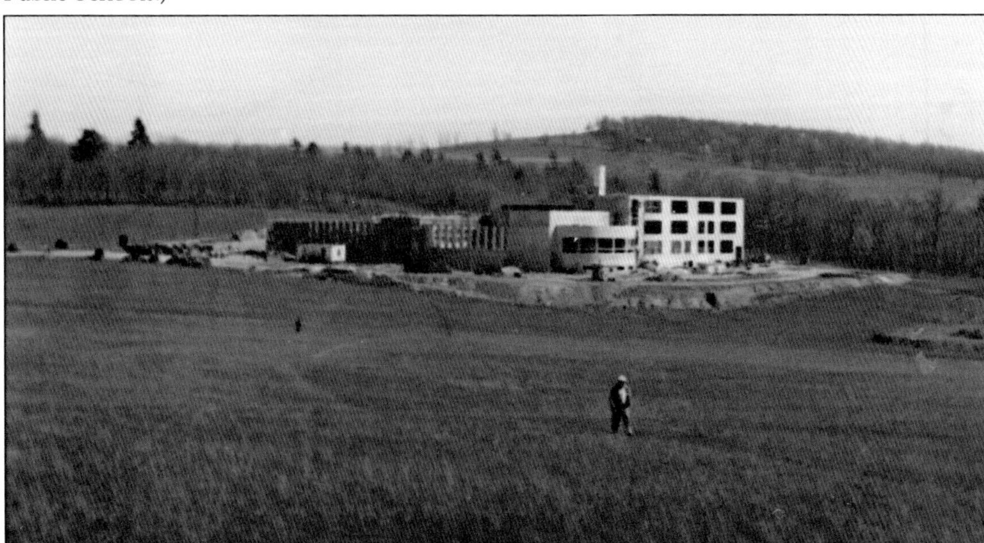

The first Beall School was built in the 1890s along College Avenue. After that facility became inadequate, construction of a new Beall High School began in 1939 on a plot of ground known as Eckhart Flats, shown in this photograph. In 2007, a new high school, called Mountain Ridge, opened on the grounds of the existing Beall High School.

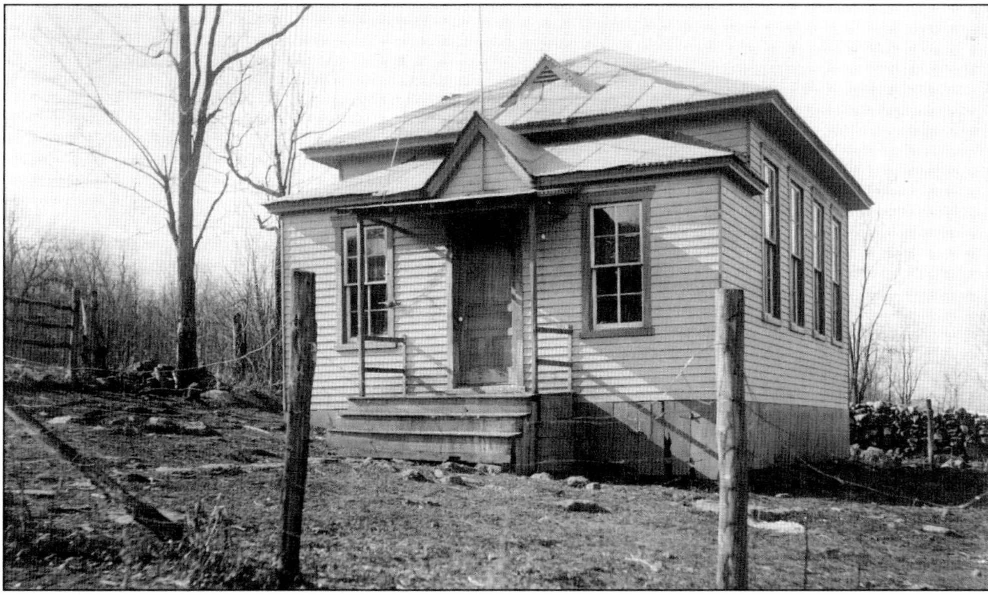

Loarville School, also referred to as Loartown, was located near Vale Summit. The building opened around the turn of the 20th century and closed in the 1920s. The Loarville School building remained abandoned and was later sold in 1946 for $300. Nearby schools in the 1880s were Eckhart Mines (Nos. 1 and 2), Hoffman Hollow, and Pompey Smash. (Courtesy Allegany County Public Schools.)

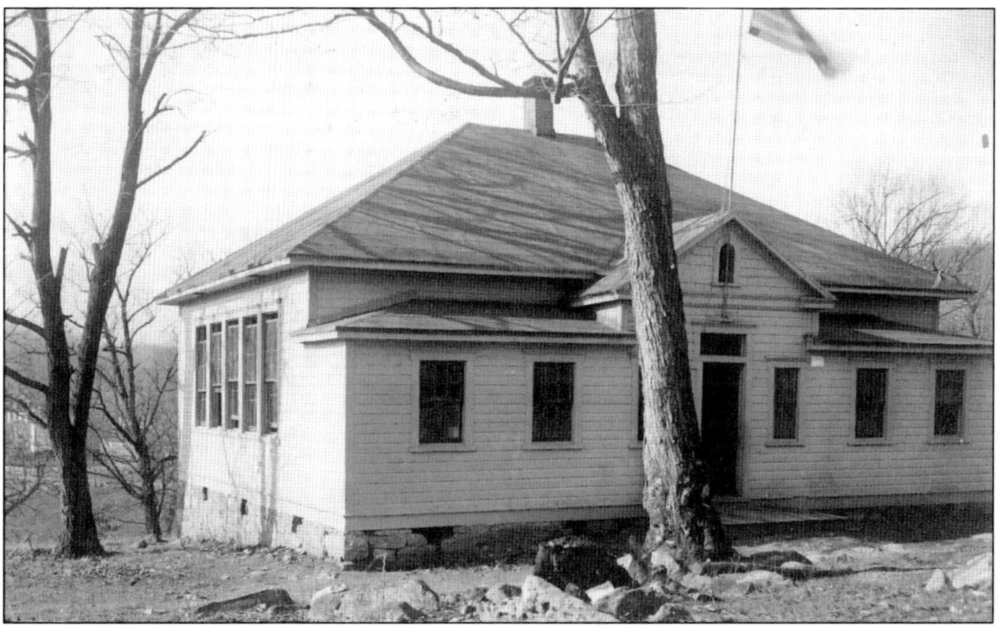

In 1881, Hoffman Hollow students attended classes directed by one teacher, Patrick O'Rourke. The schoolhouse was replaced by a larger one early in the 20th century. According to the *Cumberland Evening Times*, Hoffman School implemented a cafeteria lunch program in 1928 that was effective during the winter months. According to the newspaper report, this allowed "students living at any great distance to remain at the noon hour for lunch at a very low cost." (Courtesy Allegany County Public Schools.)

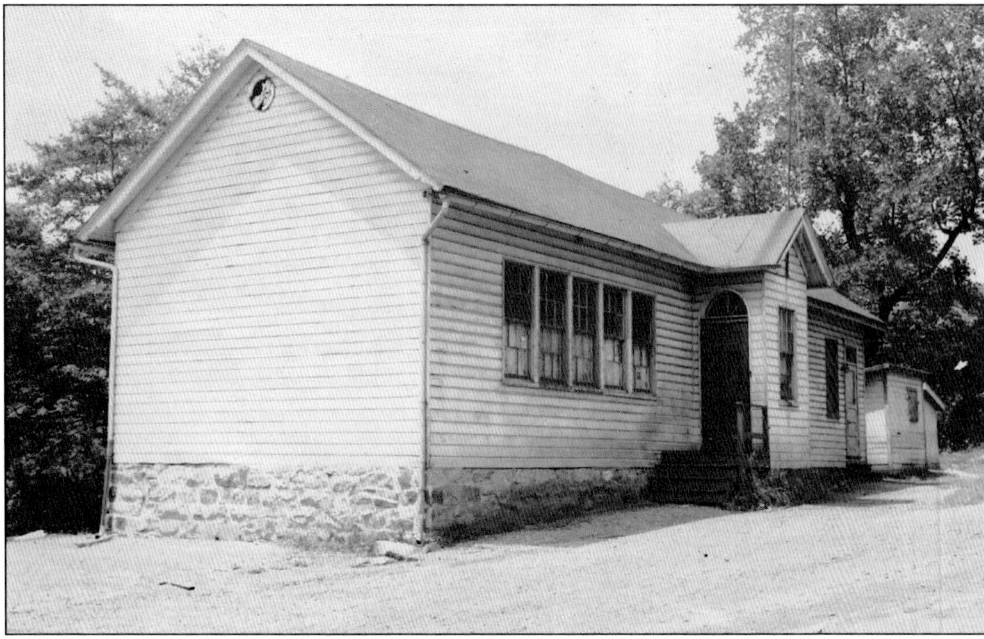

Dutch Hollow School probably opened for students in the late 1870s because it was listed by John Thomas Scharf in his 1881 survey. The teacher for that year was Sallie Campbell. A 1952 newspaper story indicated the original structure was made from logs. A larger facility constructed at a later date, shown in this photograph, remained in service until a new Mount Savage School was opened in 1952. (Courtesy Allegany County Public Schools.)

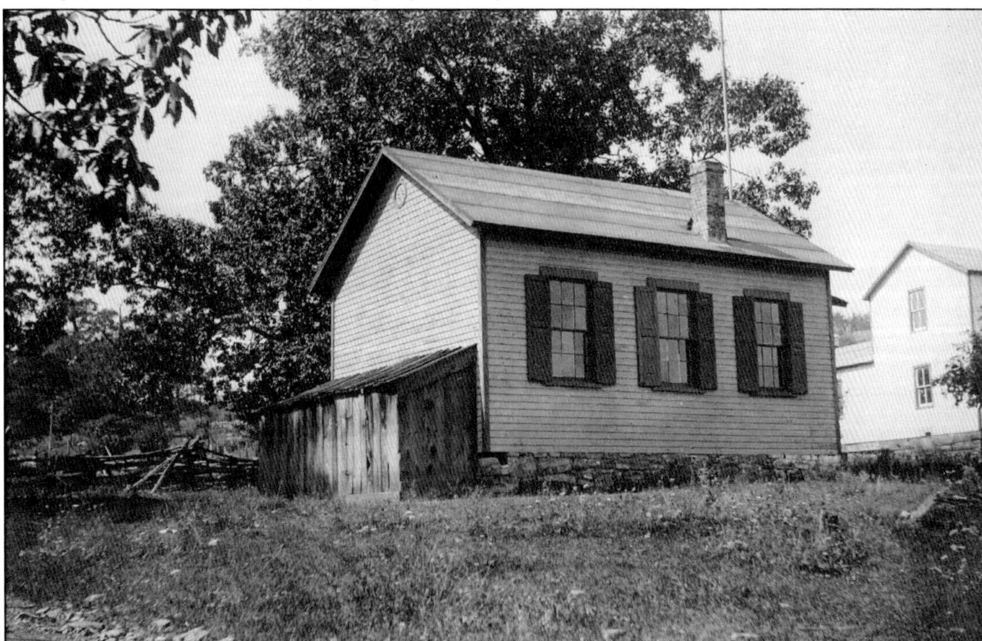

Archibald Witt conveyed property to the school board in 1870 for the purpose of building Mattingly Settlement School. The school was listed as being in Election District 13, the Mount Savage area. (Courtesy Allegany County Public Schools.)

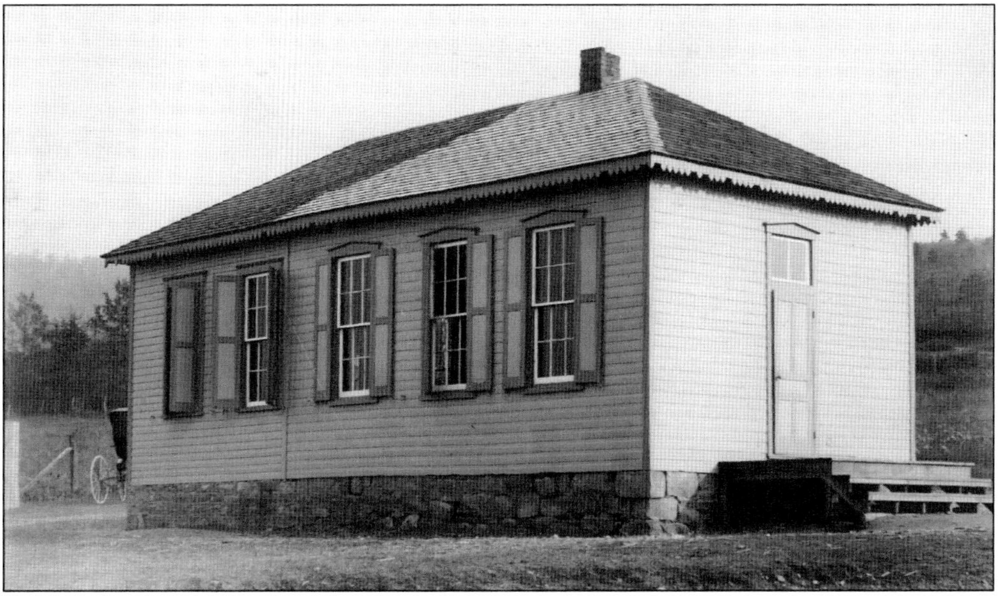

J. Marshall Porter provided a description of the Winchester Bridge School's location in his autobiography *My Time of Life*. "The little one room school was located a hundred yards below a huge wooden trestle of the George's Creek Railroad which spanned the dirt road that was then the main road to Winchester, Virginia." The school's location would be unrecognizable to 21st-century students because of commercial developments. (Courtesy Allegany County Public Schools.)

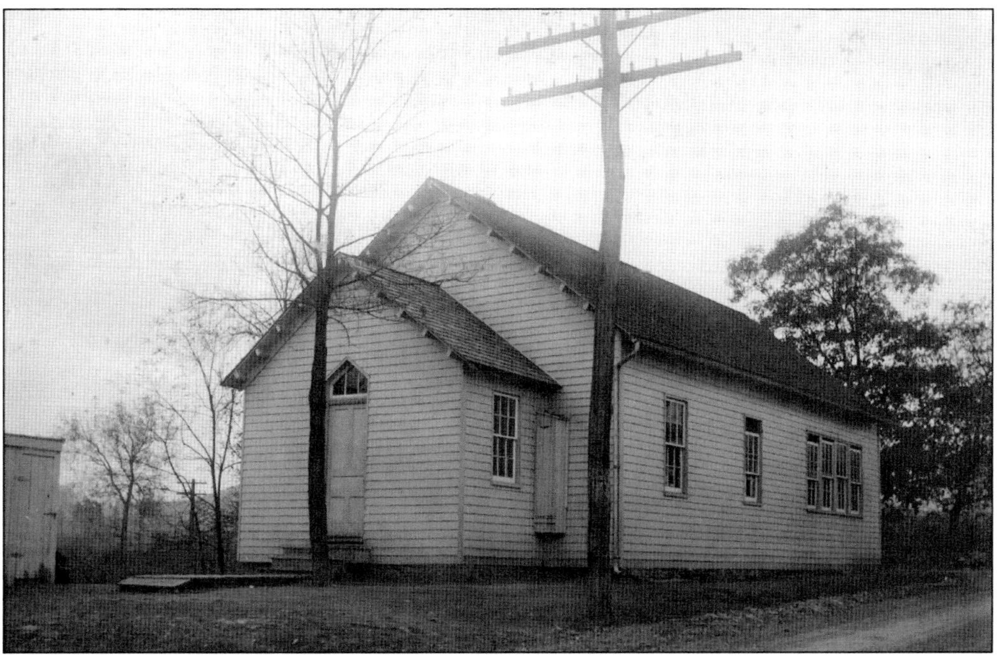

The Union Mining Company conveyed property in 1913 for the purpose of building Corrigansville School, later called Corriganville, on Kreigbaum Road. While the precise date of the structure's origin is unknown, it was likely built in the late 1870s because John Thomas Scharf listed it in 1881. The school was converted for use as a private residence in the 1920s when a larger brick school was built nearby. (Courtesy Allegany County Public Schools.)

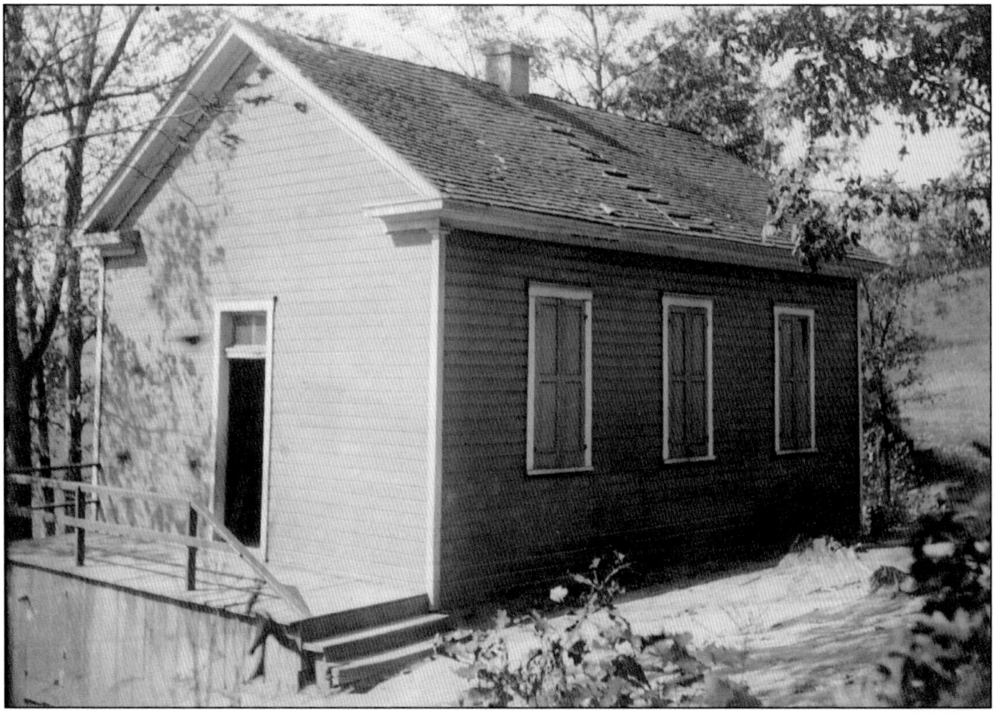

Charles Rawlings conveyed property to the school board in the mid-1890s for the purpose of erecting a school along the northeastern side of Pinto Road. In 1921, Pinto School became a news story because of a novel idea. The Women's Community Club of Pinto served the pupils hot drinks at noon as well as nutritious soup. Pinto School was closed in 1928 and later converted to a dwelling. (Courtesy Allegany County Public Schools.)

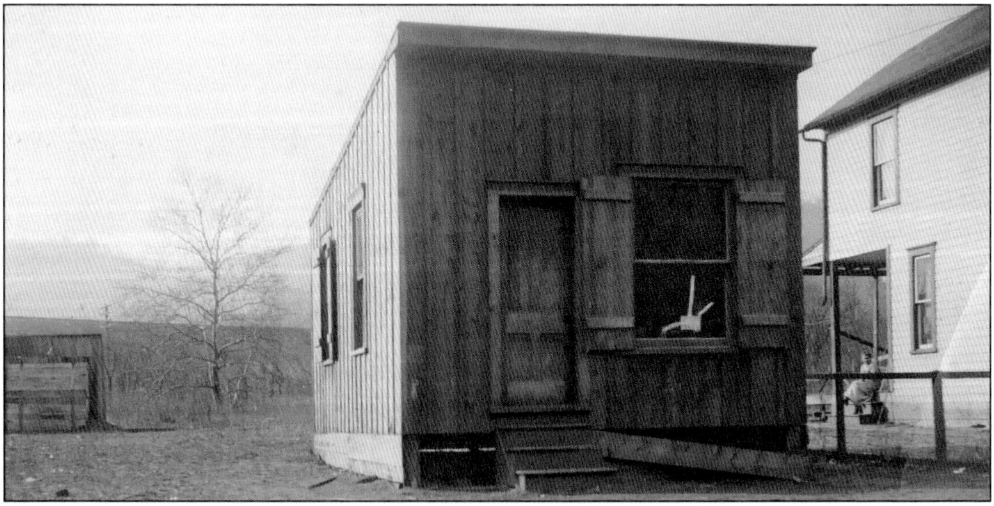

Paper Mill School, located in Locust Grove, was presumably named after the Potomac Paper Mill or successor companies operating on that location. The school building was apparently replaced because early photographs—as seen here—depicted a basic structure, while later ones showed a larger building referred to as Locust Grove School. The Locust Grove School remained in service until after World War II. In 1950, the property was transferred to the county commissioners. (Courtesy Allegany County Public Schools.)

Maryland Avenue Elementary School was built in 1874 and retired from regular school use in 1942. The building was subsequently occupied for several years as a GI trade school specializing in radio and electronics. Eventually the board of education conveyed the property to the county. In 1958, the county commissioners sold the building to Woodrow Gurley, a local car dealer, for $250. It was razed in 1962.

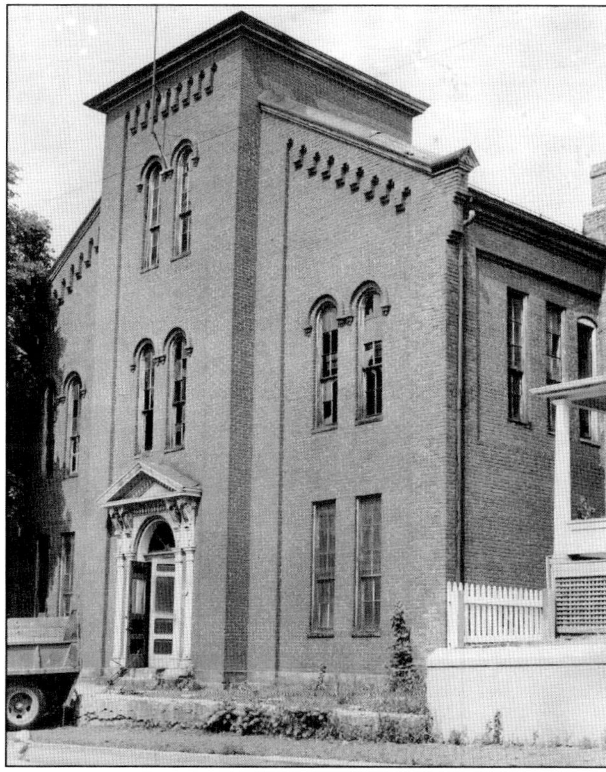

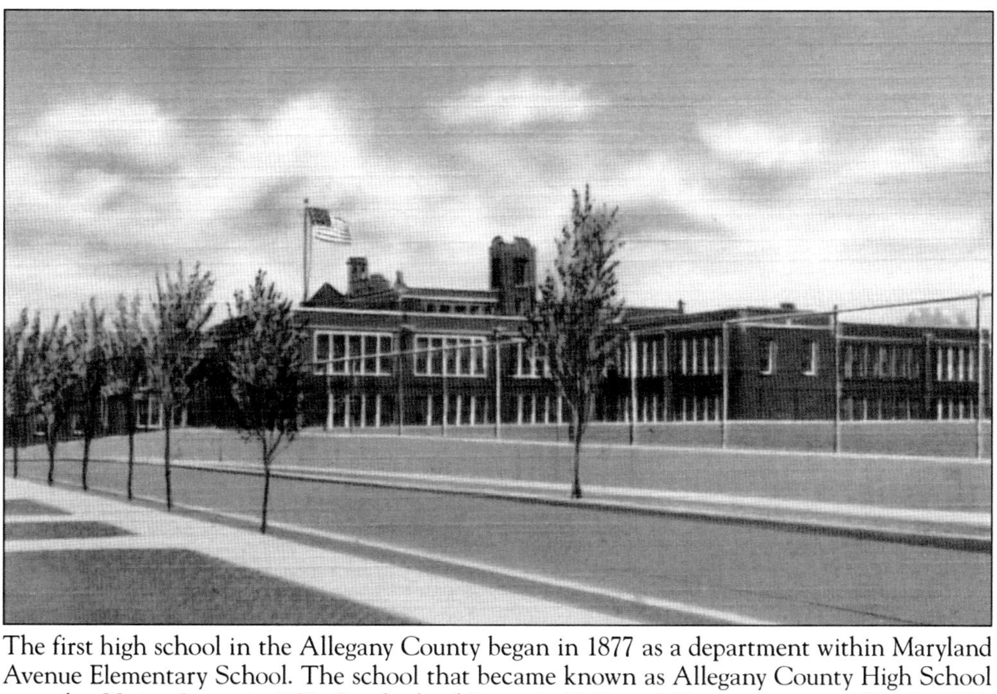

The first high school in the Allegany County began in 1877 as a department within Maryland Avenue Elementary School. The school that became known as Allegany County High School moved to Union Street in 1879, Cumberland Street in 1902, and Greene Street in 1908. In 1926, a new school building opened at Campobello and was called Allegany High School. This postcard view is from around 1955.

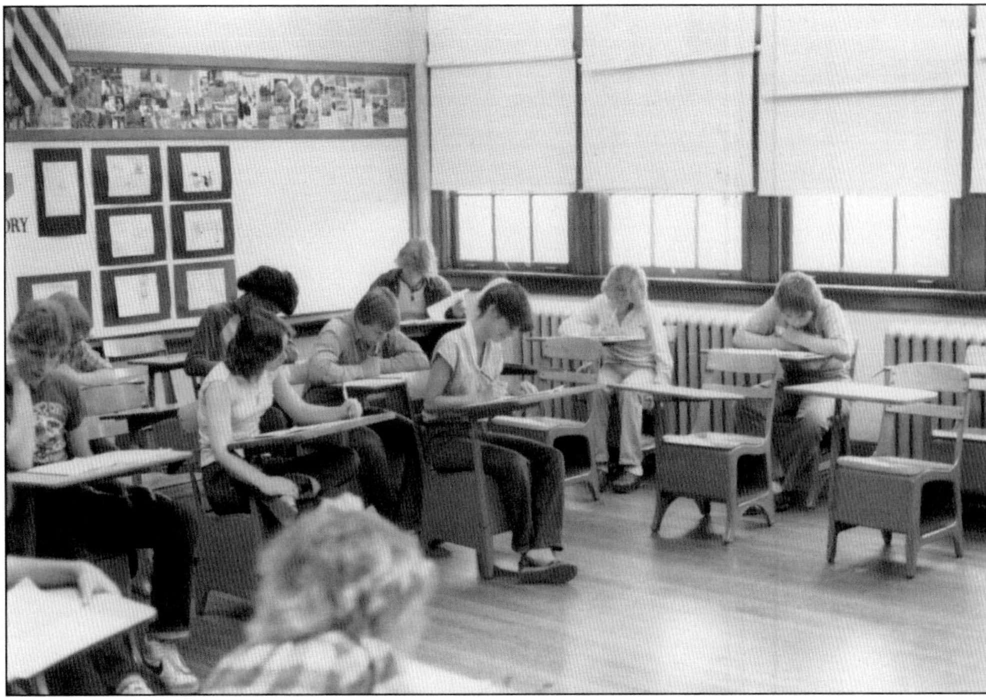

This view showed classroom No. 212, second floor, at Allegany High School in 1980. Most of the interior features of the school were significantly changed by a 1981 renovation, which required students to attend classes at Braddock Middle School for one academic year.

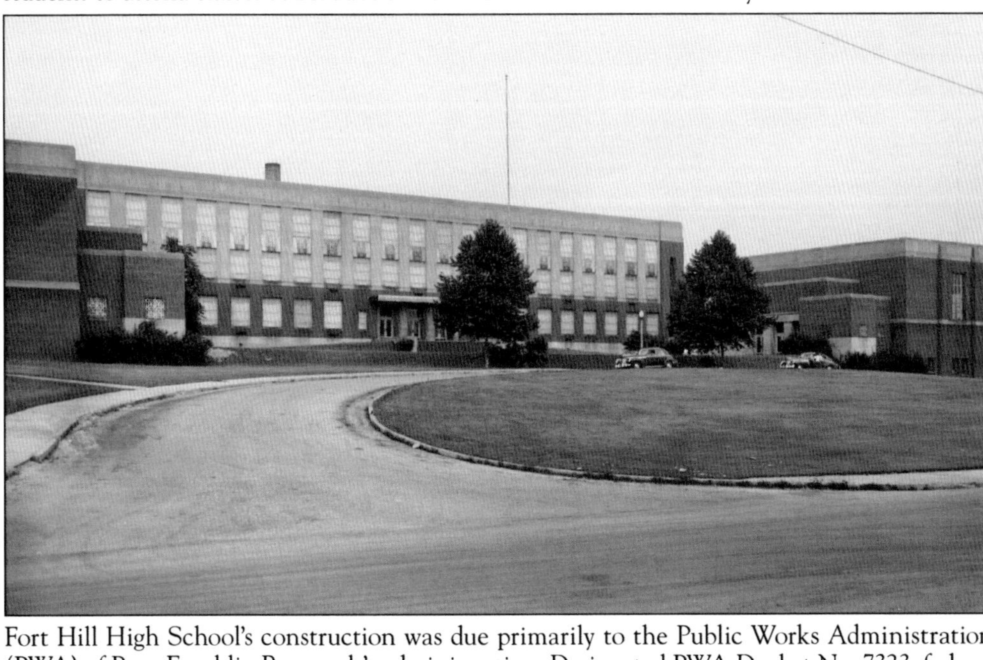

Fort Hill High School's construction was due primarily to the Public Works Administration (PWA) of Pres. Franklin Roosevelt's administration. Designated PWA Docket No. 7323, federal funds in the amount of $230,000 were set aside for construction. George Hazelwood was the contractor for the building, which opened in 1936. This photograph was taken in the 1940s. (Courtesy Allegany County Public Schools.)

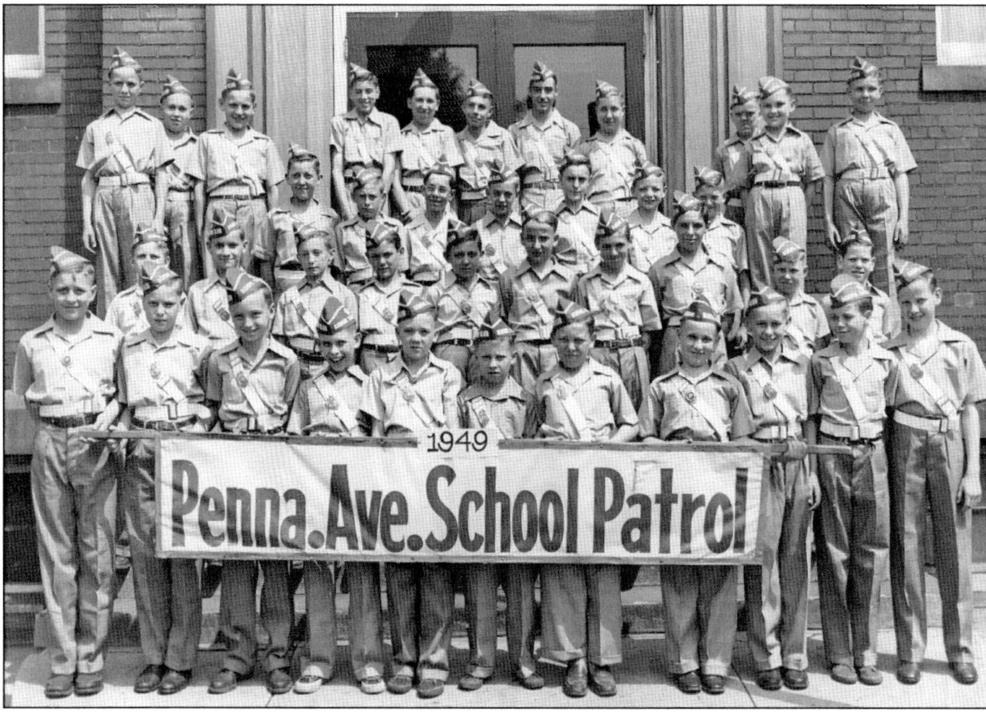

The high school wing of Pennsylvania Avenue School closed in 1936 with the opening of Fort Hill High School. The elementary program continued at the original location until the building of South Penn Elementary School. Pennsylvania Avenue elementary students regularly participated in School Patrol, a program designed to alleviate traffic concerns surrounding students walking to and from school. (Courtesy South Penn School.)

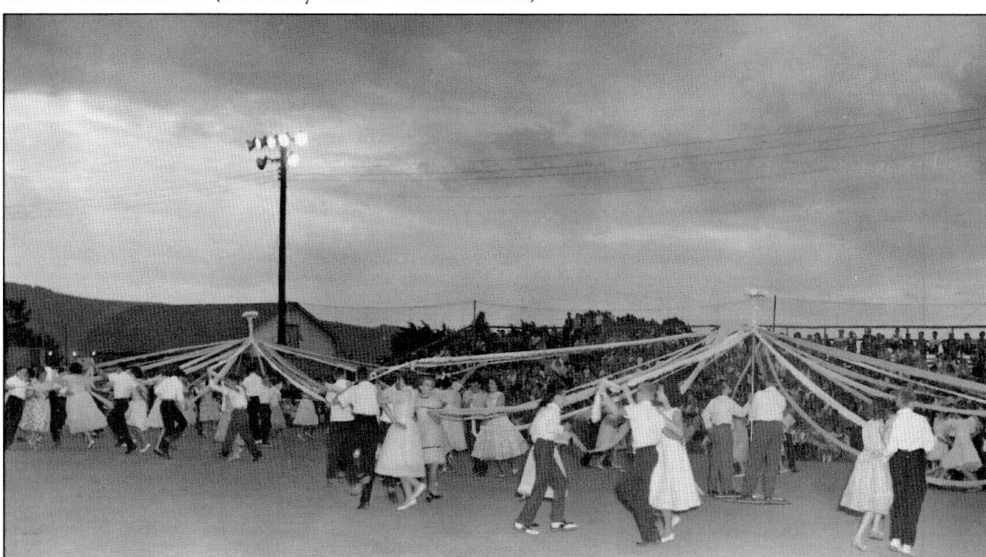

Adjacent to the Pennsylvania Avenue School building was a large playground that was used by the students for May Day activities and other events. The Pennsylvania Avenue athletic field was also equipped with lights that enabled Dapper Dan and Hot Stove baseball teams to play evening games. (Courtesy South Penn School.)

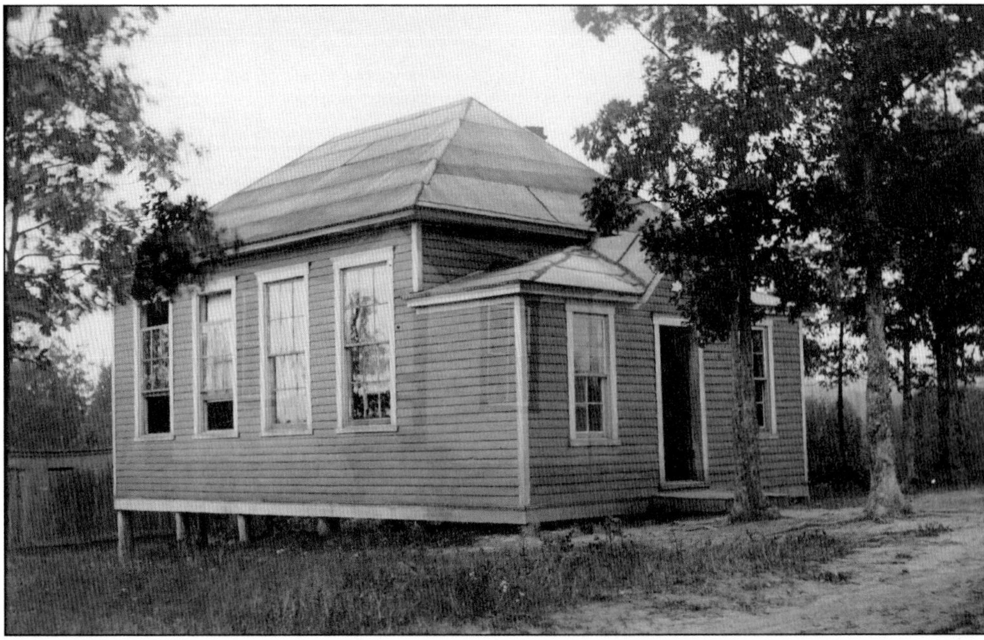

When Wilson Academy was replaced in 1920, Dicken School was built along Mason Road. Dicken School's name was later changed to Union Grove Academy. Union Grove closed in 1949, and students transferred to schools in Cumberland. By the 1970s, Union Grove was one of the few unaltered, one-room schoolhouses remaining in Allegany County. In 1977, the school was renovated by the Preservation Society of Allegany County, and again in 2010, by the Allegany County Historical Society. (Courtesy Allegany County Public Schools.)

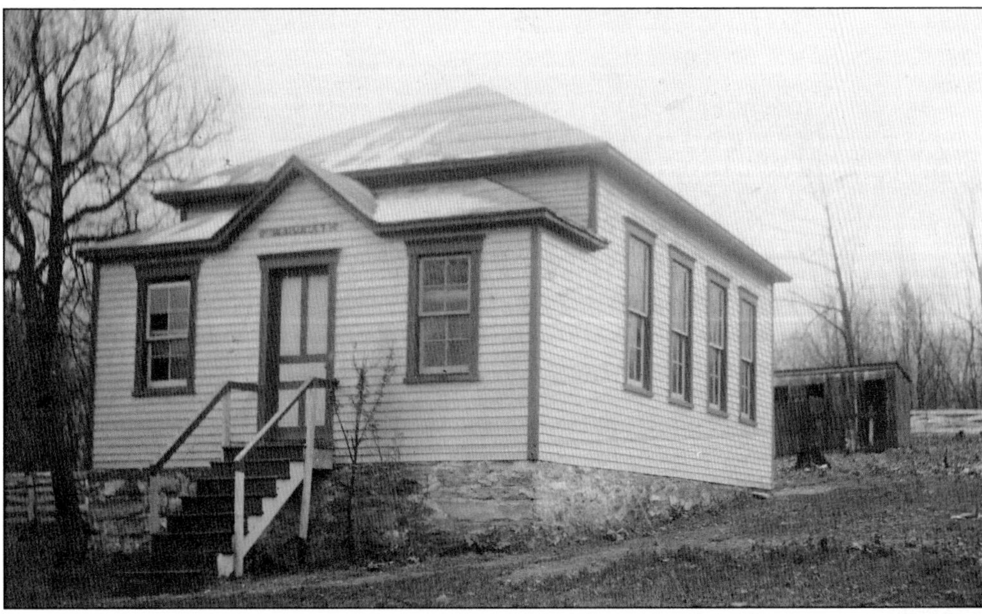

According to a 1914 newspaper report, Fairview School "is one of the largest rural schools in the county, affiliated near the fine farming location of Flintstone, Md." J. Lindley Rank served as principal of the school in 1914. Nearby schools included Murley's Branch, Twiggtown, Frazee, Bucey, Lashley, Flintstone, and Piney Plains. (Courtesy Allegany County Public Schools.)

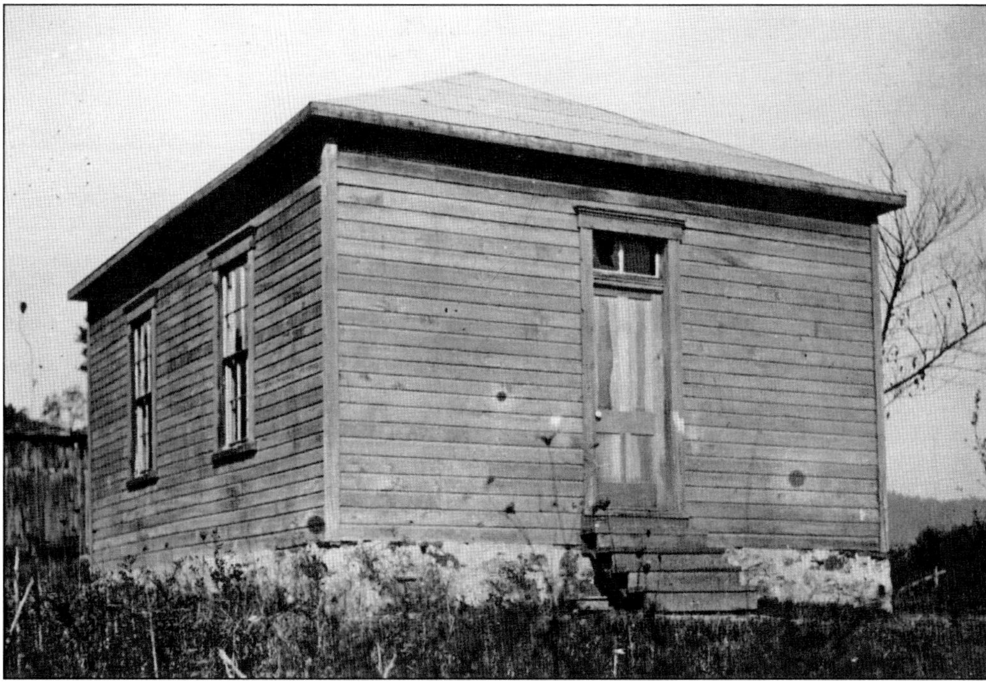

Eli Hartsock conveyed property to the school board in 1894 for the purpose of building Frazee School, located in Election District 3 in the Flintstone area. The school was likely the namesake of Daniel Frazee, trustee in 1881. Maggie McCulley was one of the first teachers. (Courtesy Allegany County Public Schools.)

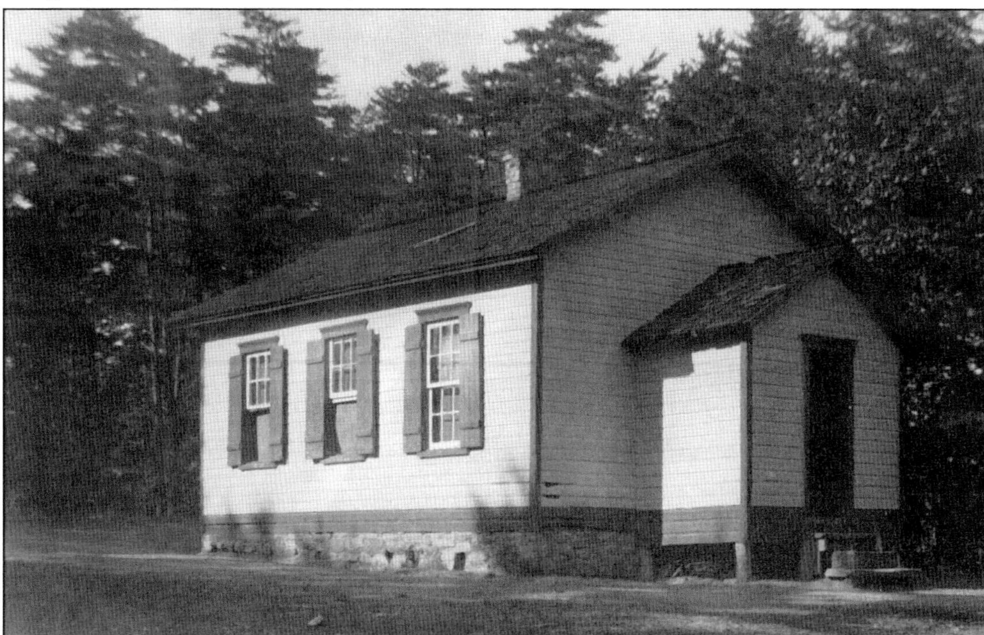

Pratt School, located on Polish Mountain, offered grades one through eight. Thomas Davis originally owned the property before its conveyance to the school board. Pratt was closed and later sold in 1924. (Courtesy Allegany County Public Schools.)

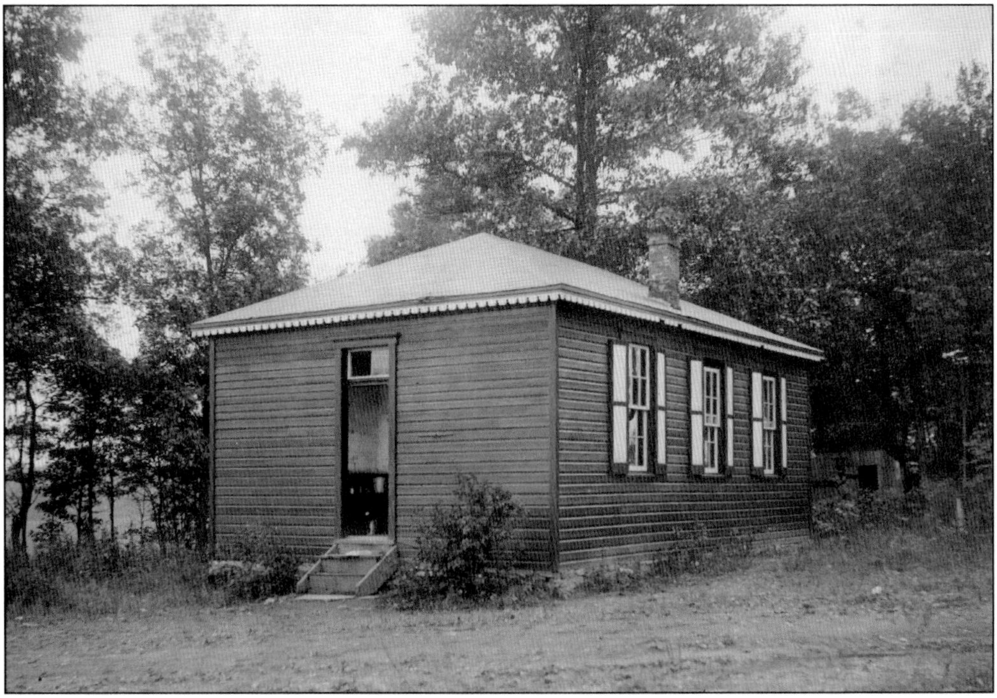

Fletcher School was located 1 mile beyond Piney Plains School on the road to Little Orleans. After being abandoned, the building was purchased by Walter Johnson, removed from the site, and converted to a cottage. Today the site is occupied by an Allegany County Roads Department facility. (Courtesy Allegany County Public Schools.)

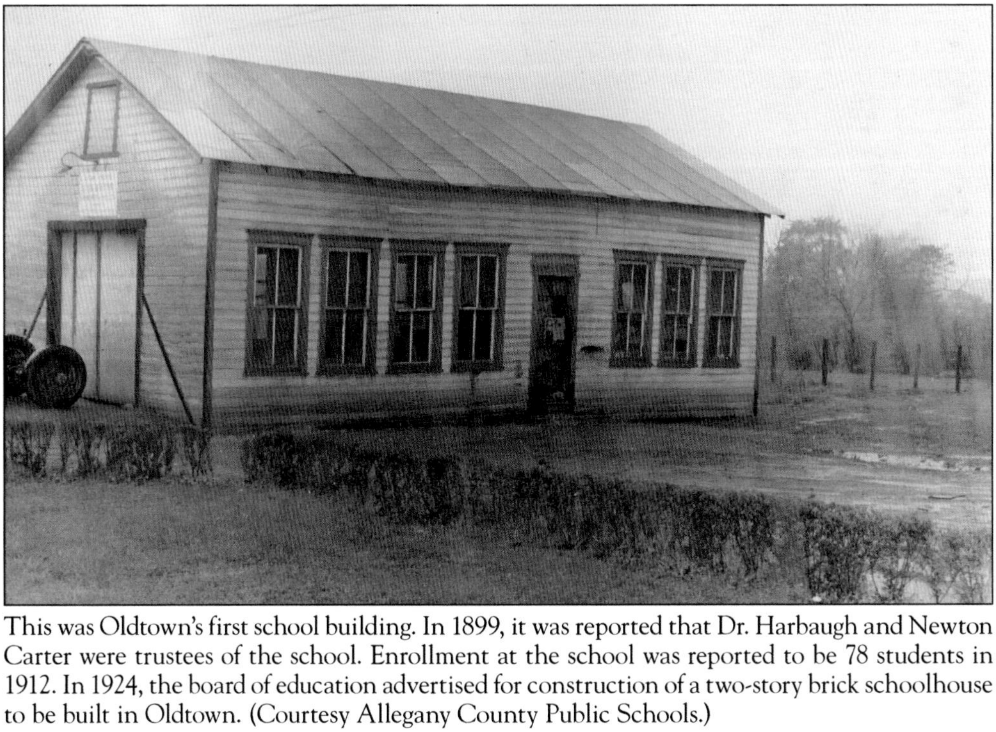

This was Oldtown's first school building. In 1899, it was reported that Dr. Harbaugh and Newton Carter were trustees of the school. Enrollment at the school was reported to be 78 students in 1912. In 1924, the board of education advertised for construction of a two-story brick schoolhouse to be built in Oldtown. (Courtesy Allegany County Public Schools.)

Two

SPORTS, RECREATION, AND ENTERTAINMENT

Industrial development and the arrival of railroads in the 19th century caused Allegany County's population to increase. As the largest population center in Allegany County and a convenient layover between Pittsburgh and Washington, Cumberland regularly offered lectures, circuses, parades, plays, patriotic rallies, horse racing, and cultural events. Theatres like the Belvidere on Baltimore Street and the Academy of Music on North Centre Street featured top quality troupes in the late 1800s. Frostburg also attracted dramatic troupes and patrons to its Paul's Hall and Independent Order of Odd Fellows' venues. As the county moved into the 20th century, scholastic competitions, automobile racing, golf tournaments, softball teams, movie theaters, drive-in theaters, horse racing, PenMar baseball, and an adult football league (until 1941) were offered as recreational opportunities. Youngsters also had a variety of recreational activities to choose from, including Dapper Dan baseball, Hot Stove baseball, recreational league baseball, marbles tournaments, soapbox derby racing, boxing, the Young Men's Christian Association (YMCA) basketball leagues, swimming, ice skating on the Chesapeake and Ohio Canal, and a large number of movie theaters to patronize.

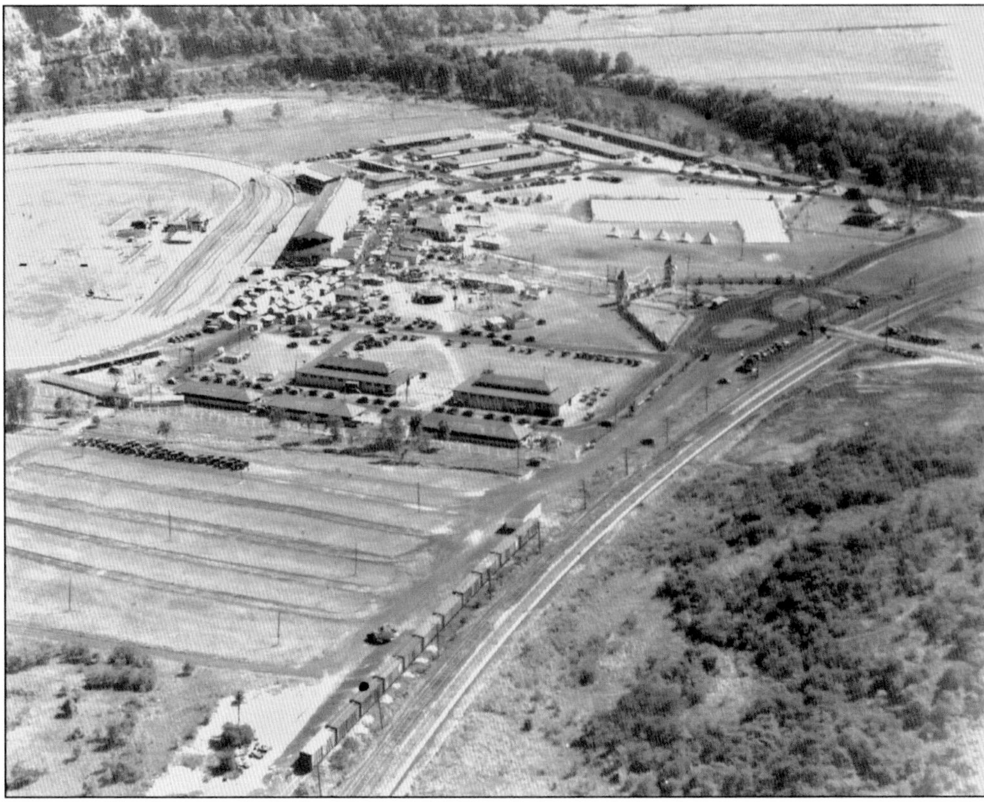

The Cumberland Fair Association formed in 1923 for the purpose of building a new agricultural fairground and horse racing track to be known as Fairgo. The new fairgrounds and half-mile racetrack were built in 1924 along the Potomac River, south of Cumberland. In addition to horse racing, the facility included an L-shaped tennis court complex visible in the upper right corner. This photograph is from around 1935.

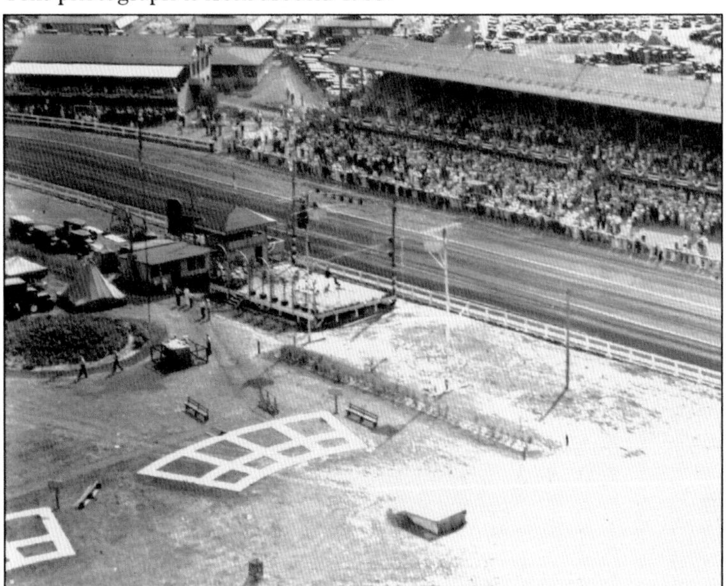

A capacity crowd packed the grandstand and clubhouse of this c. 1930 race. The wooden trackside building accommodated officials who determined places at the finish. A small tote board stood to the left of the stage (not visible in this photograph) and was later replaced by a larger one during the mid-1950s. The white web-shaped markings were part of a skeet shooting range.

Horse races were started at three different locations over the years, depending on the length of the race. The official starting this race stood on a platform near the traditional second turn.

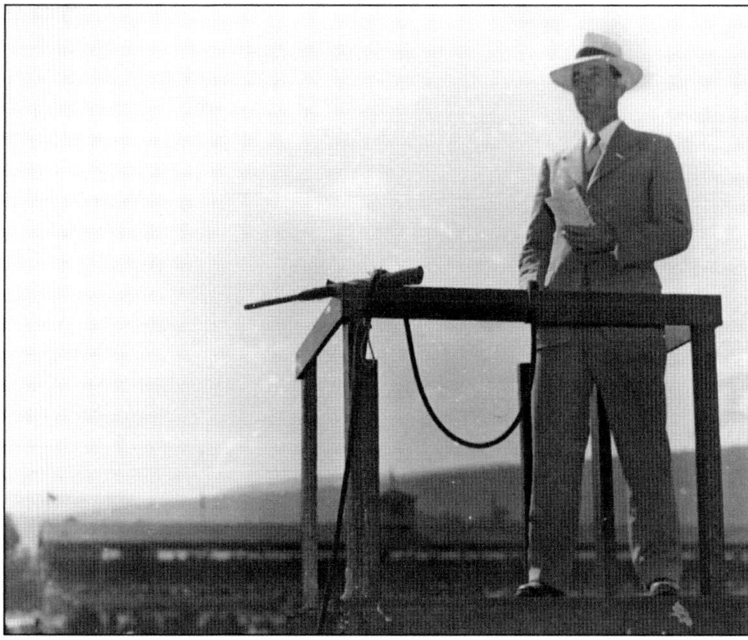

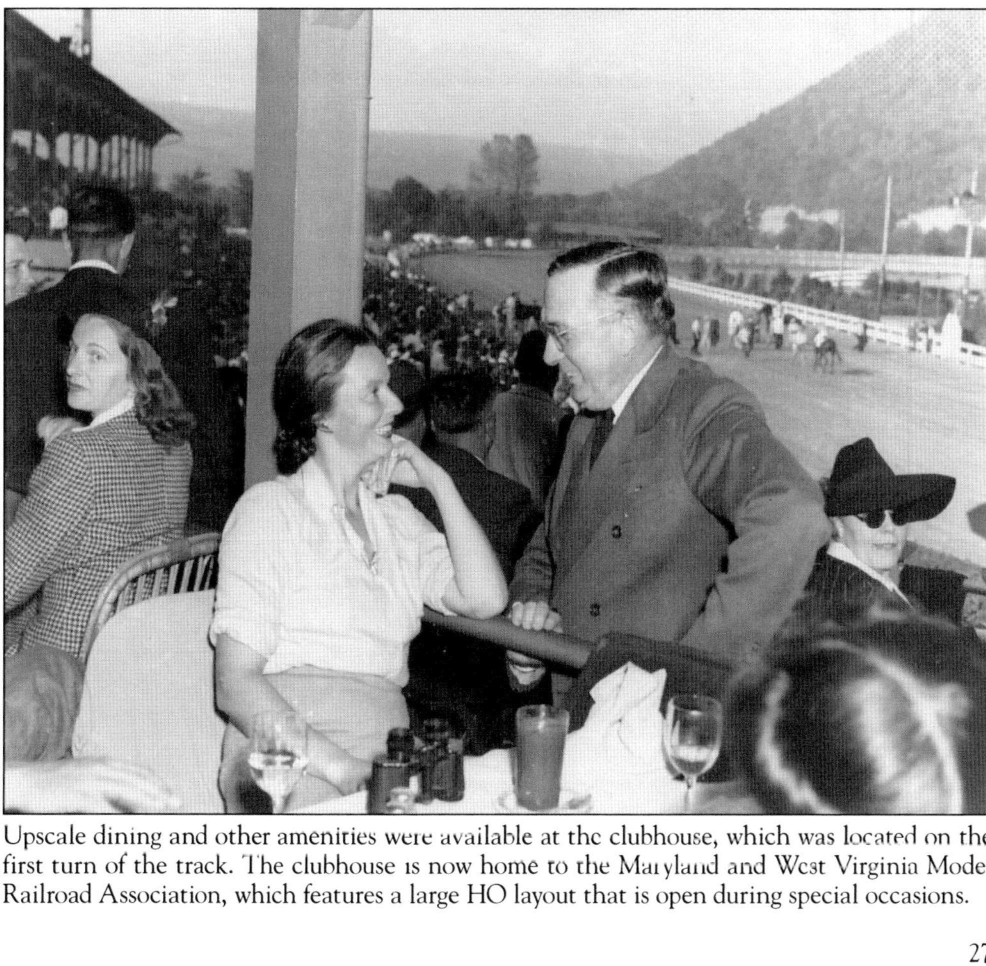

Upscale dining and other amenities were available at the clubhouse, which was located on the first turn of the track. The clubhouse is now home to the Maryland and West Virginia Model Railroad Association, which features a large HO layout that is open during special occasions.

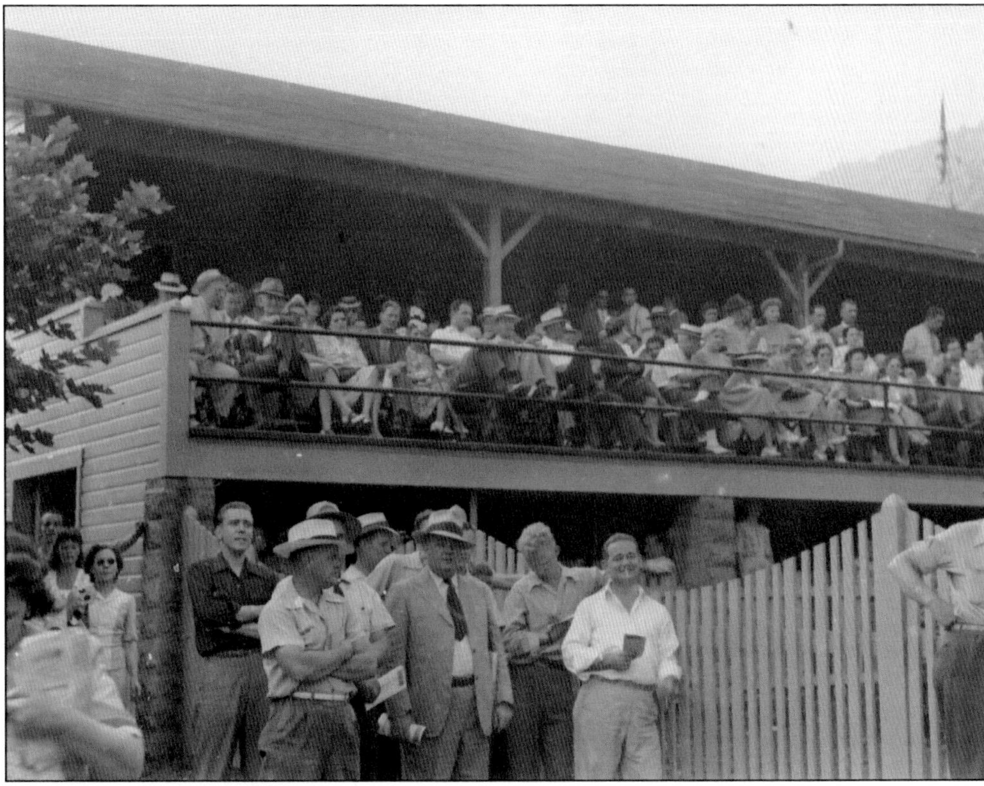

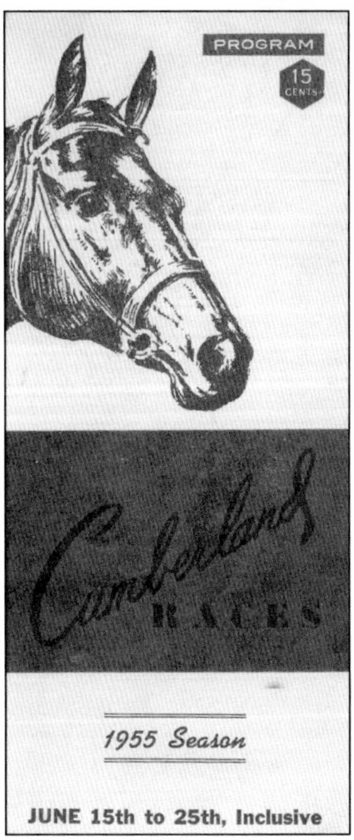

Large crowds attended the 10-day horse racing program at Fairgo during the 1950s. When regional tracks began to offer 60 racing dates, the Fairgo track could not compete and closed after the 1961 season.

The 1955 Cumberland Races program described eight races per day for the 10-day event. Information—such as names of horses, jockeys, and colors—was closely studied by fans.

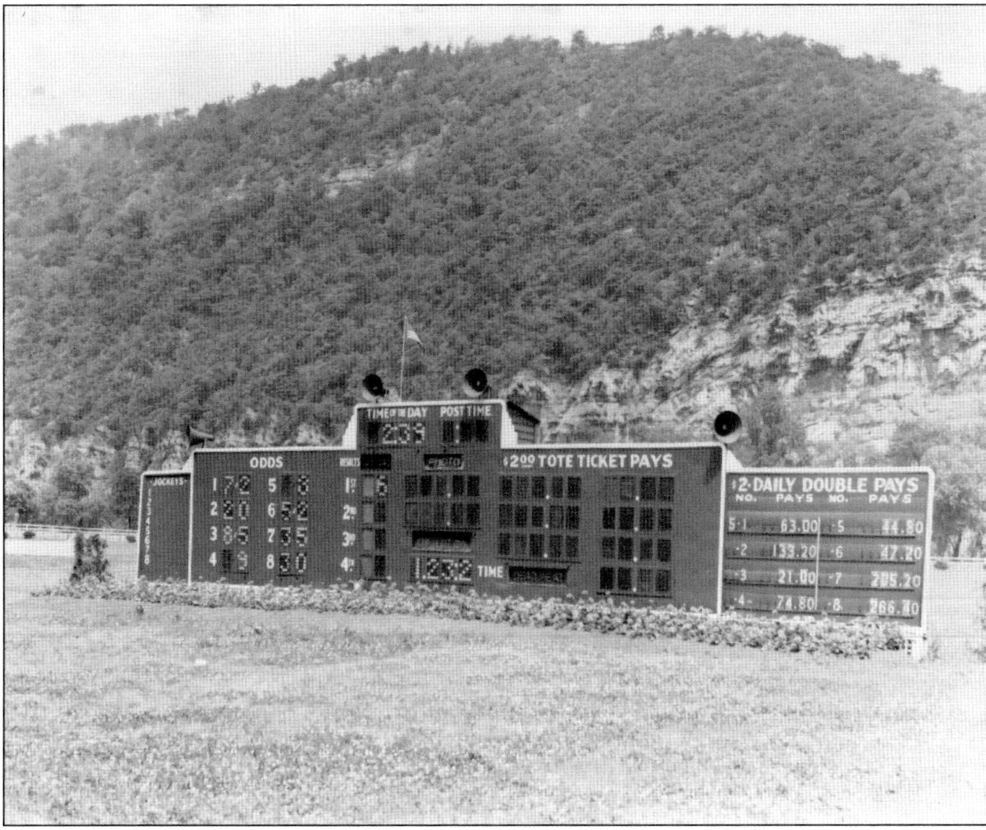

Spectators depended on the large display called a tote board for post times, odds, and payout information. Races were announced by officials working in a small press box—called a "crow's nest"—located near the top of the grandstand. The announcements were broadcast through loudspeakers mounted atop the tote board. Longtime residents of Fairgo and Potomac Park recalled that the loudspeakers could be heard throughout local neighborhoods.

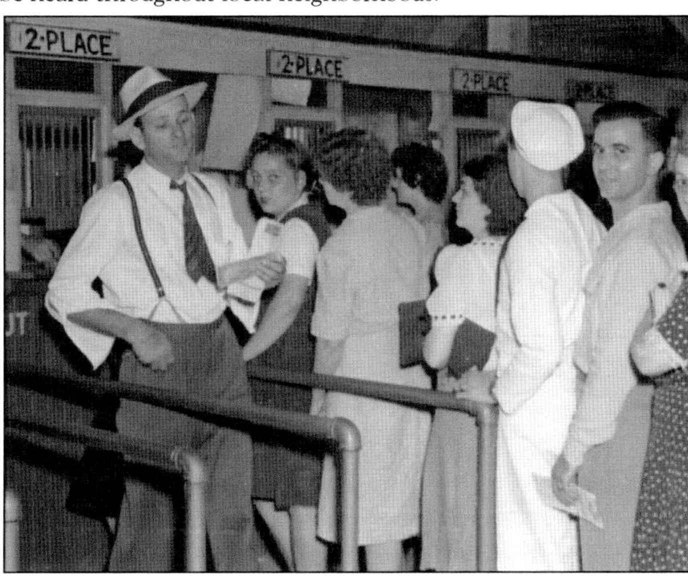

This photographer captured a busy day at the Fairgo horse races. Wagers were placed at a building located adjacent to the grandstands.

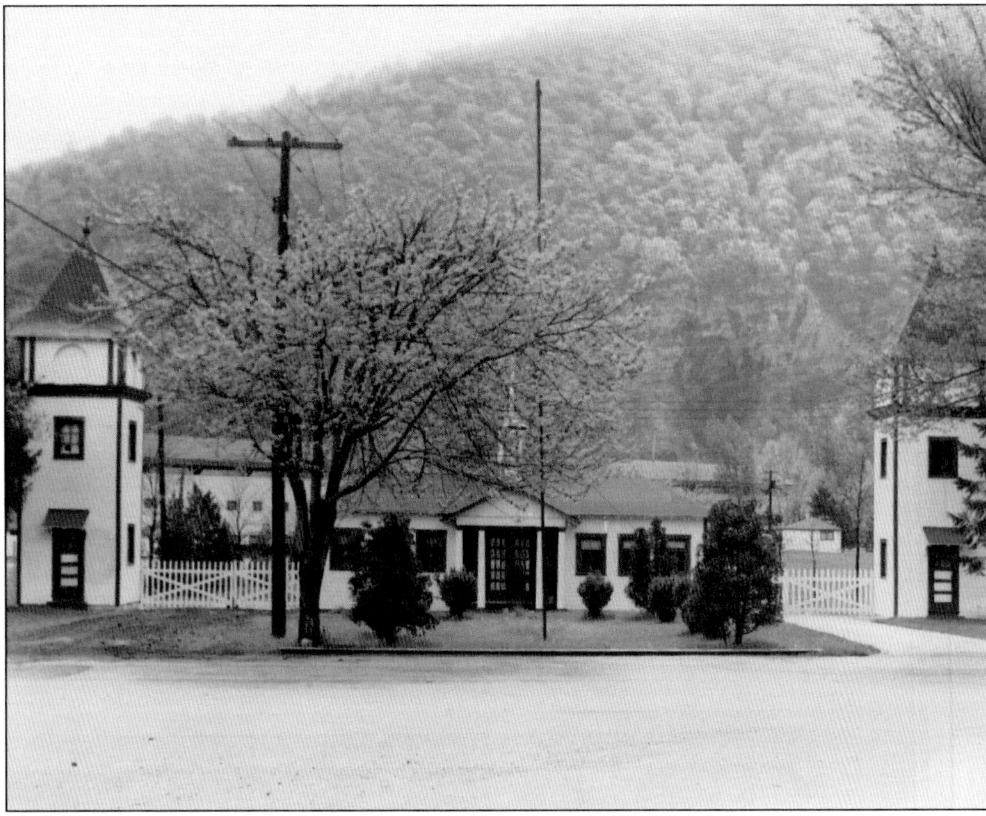

Visitors to fairground events passed through an attractive gatehouse flanked by two small wooden towers. The one-story, seven-bay gatehouse was framed with German siding. High winds destroyed one tower in 1987, while the other one gradually deteriorated over time and was removed. This photograph was taken around 1955.

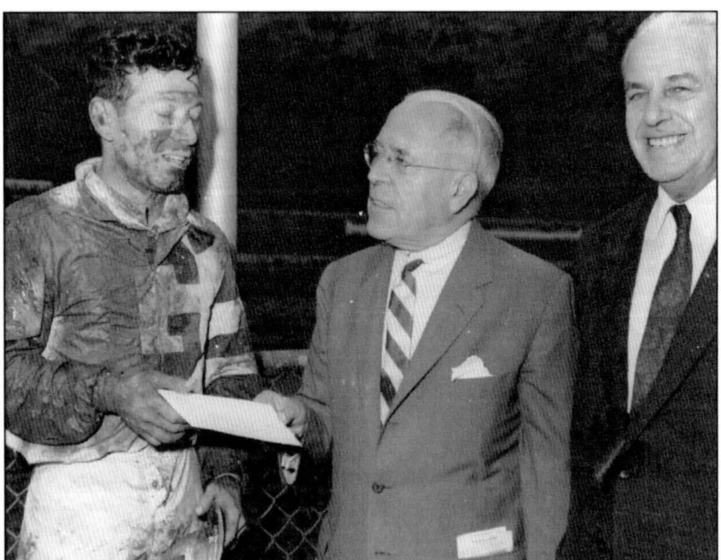

Harry Manley (center), Cumberland Fair Association general manager, offered congratulations to a winning jockey. Sen. J. Glenn Beall Sr., right, was a longtime supporter of the fairgrounds, and his son, J. Glenn Beall Jr., served as president of the Cumberland Fair Association. Manley died unexpectedly in 1943, and subsequent horse racing events were named in his honor.

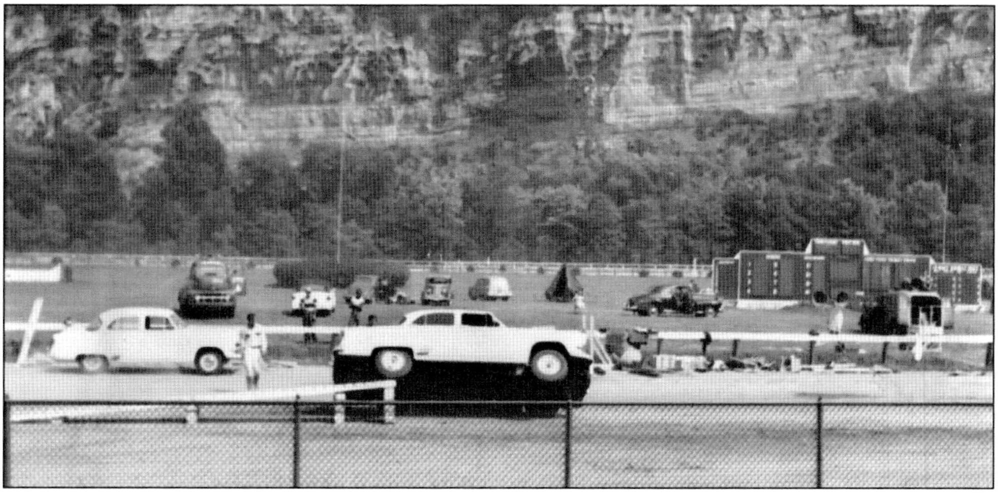

Automobile stunt drivers appeared at the fairgrounds. The Indianapolis Daredevil's "Tournament of Thrills" enthralled spectators as seen in this mid-1950s photograph. Race car driver Joey Chitwood also appeared with his "Joey Chitwood Thrill Show" that was sometimes referred to as "Hell Drivers."

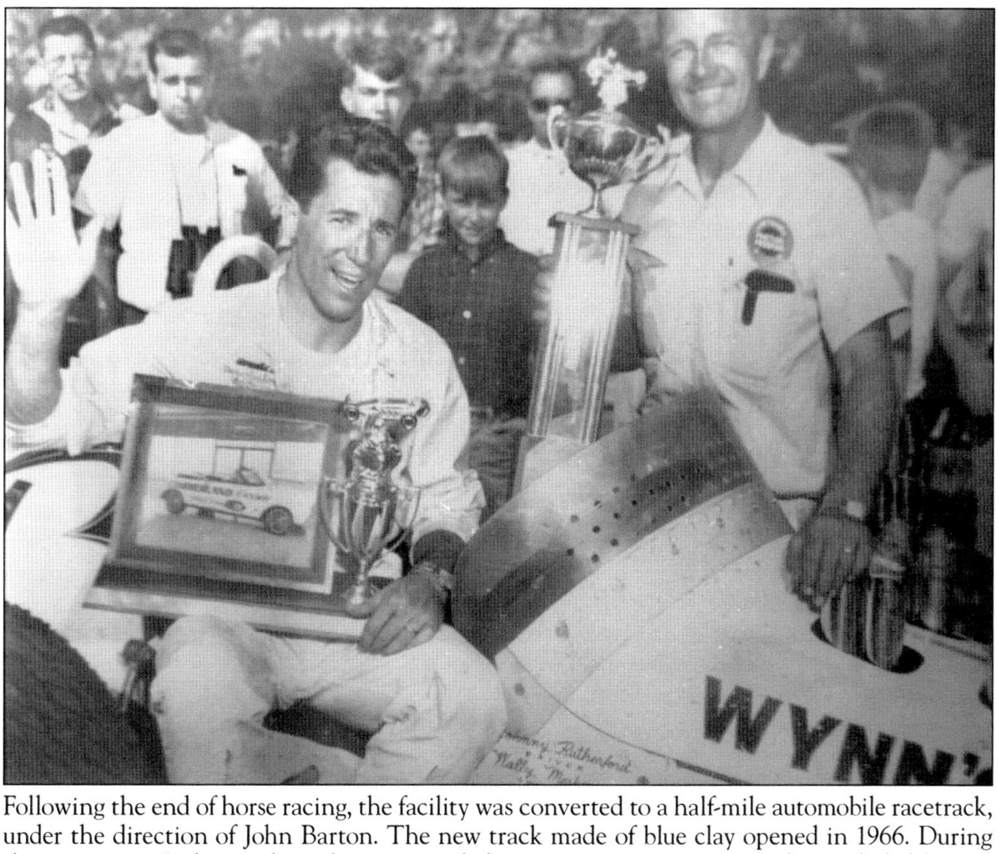

Following the end of horse racing, the facility was converted to a half-mile automobile racetrack, under the direction of John Barton. The new track made of blue clay opened in 1966. During that same year, Indianapolis-style cars provided sprint racing competitions that included famous driver Mario Andretti driving a Johnny Rutherford car. Andretti, seated and holding the trophy, placed first in the Fairgo event. (Courtesy Kevin Kamauff.)

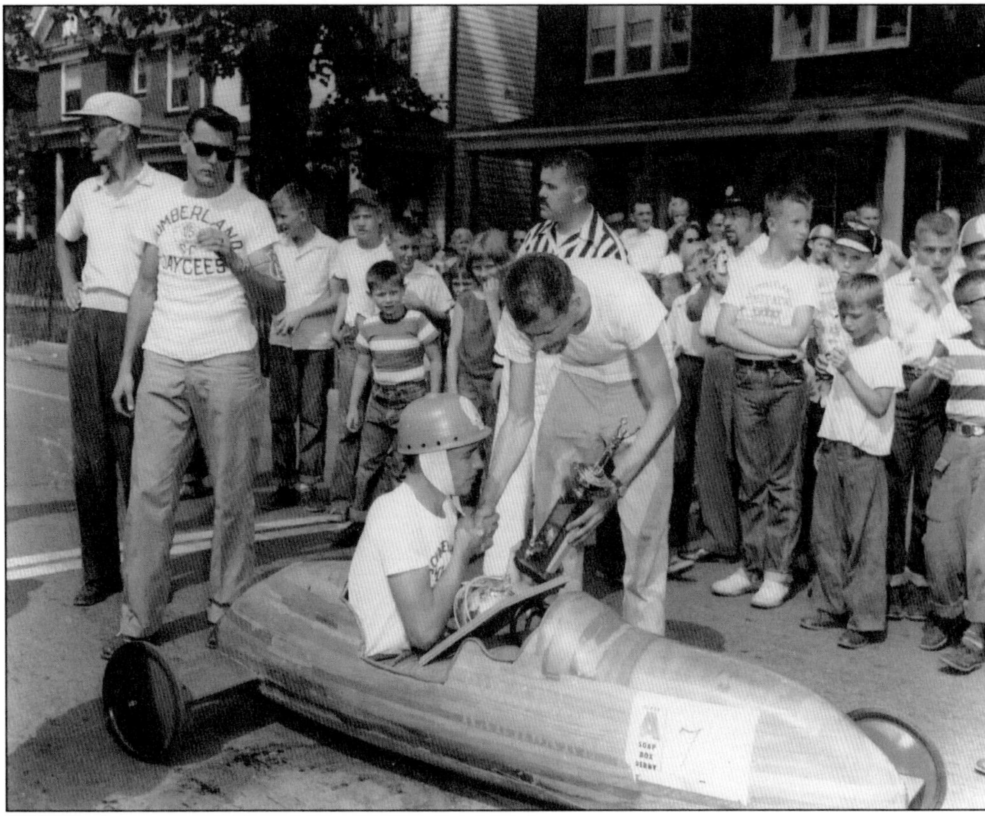

The driver in car No. 7 received congratulations and a trophy following a race held on Pennsylvania Avenue in South Cumberland. Building soapbox derby racing cars was a popular hobby in the decade following World War II. Cumberland's official competition began in 1948 when Chevrolet's national sponsorship was augmented locally by the *Cumberland Times-News*. Sanctioned races were held on Greene Street in 1948–1949, on McMullen Highway in 1950, and on Pennsylvania Avenue from 1952 to around 1955.

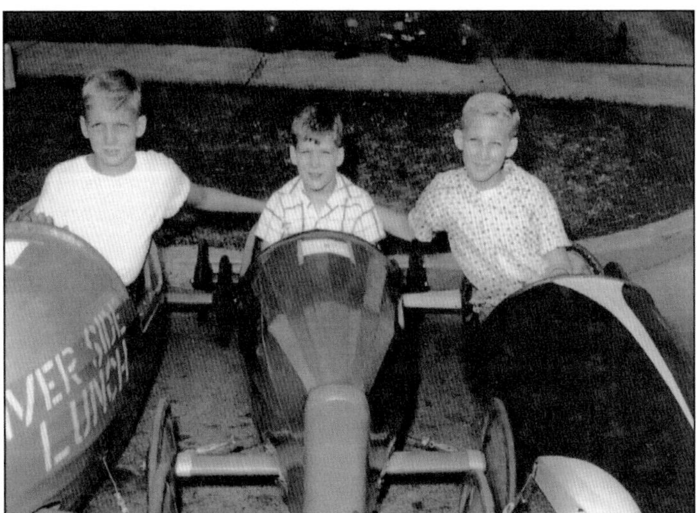

Riverside Lunch was a Westernport restaurant that sponsored soapbox drivers.

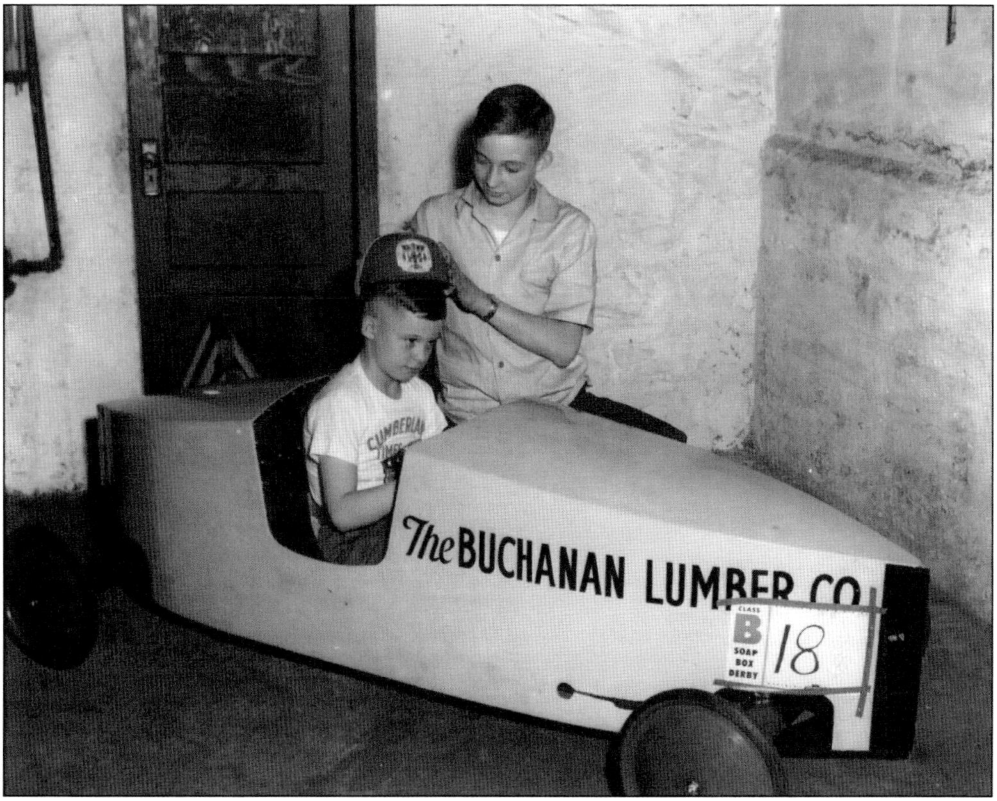

Buchanan Lumber Company, located at 549 North Centre Street in Cumberland, supplied soapbox drivers with building materials.

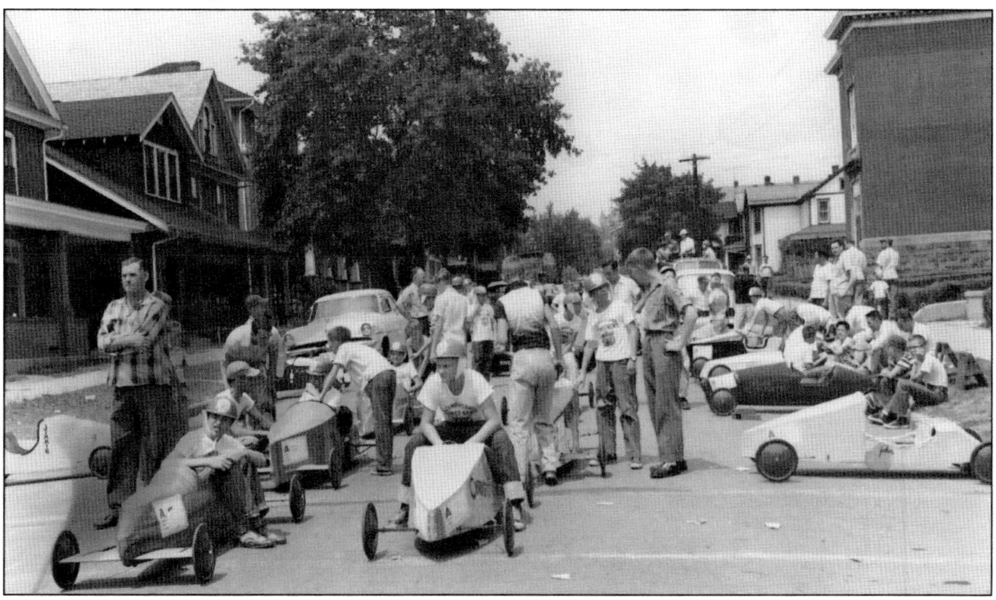

Race officials prepared drivers at the starting line near Pennsylvania Avenue School, shown in the background on the right. Drivers dueled down the avenue toward present-day Industrial Boulevard. A variety of soapbox body styles are noticeable.

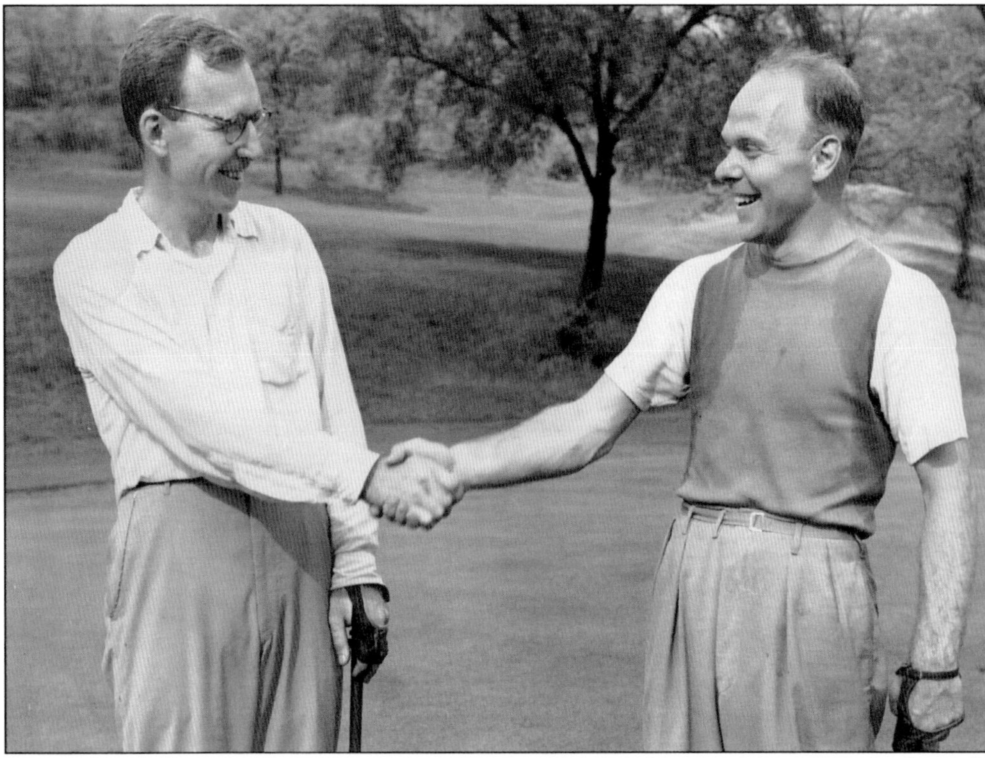

The Cumberland Country Club Spring Championship was held on May 25, 1947. Charles "Bill" Catherman, left, defeated Clifton Van Roby, right, by the score of 5-4. The contest was played in a driving rain.

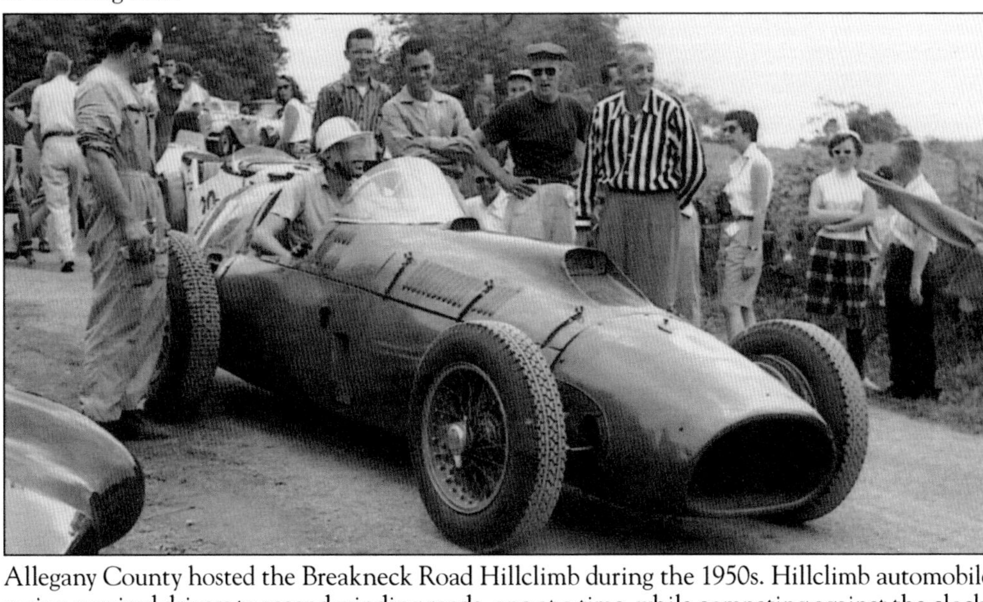

Allegany County hosted the Breakneck Road Hillclimb during the 1950s. Hillclimb automobile racing required drivers to ascend winding roads, one at a time, while competing against the clock. The first Hillclimb was held on May 29, 1955, at Breakneck Road east of Cumberland. Subsequent events drew nationally known drivers, including the legendary Carroll Shelby, shown in this photograph with his Formula One car. (Courtesy Bob Poling.)

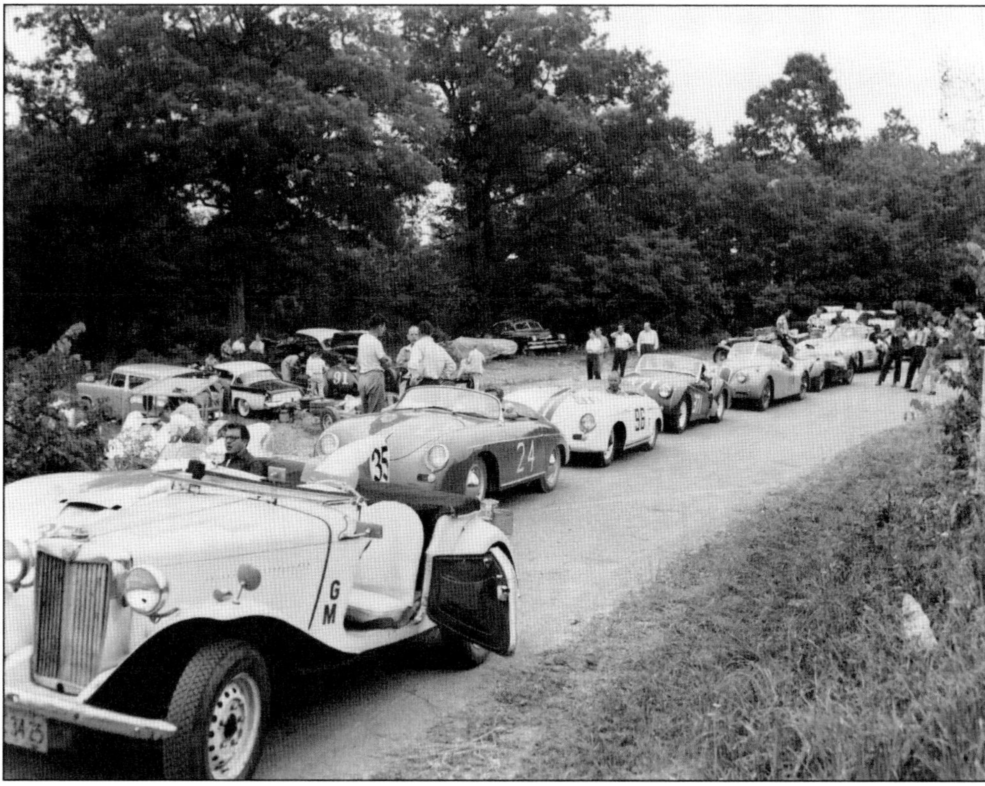

The 1956 Breakneck Road Hillclimb featured Carroll Shelby and his No. 93 Ferrari GP. Shelby won the race in a time of 1:12.41. Others pictured were, from front left to right, car No. 35, Lotus, Frank Baptista; No. 24, Jaguar, Bengtg Soderstrom; No. 96, Porsche, J. W. Thomas; and car No. 371, Triumph TR3, R. Lantz.

The Cumberland Sports Car Races began in 1953 and were held at the Cumberland Municipal Airport. Sanctioned by the Sports Car Club of America, 20,000 to 30,000 spectators typically attended the three-day event. An estimated 45,000 spectators watched the races in 1958, making it the biggest turnout. The racecourse was 1.6 miles in length and featured heats in production, modified, and formula classes. The local Lions Clubs were major sponsors.

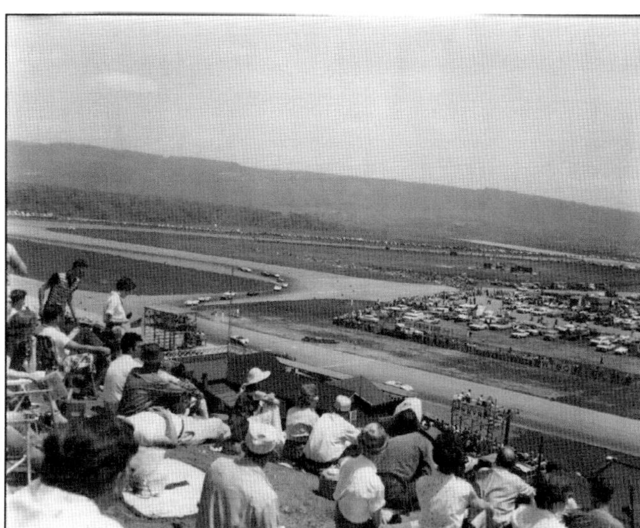

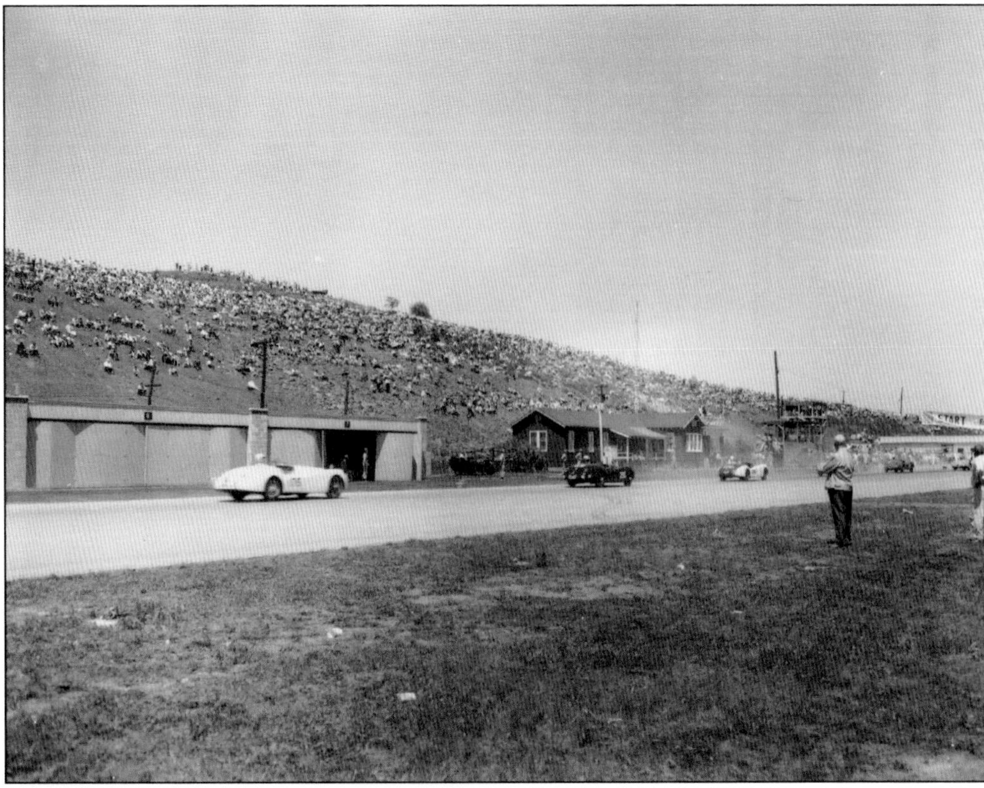

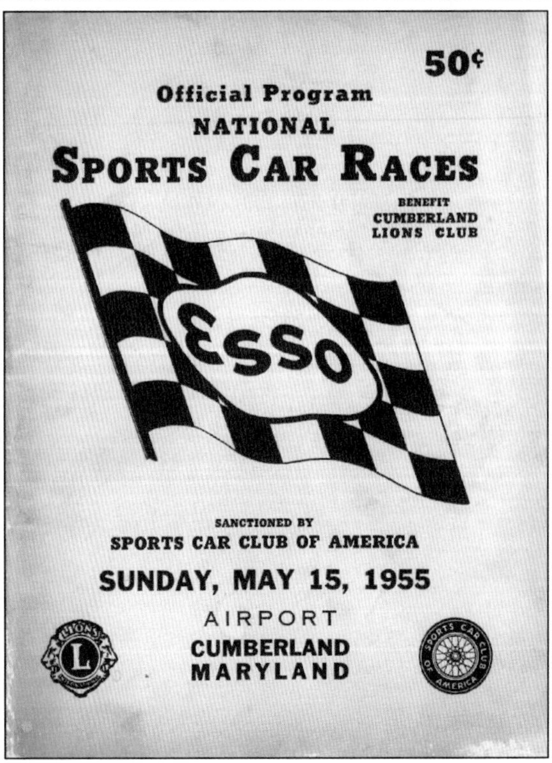

Drivers would trailer or drive their cars into the Cumberland area much to the liking of enthusiasts who watched the parade of legendary cars, including Cobras, Mustangs, Camaros, Jaguars, Ferraris, and Austin Healys, among others. Spectators seated themselves on the hills surrounding the airport. One of the biggest sports car races ever held in the United States happened at the 1955 event when 284 cars entered the competition.

This is an official program of the National Sports Car Race held at the Cumberland Airport, May 1955.

This photograph, labeled "Governor Ritchie," revealed a rare view of the playing field at Community Ballpark, located along Wineow Street in South Cumberland. The Footer Dye Company is visible in the background. Albert Ritchie served as 49th governor of Maryland from 1920 to 1935 and unsuccessfully campaigned for the Democratic presidential nomination in 1924 and 1932.

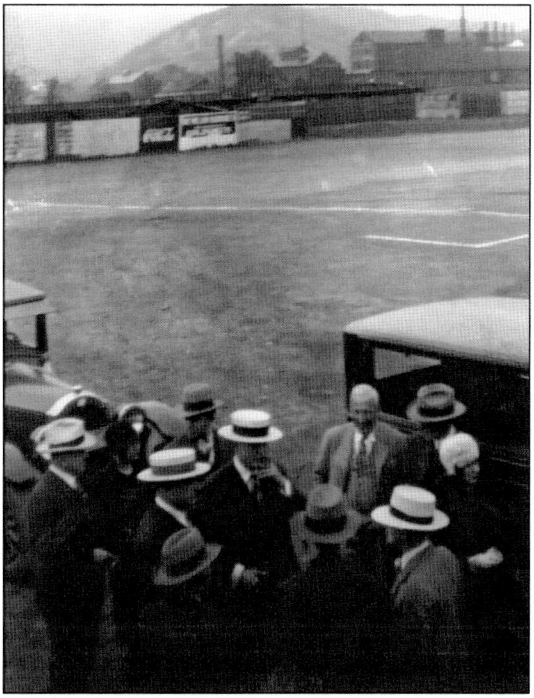

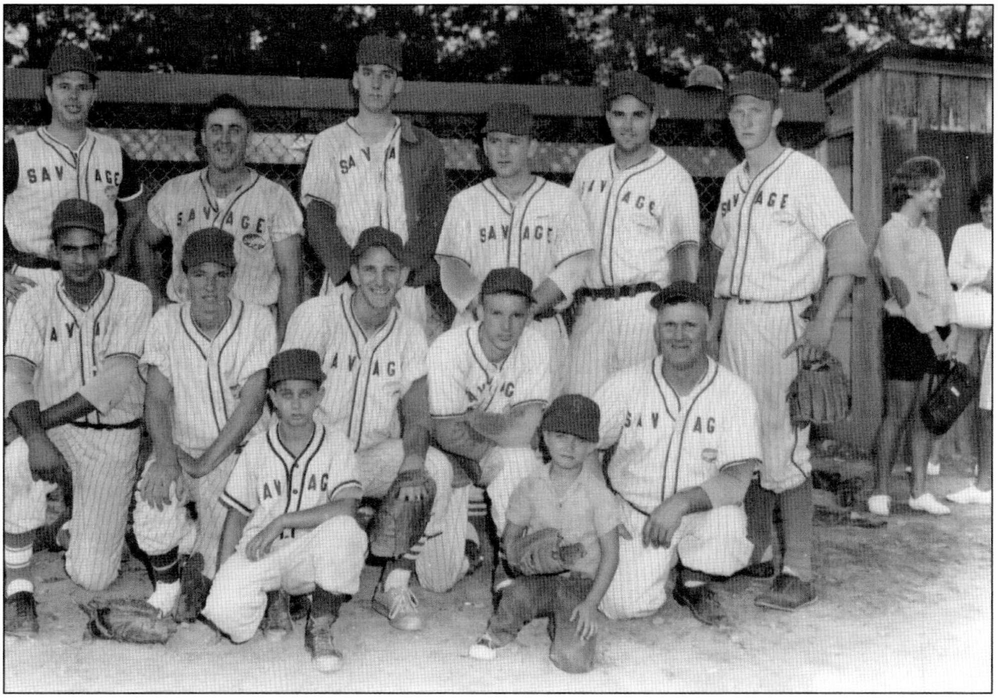

In 1965, the Mount Savage PenMar baseball team posed for a photograph. From left to right are (first row) bat boys Dennis Johnson and Kenny Johnson; (second row) Ted Femi, Ray Blank, Fay Often, Bobby Green, and Ralph Dickel; (third row) Bobby Dawson, manager Kenny Johnson, Ralph Wilson, Steve Faulkner, Rich Lybarger, and Bobby Robertson. Bobby Robertson later played 11 seasons of major league baseball with Pittsburgh, Seattle, and Toronto.

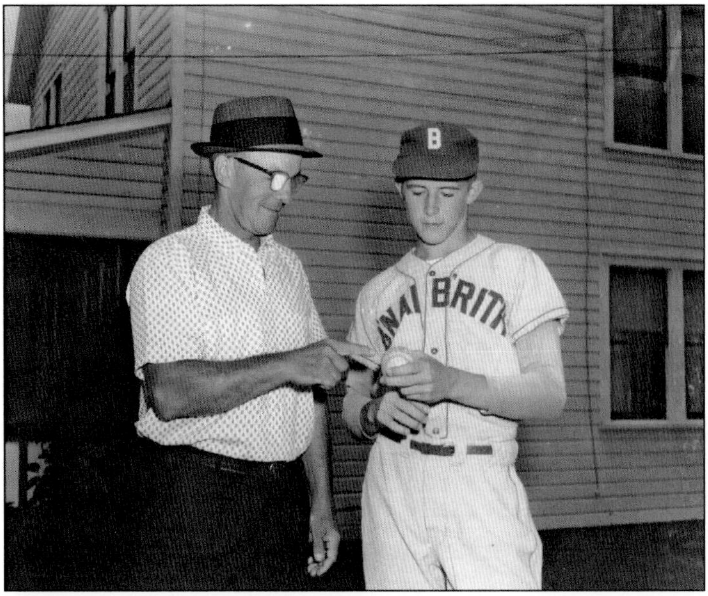

"Boots" Sap retrieved the baseball that legendary slugger Babe Ruth hit over the fence at Community Park when the New York Yankees appeared in Cumberland in September 1931. The Yankees exhibition game against the Cumberland Colts minor league team drew an overflow crowd of 4,000 fans. Greg Shaffer, who played for the team sponsored by the Jewish civic organization B'Nai B'rith, enjoyed holding the special baseball.

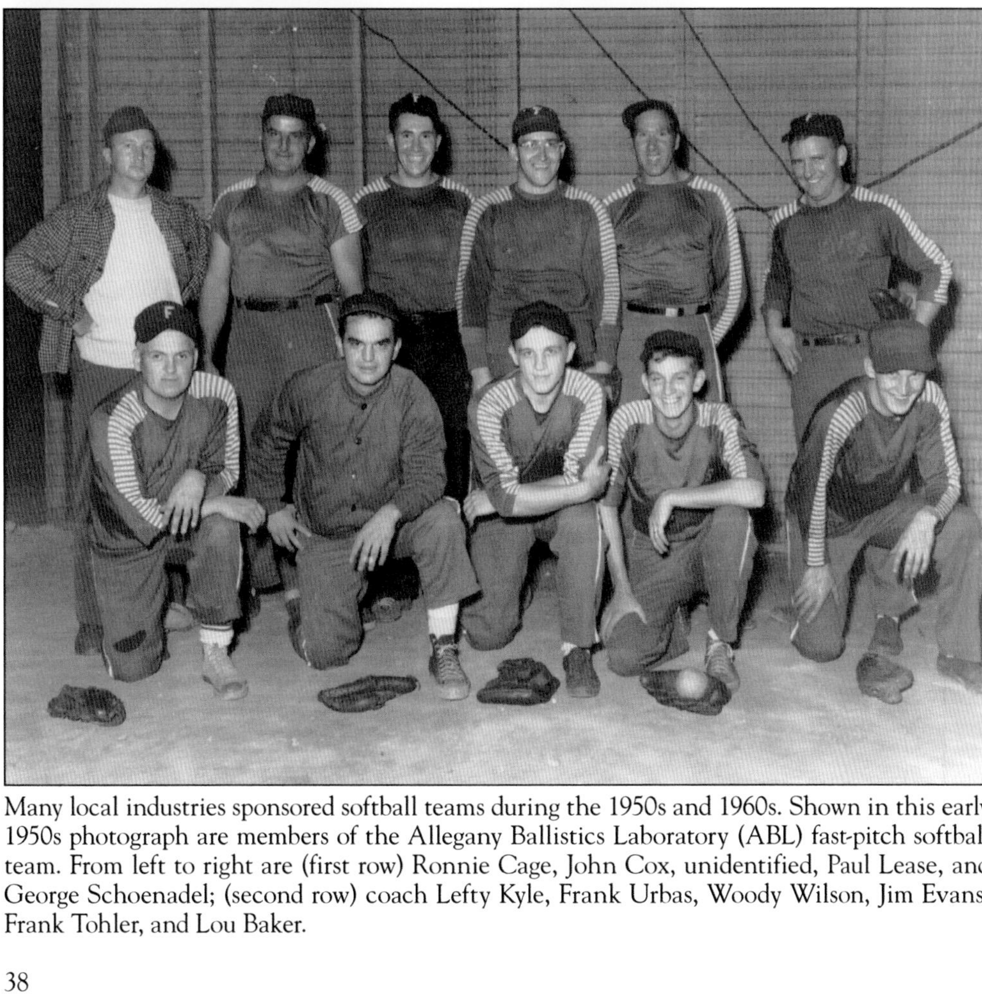

Many local industries sponsored softball teams during the 1950s and 1960s. Shown in this early 1950s photograph are members of the Allegany Ballistics Laboratory (ABL) fast-pitch softball team. From left to right are (first row) Ronnie Cage, John Cox, unidentified, Paul Lease, and George Schoenadel; (second row) coach Lefty Kyle, Frank Urbas, Woody Wilson, Jim Evans, Frank Tohler, and Lou Baker.

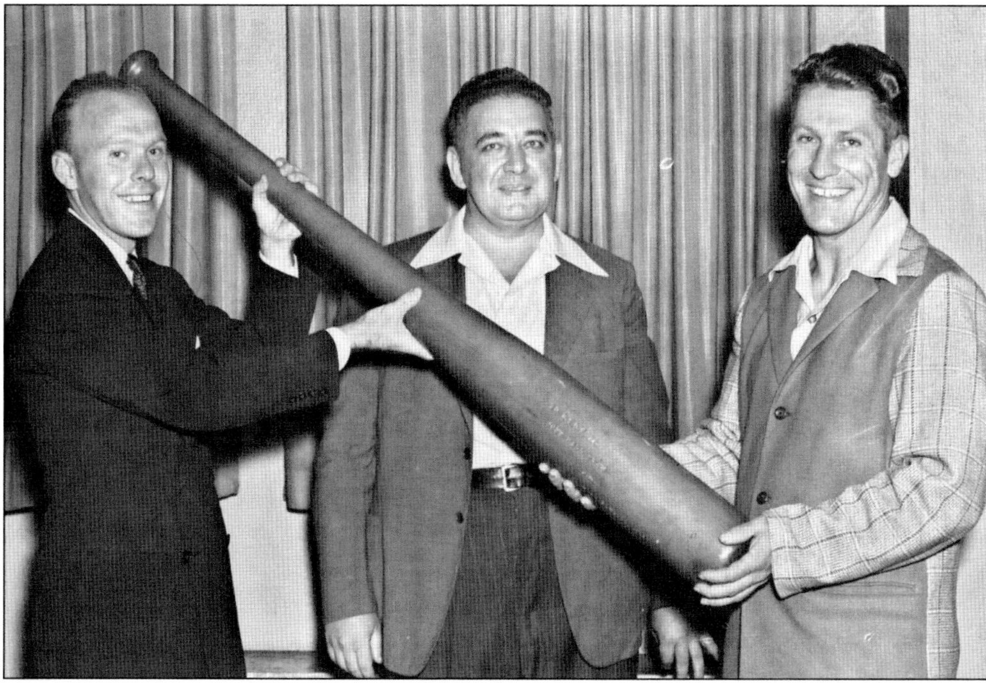

The Rocking Chair League featured fast-pitch softball games. Clifton Van Roby, left, presented the token Rocking Chair Award to "Jim Browning, right, manager of the championship Knights of Columbus team, while Lob" Brant, center, president of the league, looks on in this 1946 photograph.

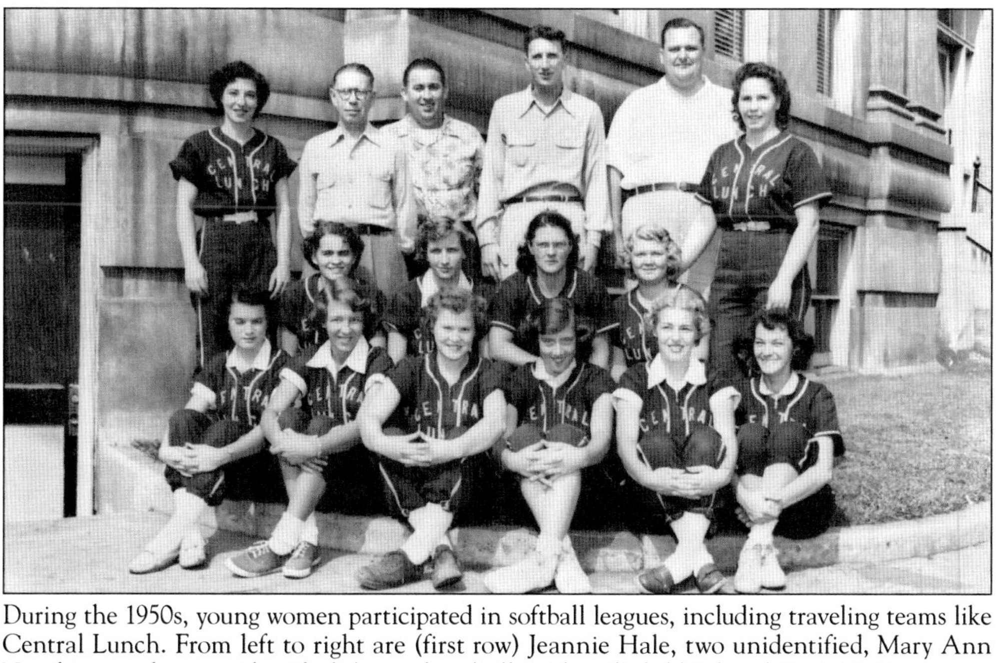

During the 1950s, young women participated in softball leagues, including traveling teams like Central Lunch. From left to right are (first row) Jeannie Hale, two unidentified, Mary Ann Naughton, and two unidentified; (second row) all unidentified; (third row) Rosie DeHaven, two unidentified, coach Gene Scaletta, Ed McGee, and Elsie McGee. The sponsor of the team was Central Lunch Restaurant, located at 71 North Centre Street.

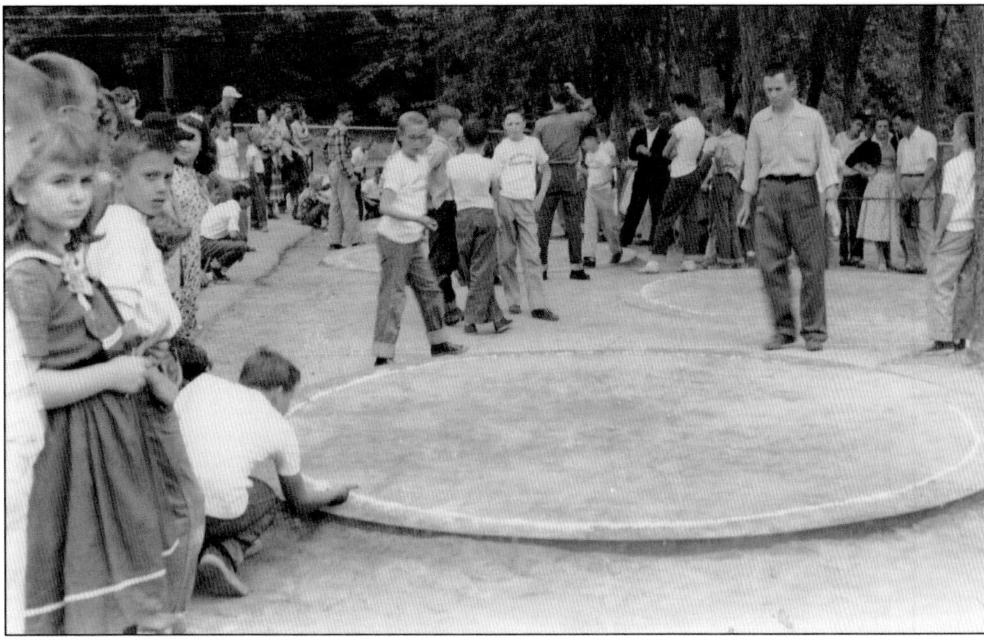

Marbles competition was a popular activity for students during the 1950s and 1960s. The championship tournaments drew spectators to Gephart School on Frederick Street. Marbles tournaments have continued and the city of Cumberland has been well-represented at the national competitions held in New Jersey.

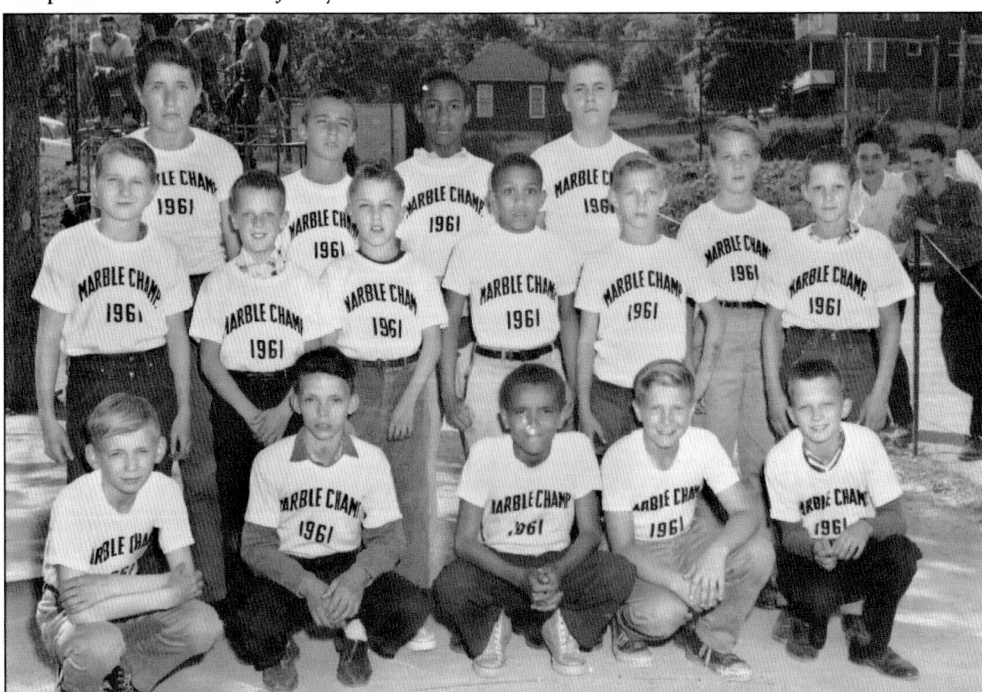

This photograph depicted elementary school winners who competed in the 1961 Allegany County championship tournament held at Gephart School on Frederick Street.

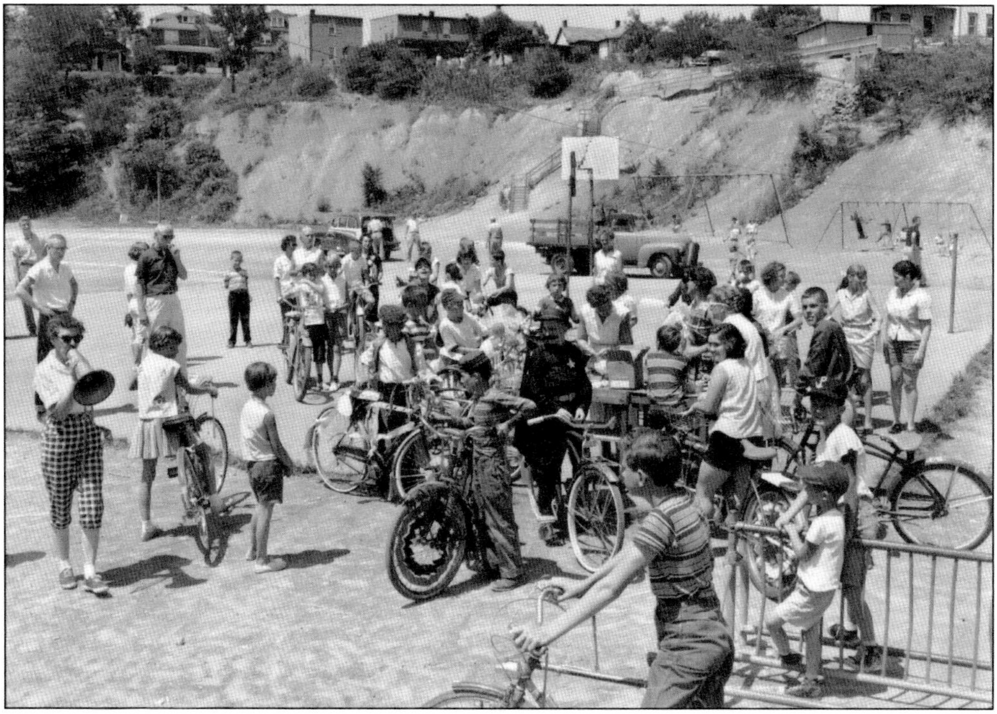

The East Side School playground hosted a variety of activities during the summer months. The playground was removed during construction of Interstate 68, but the school building remained intact. East Side School has been closed for several decades.

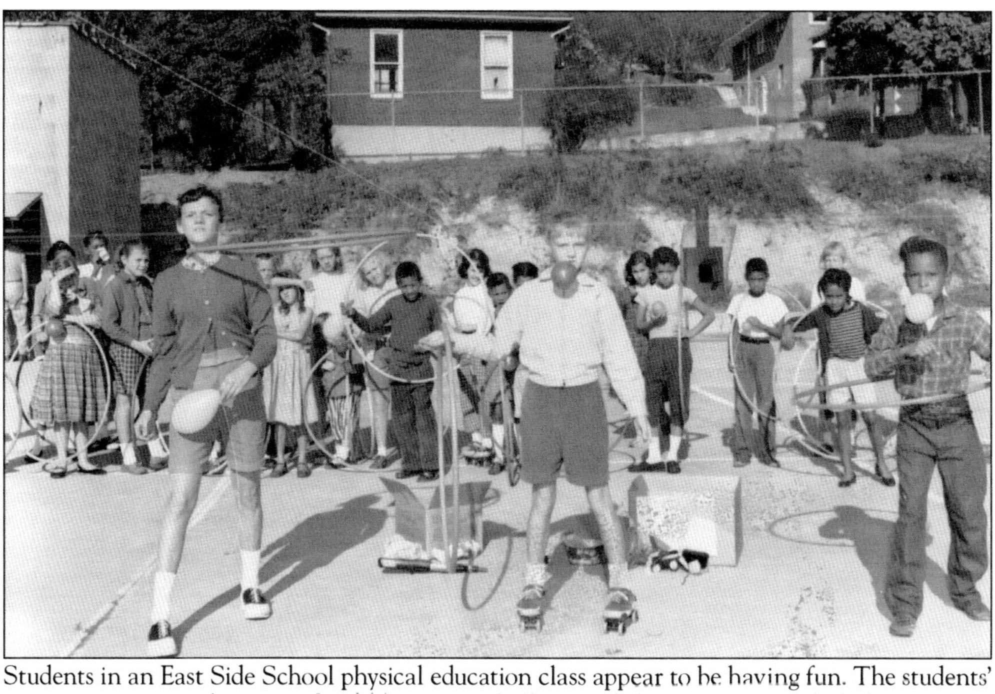

Students in an East Side School physical education class appear to be having fun. The students' activity appears to have involved blowing up balloons while maneuvering hula hoops. This photograph is from the mid-1950s.

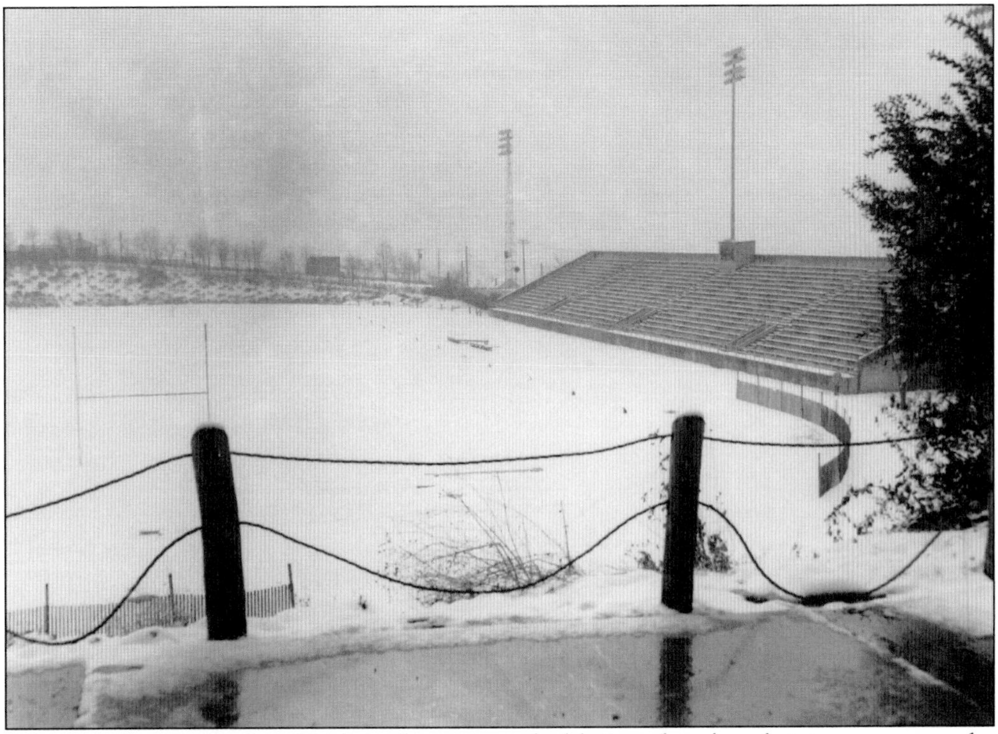

Greenway Avenue Stadium has hosted a variety of athletic, cultural, and civic events over the years. This 1950s view of the stadium will bring back memories for many area residents who participated in events at the location. The concrete bleachers were razed in 2010 for safety reasons and were later replaced.

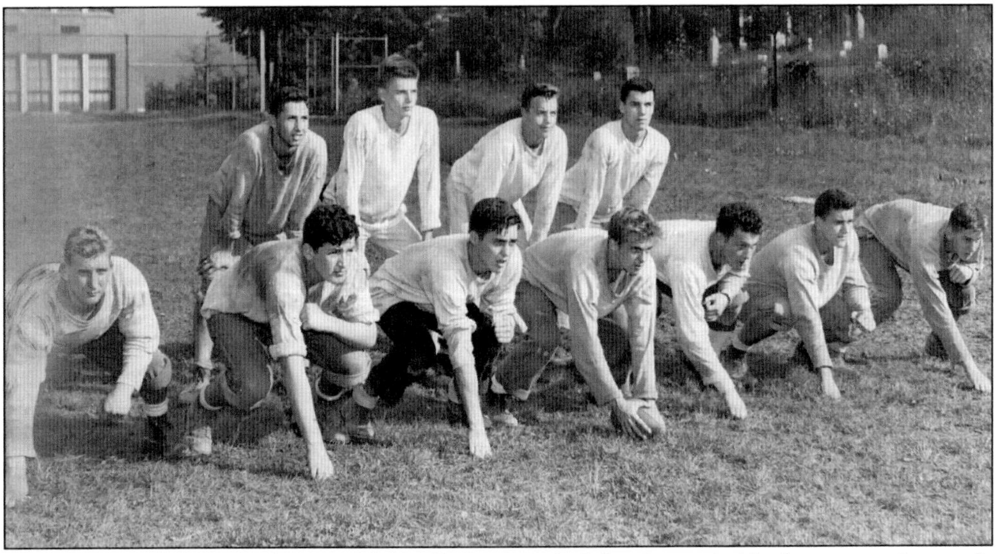

During the 1940s, football practices at Allegany High School were held adjacent to the north wing of the school. In 1959, a new gymnasium was constructed near the location of the players shown in this photograph. From left to right are (first row) Bill Bartlett, Olin Yoder, Wilburt Robinson, Burkey Smith, Linaburg Cook, Vic Awil, and Glenn Brant; (second row) Ed Strock, Bob Price, Tom Powers, and Jim Radcliff. This photograph was taken in 1946.

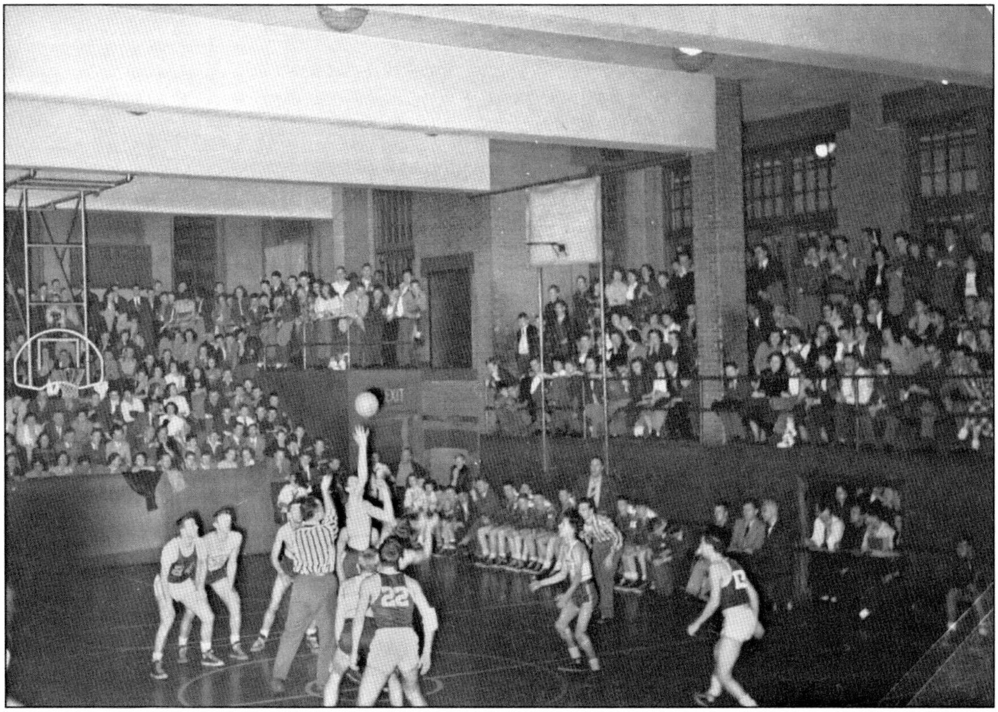

The Allegany High School gymnasium was originally located in the center of the building. The bleacher seating was close to the perimeter of the basketball court, creating dangerous conditions for the players. In 1959, a new gymnasium was constructed and the former facility became the location of the school's library.

West Virginia University basketball coach Lee Patton, right, directed an officiating clinic at the Cumberland YMCA in 1946. The clinic was arranged by Clifton Van Roby, left, director at the YMCA and a local official. Appearing with Patton was Harold "Bunny" Levitt, holding the basketball, recognized at the time as the world's free throw champion. Levitt was credited with making 490 consecutive free throws, a feat which landed him in *Ripley's Believe It or Not!*

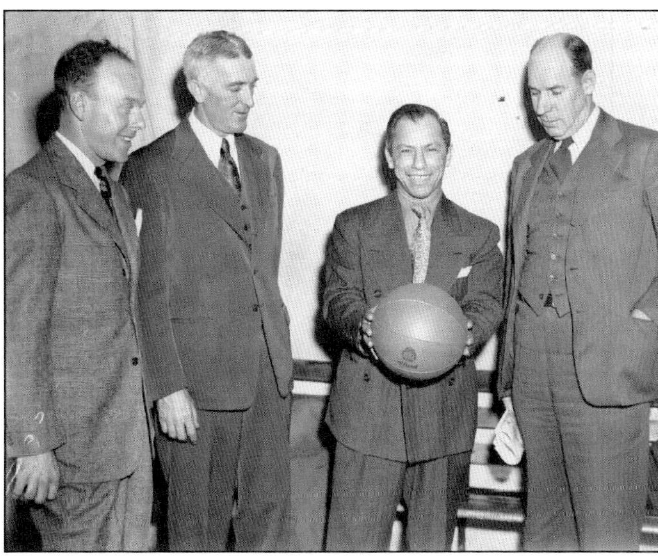

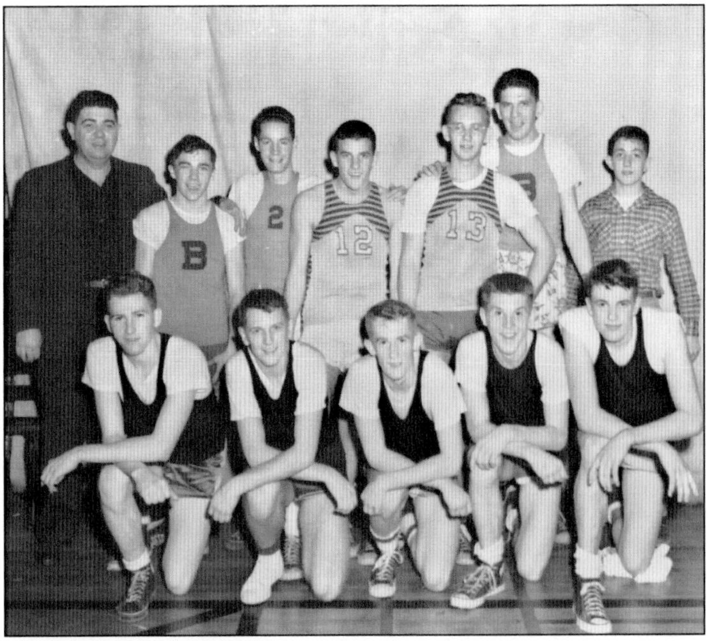

This Gold Medal Tournament basketball team around 1953 featured George's Creek players. From left to right are (first row) Bob Kirk, Gene Biggs, Peter Tomlinson, unidentified, and Ronnie Brenneman; (second row) coach Cliff Fearer, two unidentified, Mac Smith, two unidentified, and an unidentified manager. Gold Medal Tournaments were typically sponsored by local businesses and played at the YMCA in Cumberland.

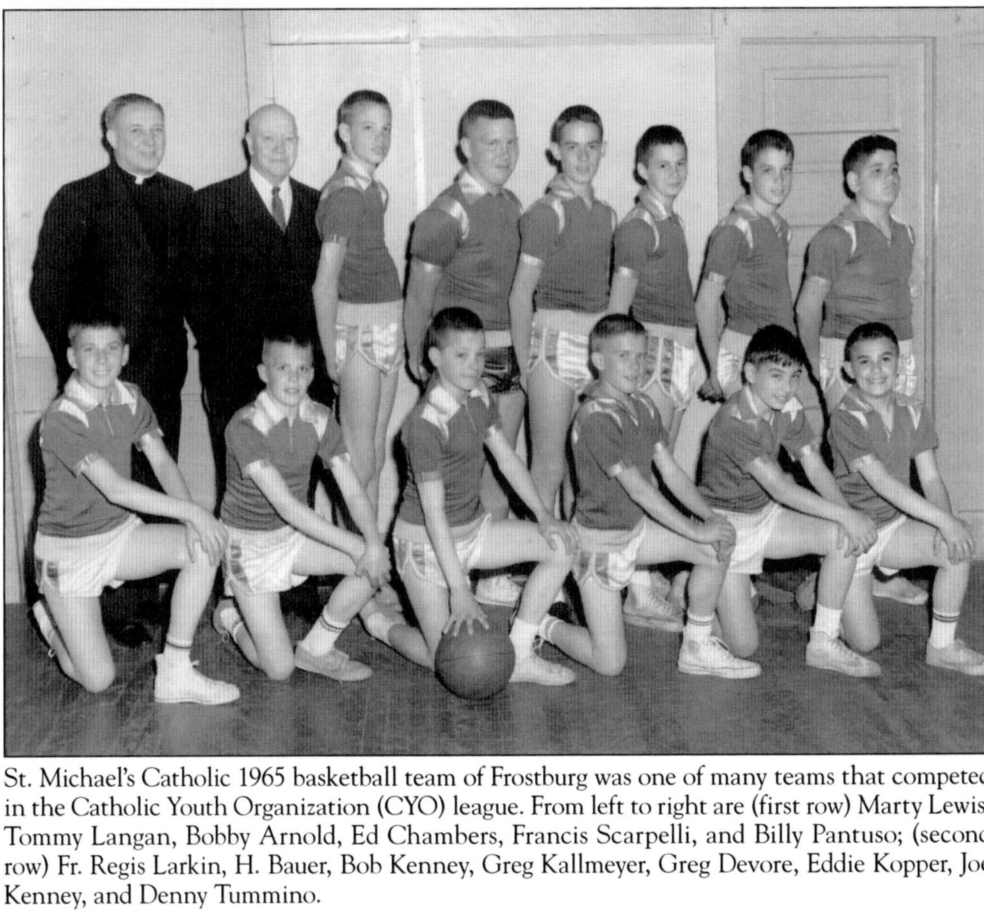

St. Michael's Catholic 1965 basketball team of Frostburg was one of many teams that competed in the Catholic Youth Organization (CYO) league. From left to right are (first row) Marty Lewis, Tommy Langan, Bobby Arnold, Ed Chambers, Francis Scarpelli, and Billy Pantuso; (second row) Fr. Regis Larkin, H. Bauer, Bob Kenney, Greg Kallmeyer, Greg Devore, Eddie Kopper, Joe Kenney, and Denny Tummino.

Holy Cross's basketball team won the Sunday School League championship in March 1966.

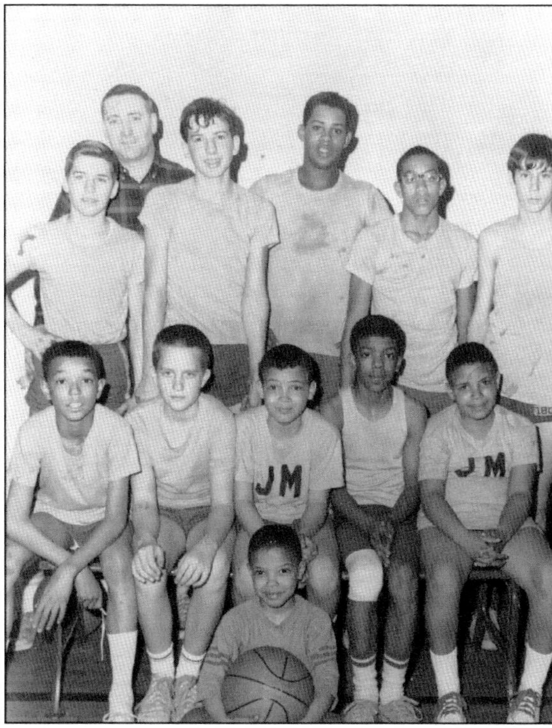

Charles Washington, left, of Cumberland, successfully landed a blow to his opponent in a 1958 bout. Washington registered in the lightweight class. Amateur boxing enjoyed popularity in the immediate post–World War II era. After a brief hiatus, boxing resumed in the mid-1950s under the sponsorship of the local Police Boys Club, which organized its activities at 38 North Mechanic Street.

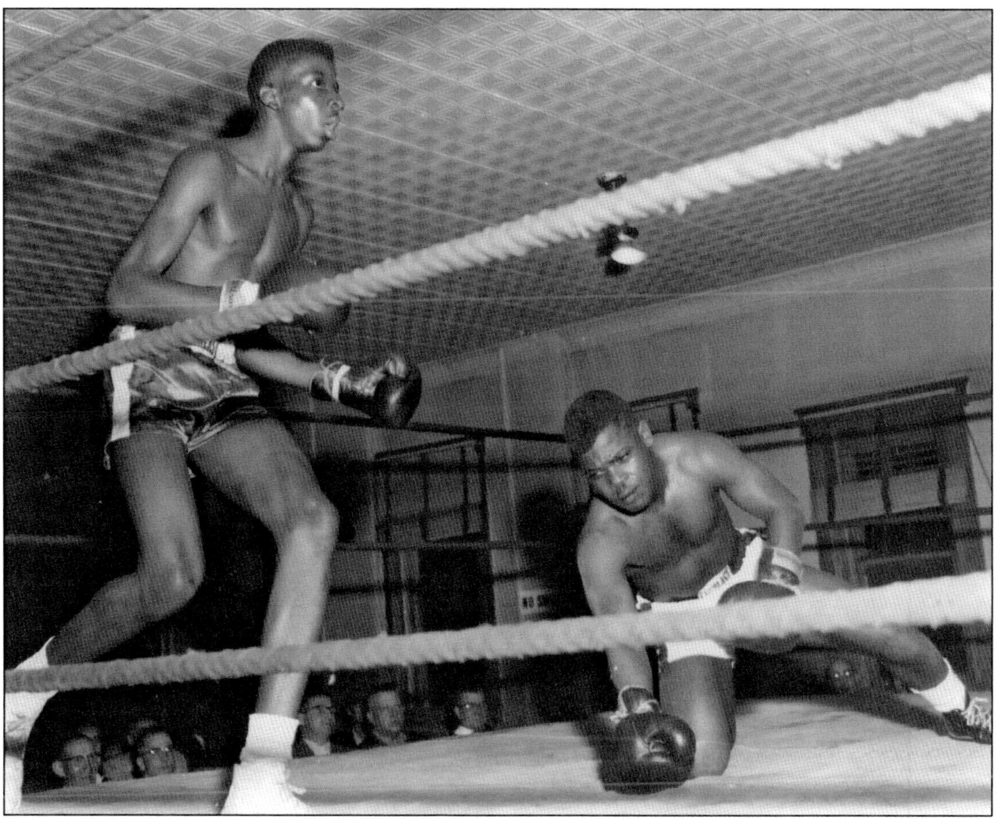

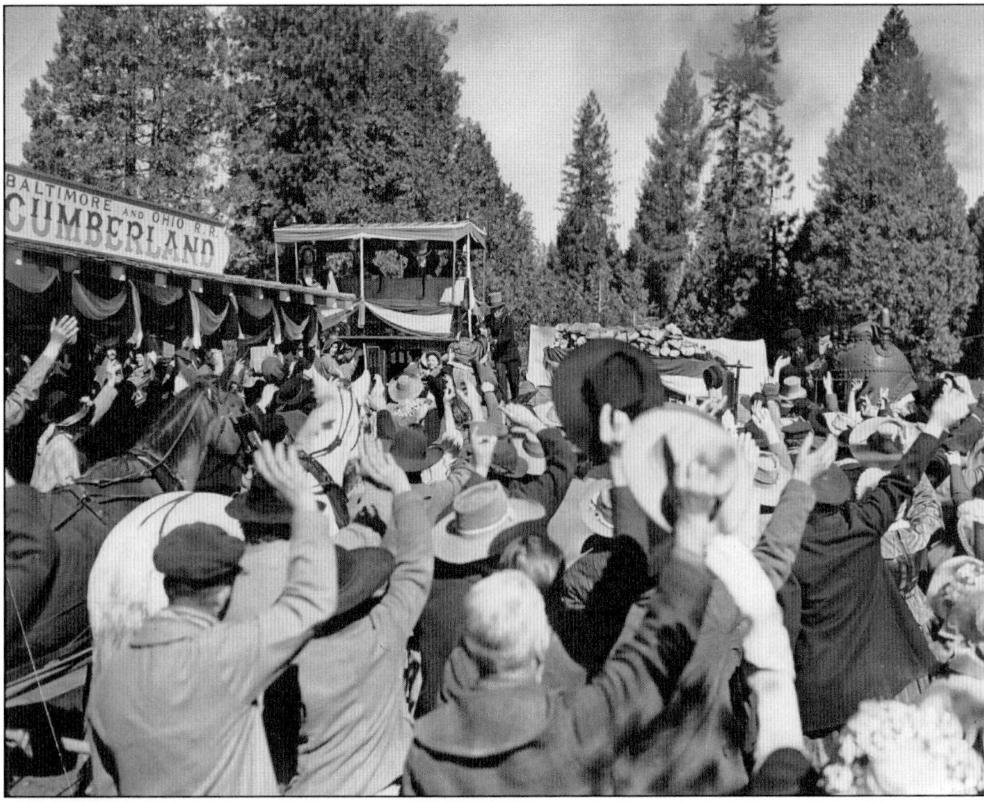

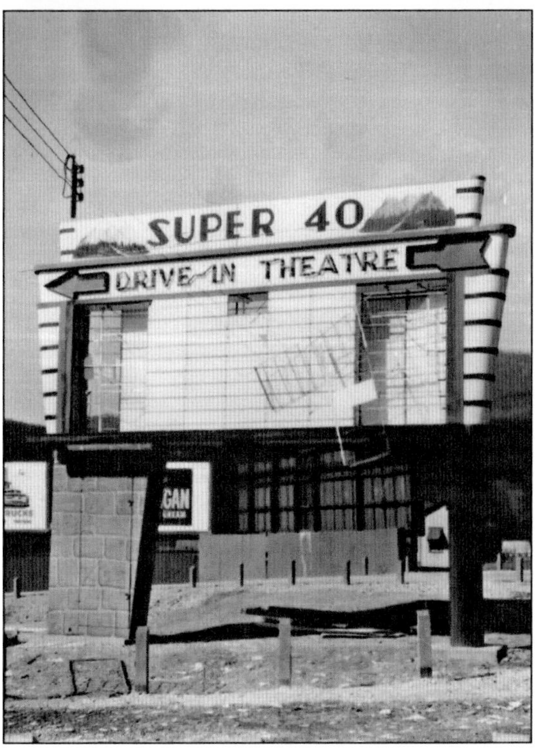

In January 1939, thousands of county residents witnessed a Baltimore and Ohio Railroad steam locomotive racing a four-horse stagecoach along Henderson Boulevard. The race was arranged through the cooperative efforts of the Allegany County Chamber of Commerce and Metro-Goldwyn-Mayer. The studio's *Stand Up and Fight* (1939) reproduced the competition between the stagecoach and an iron horse a century earlier. This 1939 promotional photograph was not taken in Cumberland.

This photographer was apparently interested in documenting damage to the sign at the Super 40 Drive-In. Located adjacent to the Super 40 was the Crystal Drive-In. The Super 40 opened in 1951, followed by the Crystal in August 1952. The drive-ins operated at the present-day locations of Wendy's, CVS Pharmacy, Staples, and McDonald's along U.S. Route 40 in LaVale.

The Potomac Drive-In operated along Winchester Road at the present-day location of the Maryland Vehicle Administration. In the pamphlet at right, *Ma and Pa Kettle Go to Town*, *Tarzan Triumphs*, and Ginger Rogers and Dennis Morgan in *Perfect Strangers* were coming attractions. The 50¢ admission included a "kiddies' playground," modern snack bar, and car service.

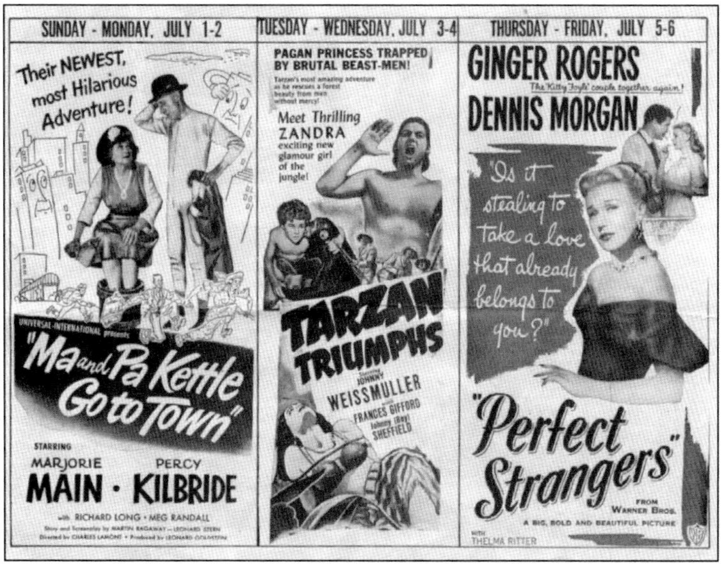

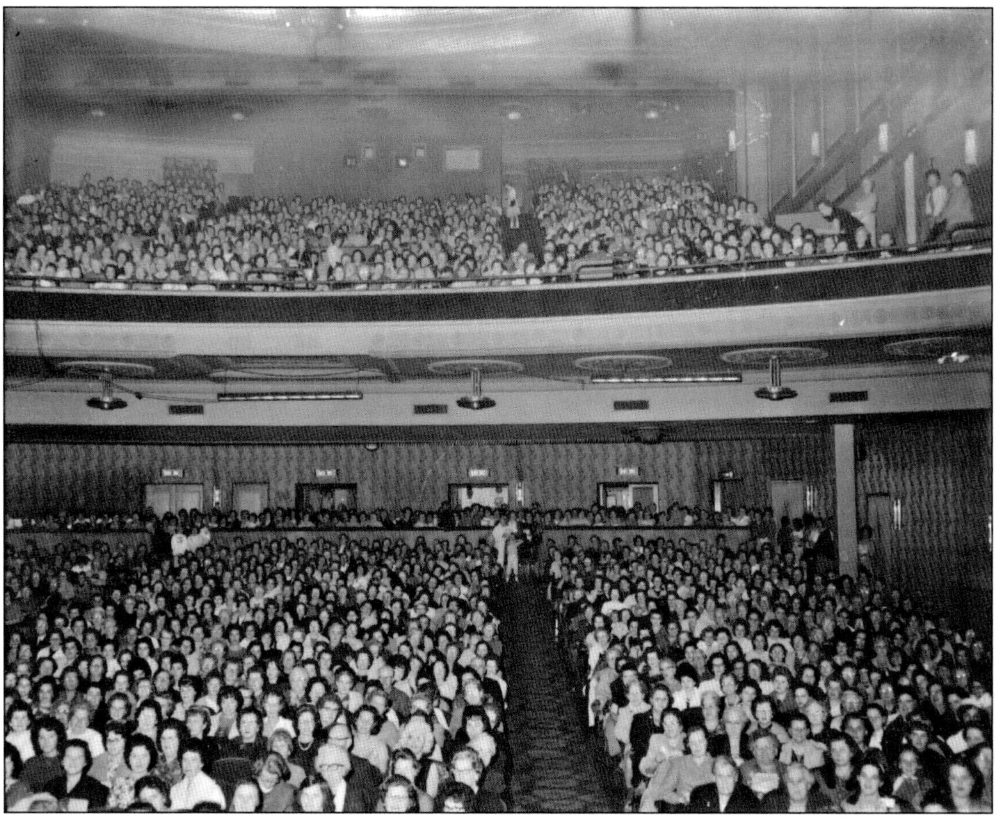

The Strand Theatre opened September 3, 1920, to a full house of 2,000 patrons. The theater hosted local and national stage performances, nationally known musicians, and first-run movies. Competition from television caused a decline in patronage and the eventual closing of the theater in 1972. Strand patrons in this photograph were participating in the popular Cooking School, which attracted sellout crowds during the 1950s.

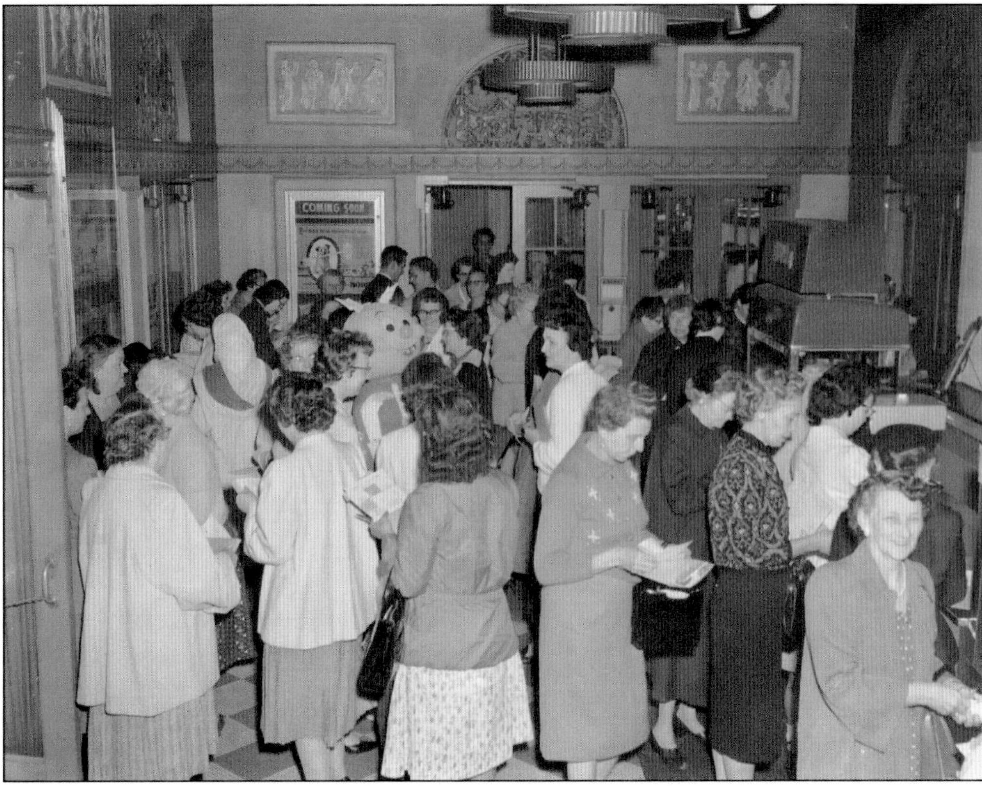

Women filled the lobby of the Strand for the Cooking School program. To be noted were the elaborate classical reliefs decorating the lobby. During the last years of the theater, the motifs' features were diminished by workers painting over them.

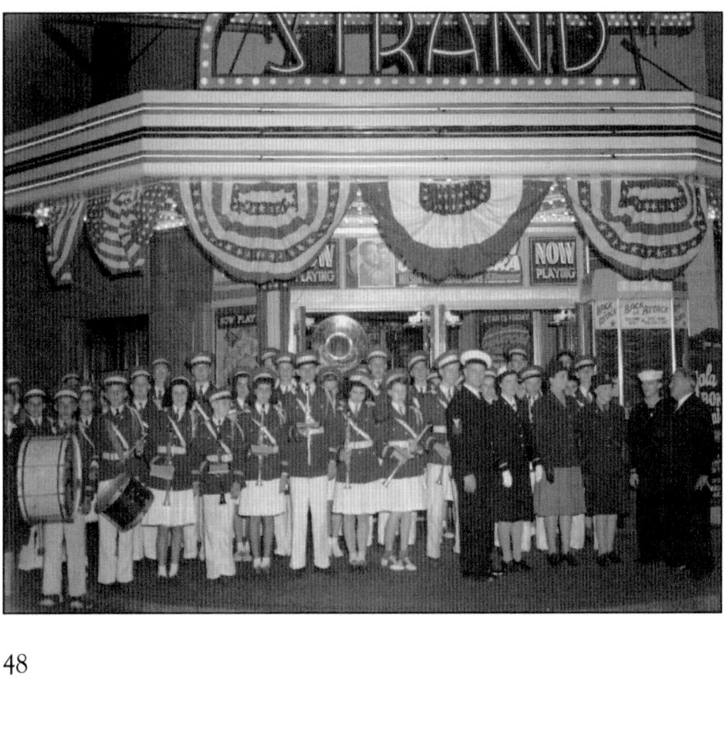

The Strand Theatre featured patriotic performances, movies, and special events during World War II, including U.S. war bond drives. The Allegany High School Band, under the direction of Dorothy Willison, performed at this 1944 event.

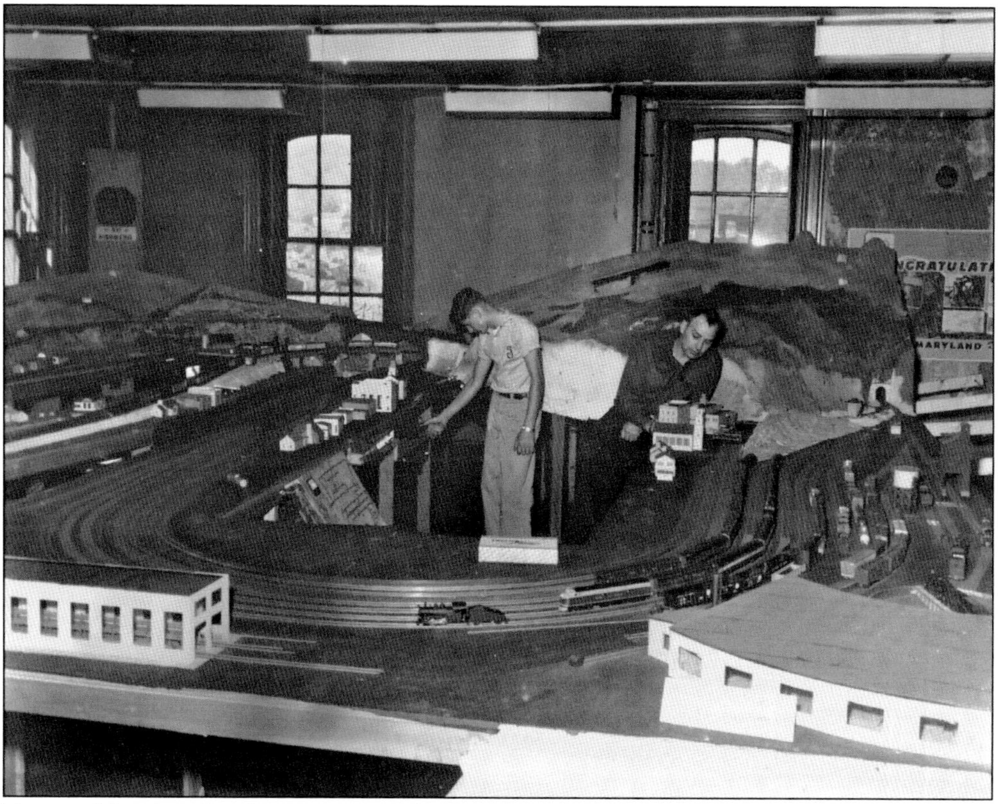

Two model railroad enthusiasts enjoyed operating two-rail, O-gauge trains on the top floor of Queen City Station during the 1950s. Many rooms of the Queen City Hotel and Station were taken out of service during the 1950s and 1960s.

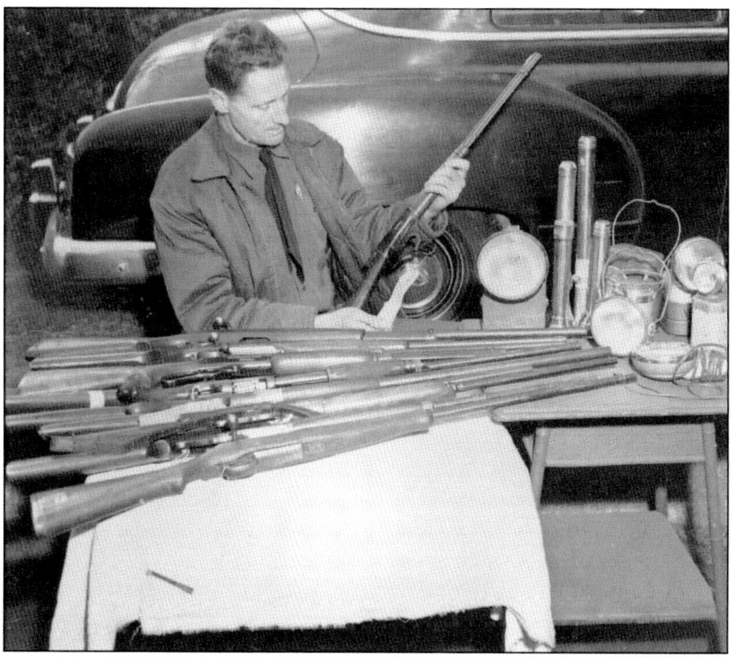

Well-known regional game warden Joseph Minke apparently encountered "spot lighters," as suggested by the cache of weapons and flashlights. Minke conducted educational programs for elementary school students in addition to his outdoor regulatory duties. He retired in 1966 after 40 years of service with the state of Maryland.

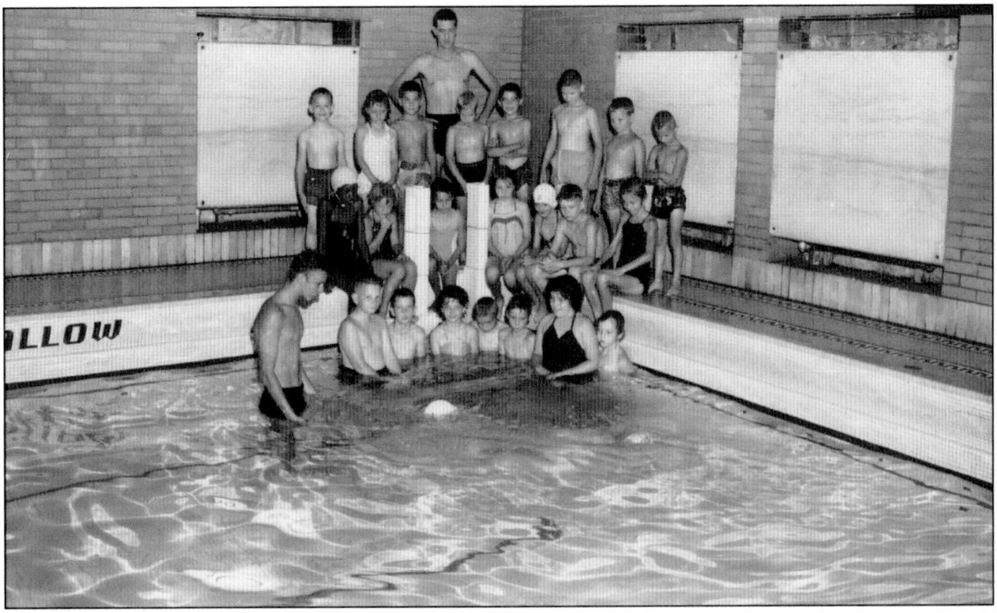

Swimming and lifeguarding classes were regularly scheduled programs at the Young Men's Christian Association (YMCA) facility on Baltimore Avenue in Cumberland. Saturday events were especially well attended by elementary students.

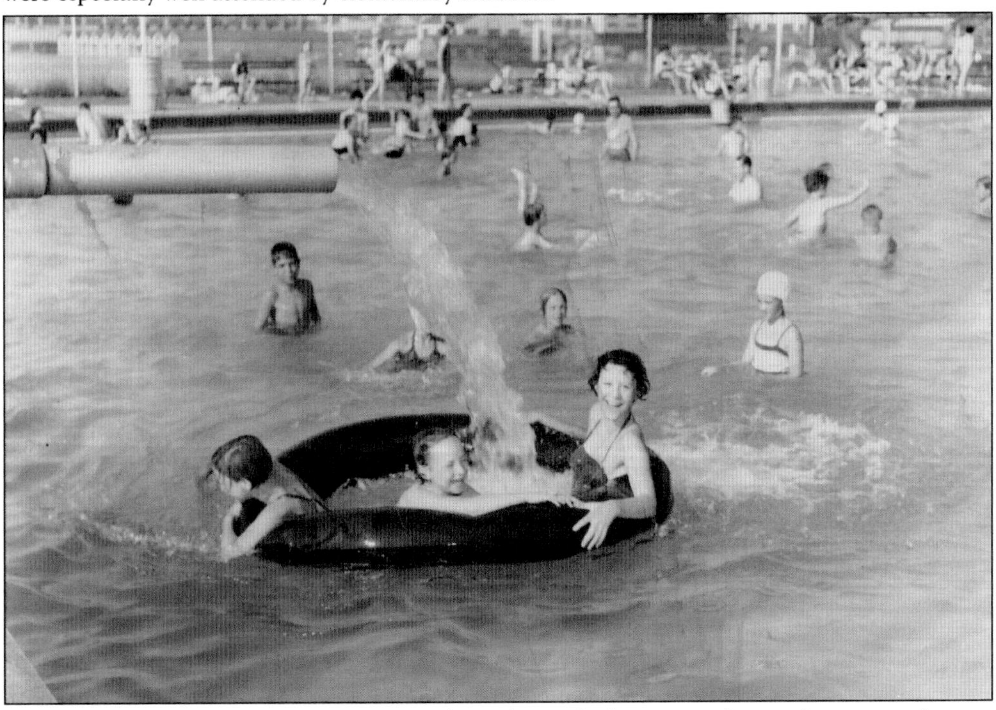

The Celanese Corporation swimming pool was located adjacent to the synthetic yarn factory, along U.S. Route 220 in Cresaptown. While Celanese Corporation employees contributed financially to the pool's construction and maintenance, it was open to the general public for a nominal admission fee. Large crowds gathered at the pool and picnic grounds, making it one of the most popular summertime attractions in the county.

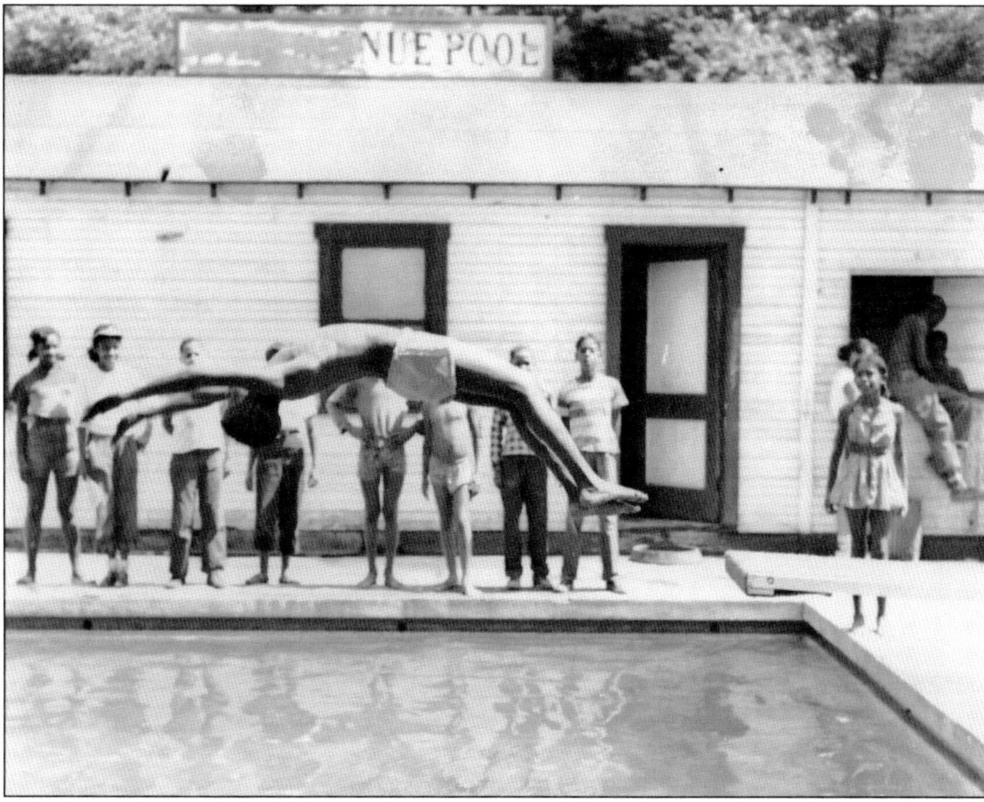

Allegany County experienced racial discrimination that restricted African Americans from gaining admission to public venues, including swimming pools and playgrounds. The Pine Avenue Playground included a swimming pool that was built by residents for the enjoyment of all races and ethnicities. The playground also hosted an active summer playground program. After Constitution Park and other swimming pools integrated, the Pine Avenue pool was closed and backfilled.

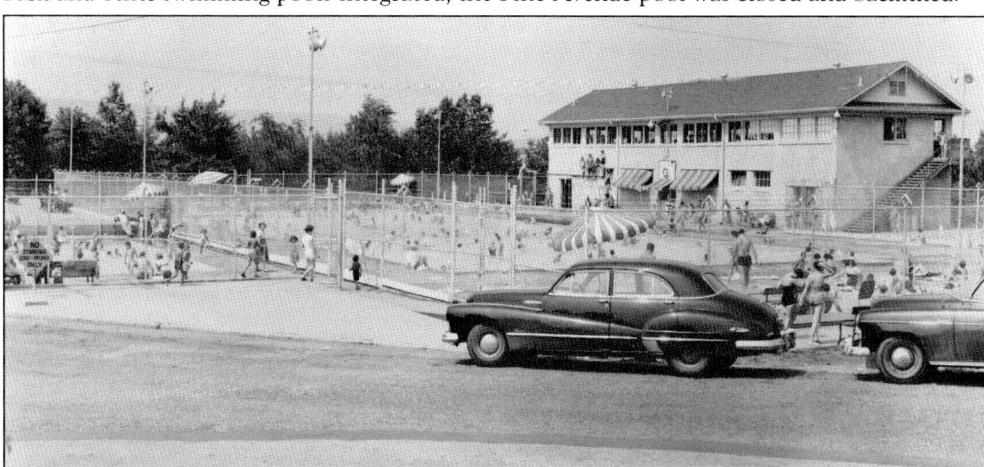

The most noted Works Progress Administration (WPA) project in the city of Cumberland was Constitution Park. Most work was completed by using hand tools, including picks, shovels, and rakes. In addition to the swimming pool shown in this photograph, wooden benches, fish ponds, deer and bear pens, and pavilions were erected. The park opened on June 25, 1939.

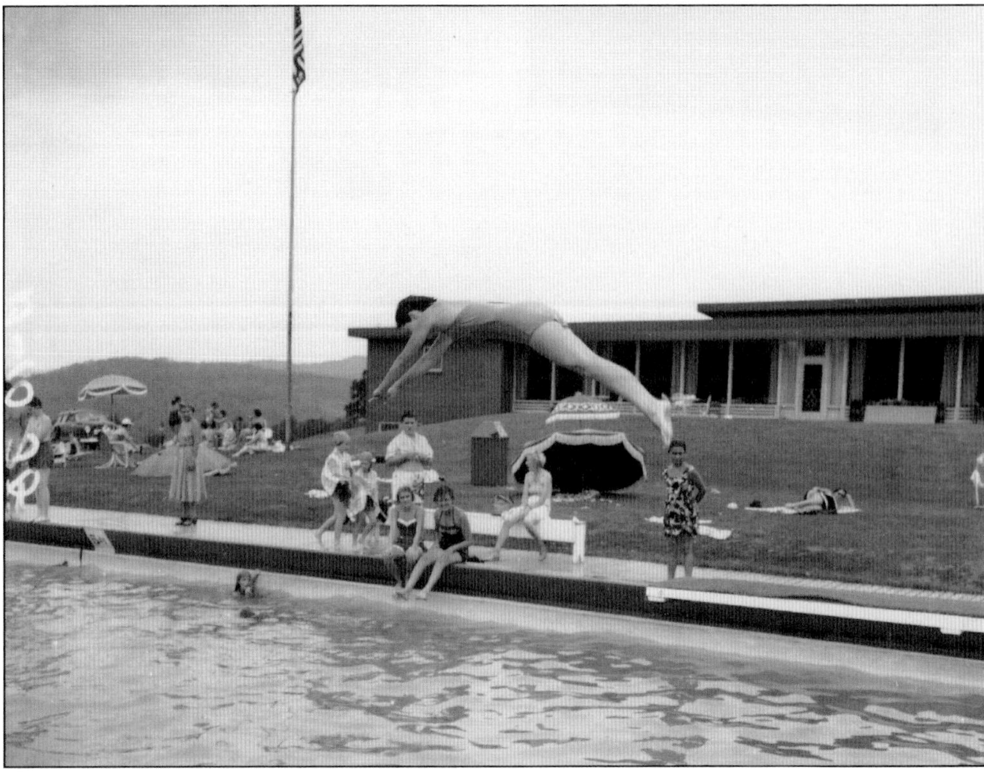

This photograph of the Cumberland Country Club swimming pool was taken around 1960.

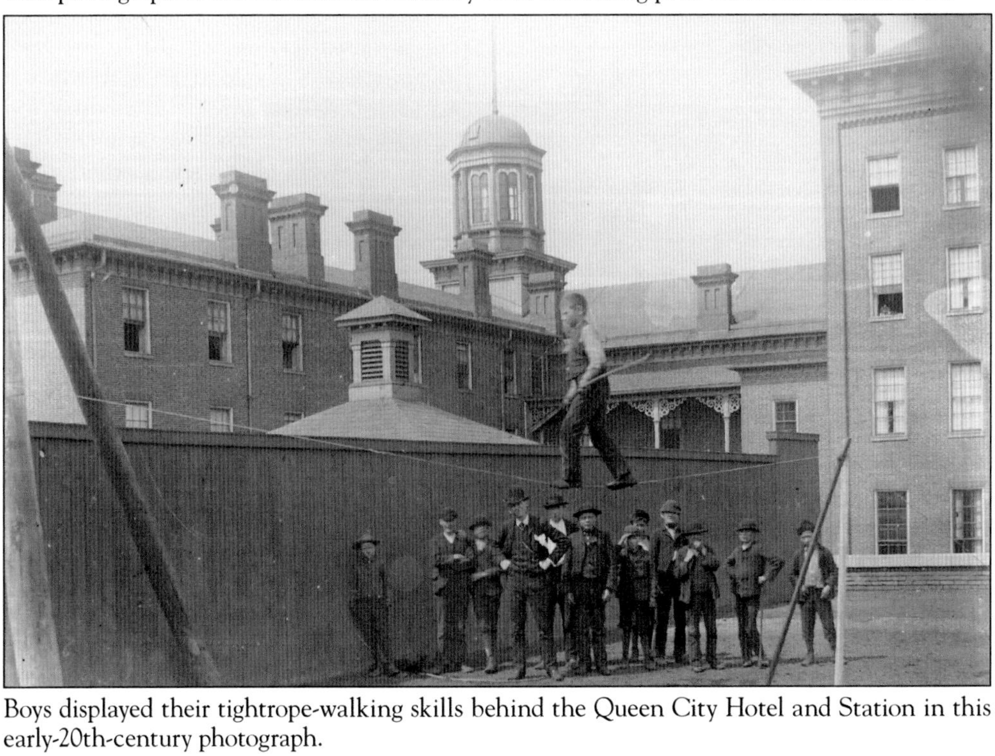

Boys displayed their tightrope-walking skills behind the Queen City Hotel and Station in this early-20th-century photograph.

Three

TRANSPORTATION

Transportation advantages were the primary reasons for the commercial development of Allegany County in the 18th and early 19th centuries. A water gap known as the Cumberland Narrows, abundant natural resources, and laborers imbued with an entrepreneurial spirit combined to make Allegany County a major transportation center.

When British general Edward Braddock was dispatched to Fort Cumberland in 1755, he quickly learned that transporting military equipment across Haystack Mountain was difficult and dangerous. One of Braddock's officers was credited with recommending an alternative route through a nearby water gap that became known as the Cumberland Narrows. The new road facilitated the movement of British troops during the French and Indian War (1756–1763), but within a short period of time the military purposes of the road diminished. Hardy pioneers, traders, and settlers continued to use the convenient passage on their way west.

The Cumberland Narrows proved to be valuable once again in 1833 when the National Highway was rerouted from Haystack Mountain to the road originally blazed by Braddock's men. The increased flow of traffic brought about by America's first federally funded highway caused Cumberland to be known as the "Gateway to the West."

The discovery of iron ore, fire clay, and coal deposits in Allegany County initiated an industrial boom in the 19th century. Railroads and the Chesapeake and Ohio Canal made their way from eastern metropolitan centers to access the rich natural resources of western Maryland. The Baltimore and Ohio Railroad's arrival into Cumberland in 1842 was especially significant because it allowed for the establishment of a luxurious hotel, passenger station, roundhouse, and repair facilities that employed hundreds of workers. The Cumberland and Pennsylvania Railroad, West Virginia Central Railroad, George's Creek Railroad, George's Creek and Cumberland Railroad, Pennsylvania Railroad, and the Western Maryland Railway also established facilities and services in the county.

During the 1920s, U.S. Routes 220 and 40 intersected in Allegany County. Both highways ran through downtown Cumberland before diverging to the southwest and west respectively. Construction of a federally funded highway through Cumberland during the 1960s, later designated as Interstate 68, improved the county's transportation system.

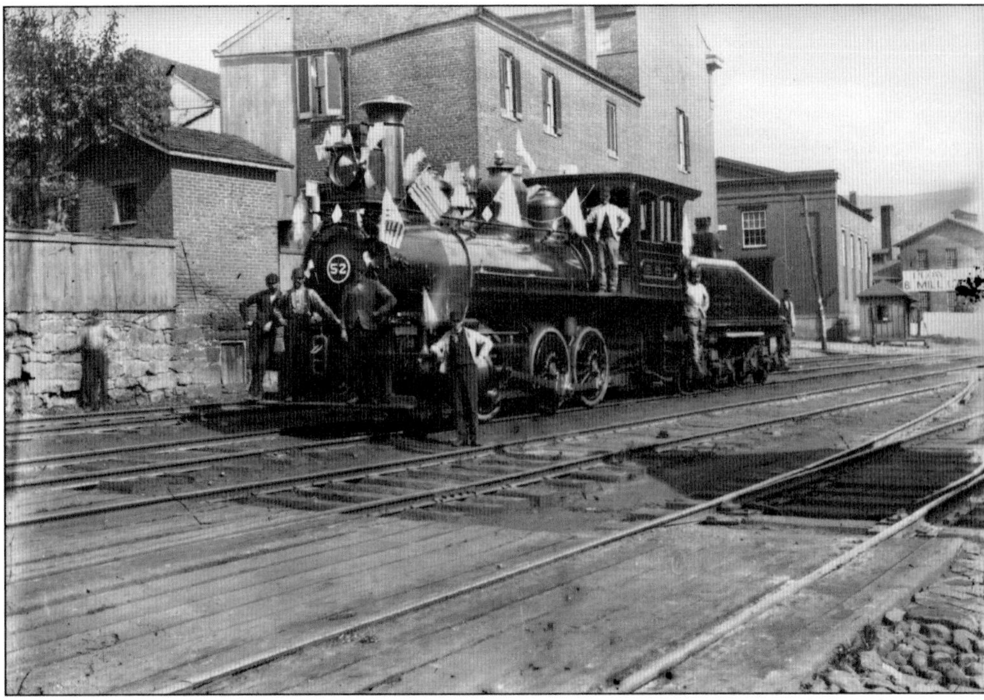

A crew of the 4-4-0 Baltimore and Ohio Railroad Winan proudly decorated their locomotive for a special event. The Winan locomotive was rare; the one shown in this photograph, named "Juno," was built in 1848, rebuilt in 1856, and retired by 1881. The 1856 rebuild included a new cab. This photographer captured the image on the Baltimore and Ohio Railroad tracks near Frederick and Bedford Streets.

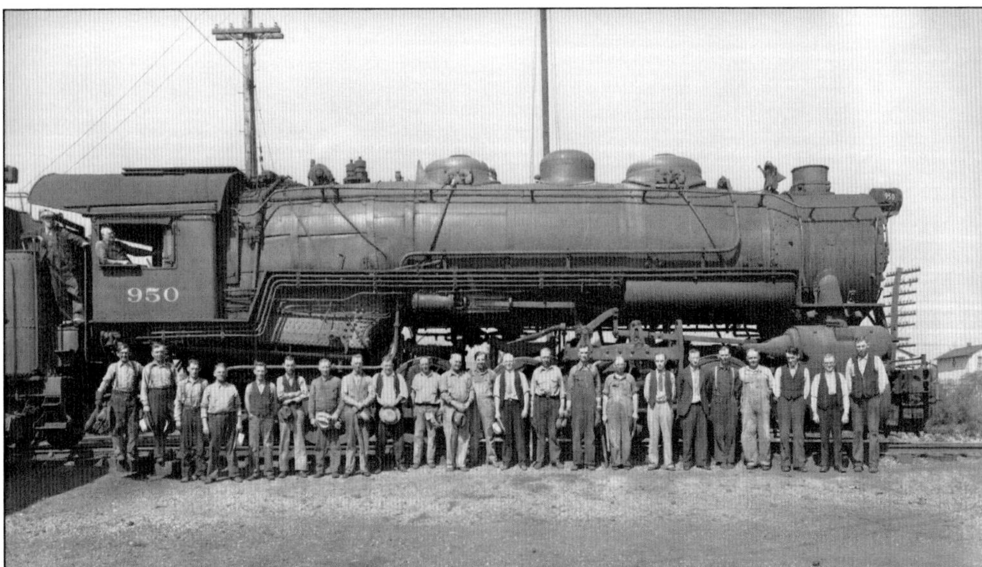

The Baltimore and Ohio Railroad locomotive shown in this photograph was built by Baldwin in 1914 and was later rebuilt and renumbered; it was the most powerful non-articulated steam engine in the United States. The engine saw limited service in Cumberland. This photograph is from the mid-1920s.

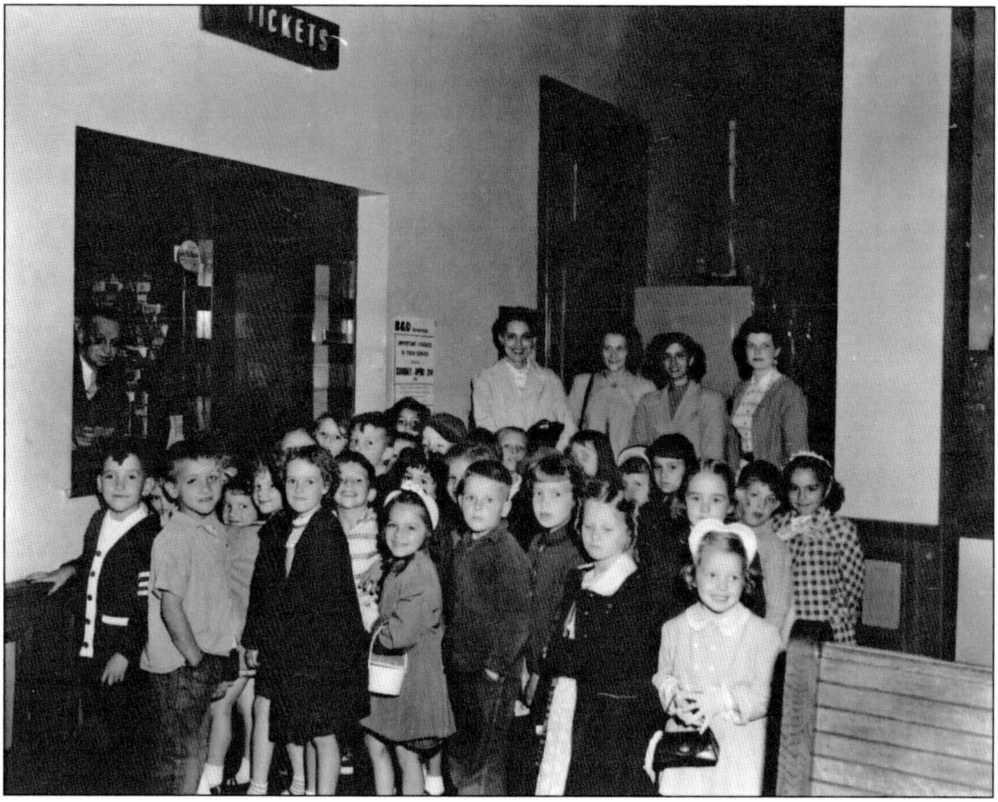

It appeared that students and teachers experienced a busy day at the Queen City Station. Ticket agent Ralph Smith assisted students as they awaited the passenger train's arrival. This photograph also provided an interior view of the station operated by the Baltimore and Ohio Railroad.

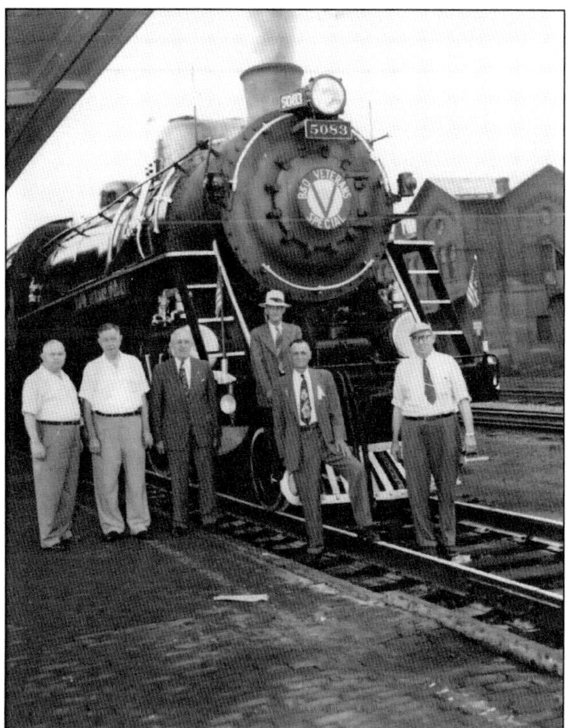

On August 3, 1949, the Baltimore and Ohio Railroad ran a special train from Cumberland to Oakland for the purpose of recognizing military veterans. The train was headed by a 4-6-2 presidential-class Pacific locomotive. More than 500 people attended the train's arrival and related festivities.

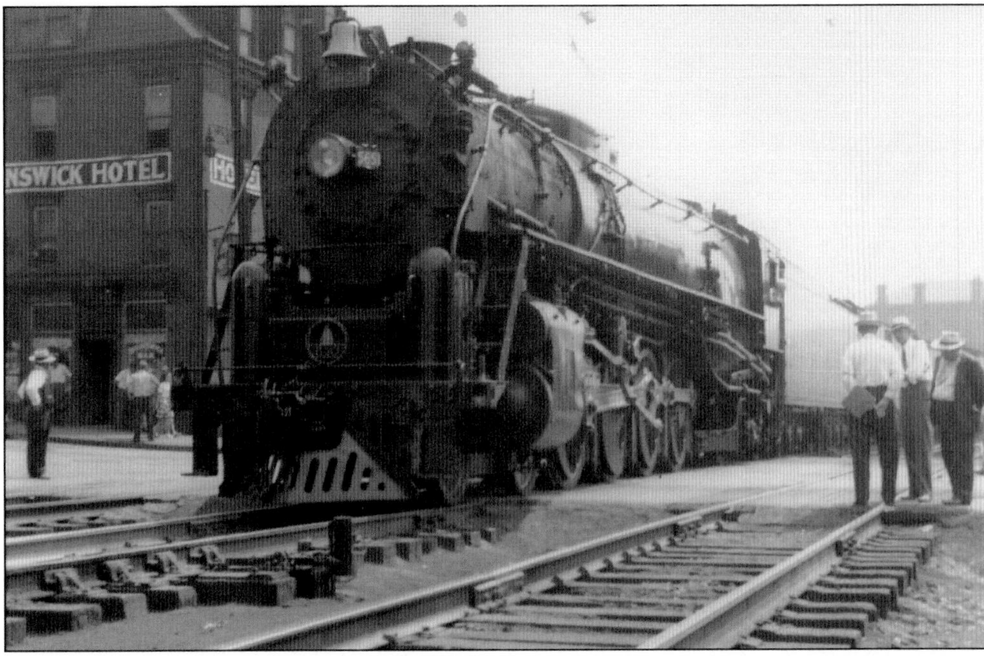

A Baltimore and Ohio Railroad steam locomotive awaited a green signal at the Baltimore Street crossing. The 4-8-2 locomotive was purchased from the Boston and Maine Railroad around 1950. The Brunswick Hotel, shown in the background, was built in 1886 and catered to railroad workers and travelers.

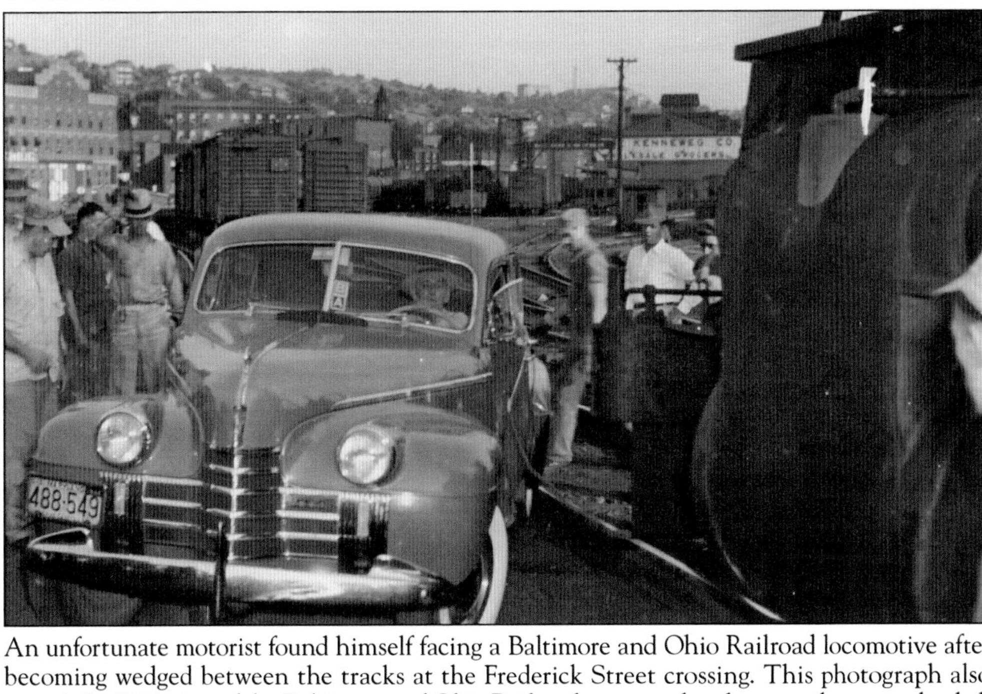

An unfortunate motorist found himself facing a Baltimore and Ohio Railroad locomotive after becoming wedged between the tracks at the Frederick Street crossing. This photograph also provided a 1944 view of the Baltimore and Ohio Railroad team tracks where goods were unloaded. The team tracks and related facilities were removed during the development of an urban renewal project that led to the opening of Gee Bee's Department Store in 1973.

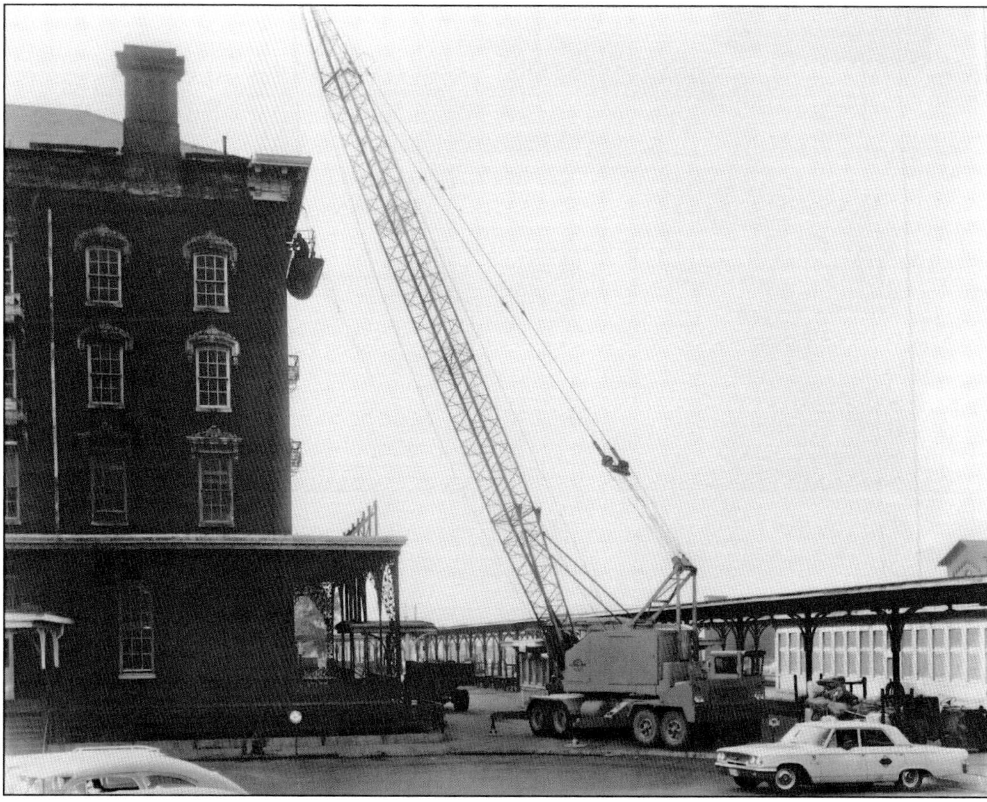

Allegany County's railroad heritage is associated with the Queen City Hotel and Station, an Italianate-style building constructed in 1871–1872. Declining rail passenger service, caused by an increased use of automobiles for long-distance travel, led to the piecemeal closing of the hotel during the 1920s. The Baltimore and Ohio Railroad closed the ticket station and began demolition of the landmark building in the fall of 1971, as shown in this photograph.

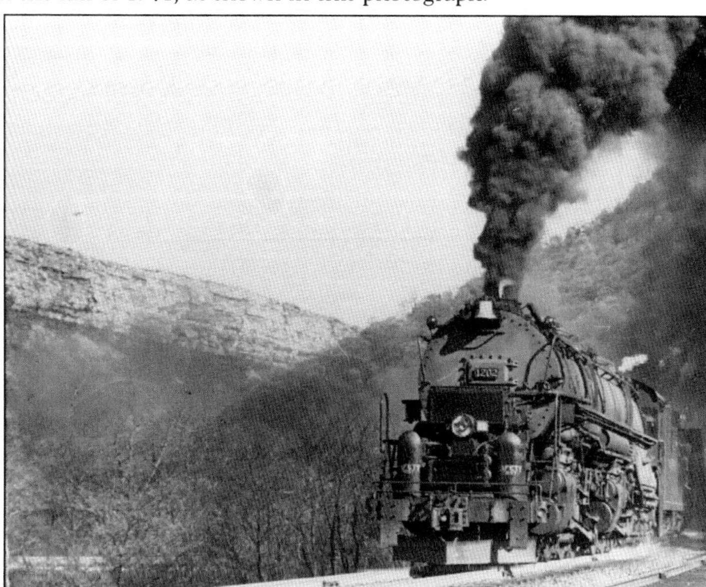

In this classic railroading scene, Western Maryland Railway Locomotive No. 1202 headed west toward Frostburg after crossing the Cumberland Narrows Bridge. The powerful Challenger locomotive made its way up Big Savage Mountain before crossing the state line into Pennsylvania.

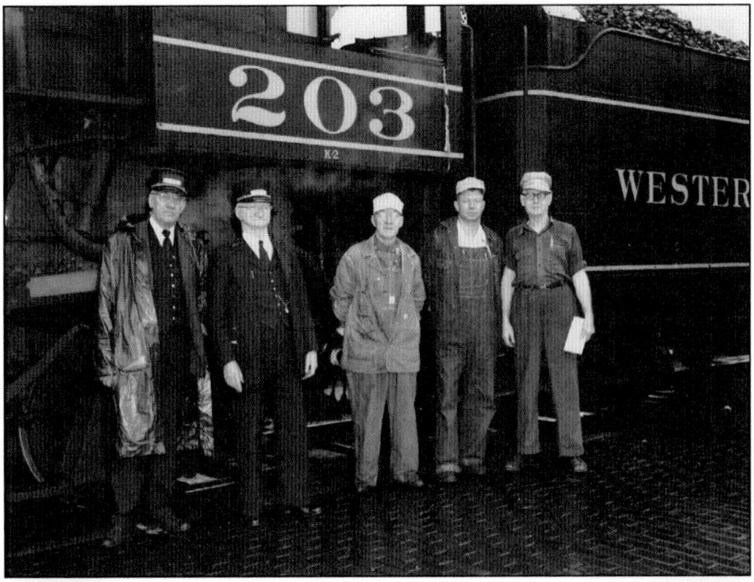

The crew of the Western Maryland Railway No. 203, a Pacific-class locomotive, carefully monitored time near the Western Maryland Railway Station in Cumberland.

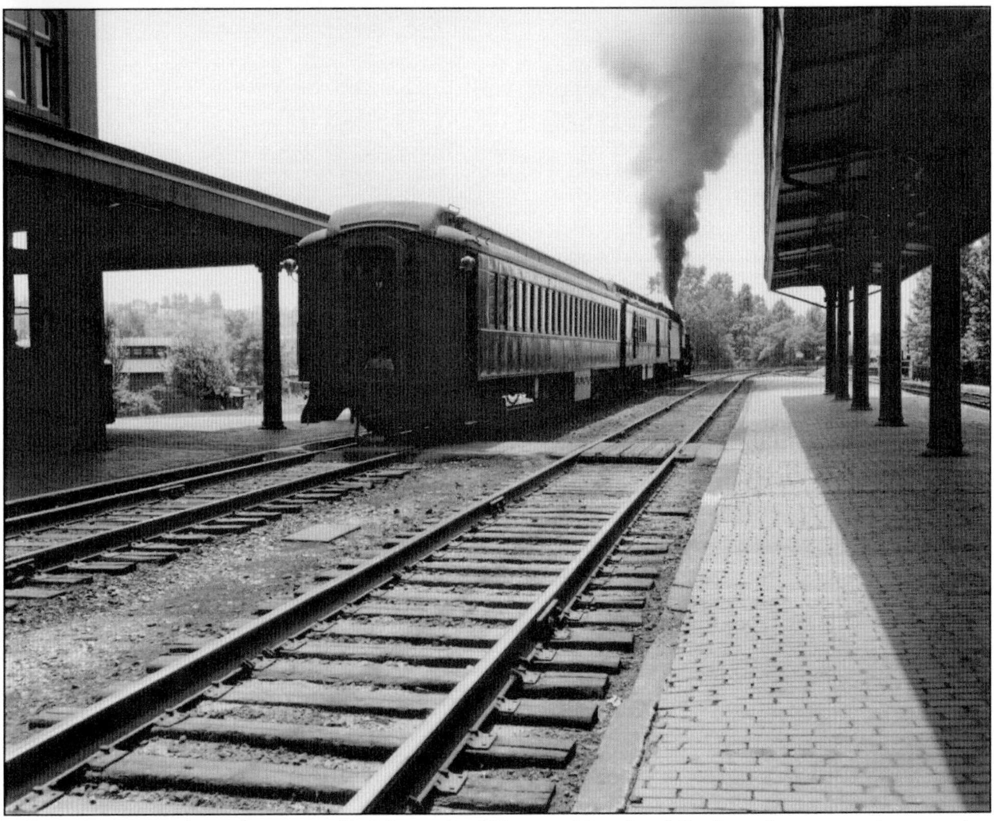

A baggage car and coach were pulled from the Western Maryland Railway by a steam locomotive on a summer day. The railroad offered passenger service by steam motive power until 1953 and then diesel power until 1958. The Western Maryland Railway Station, shown in this photograph, was built in 1913 and remained in operation until 1976. Today the station is under the direction of the Canal Place Authority.

Only longtime residents recall the watchmen and their shelters, called "shanties," that were located at all major railroad crossings in Cumberland. Each shanty, approximately 6 feet wide and 8 feet tall, provided protection during inclement weather. Note the railroad lanterns on the shelf behind the watchman. This shanty was located at the Western Maryland Railway crossing on Baltimore Street, around 1962.

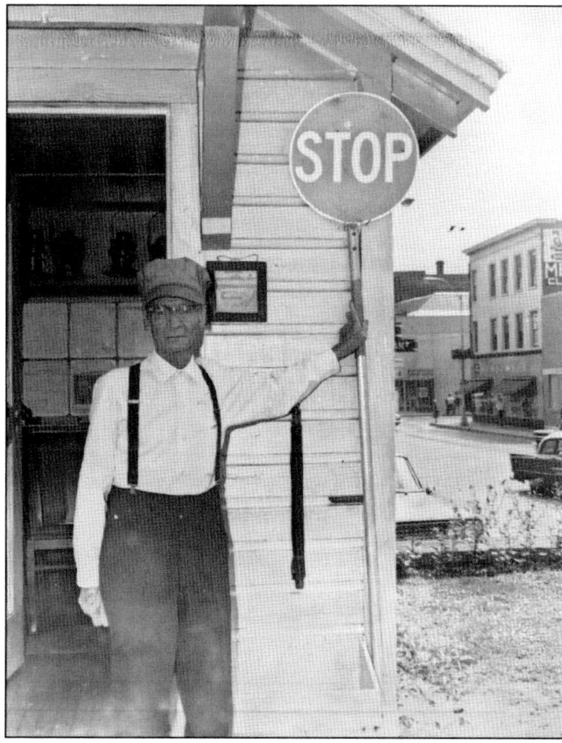

The Cumberland and Pennsylvania Railroad had become history by the time of this *c.* 1955 photograph showing the Mount Savage shops. Acquired by the Western Maryland Railway in 1944, the Cumberland and Pennsylvania shops were phased out. The motive power office was located between the roofs of the paint and car shops.

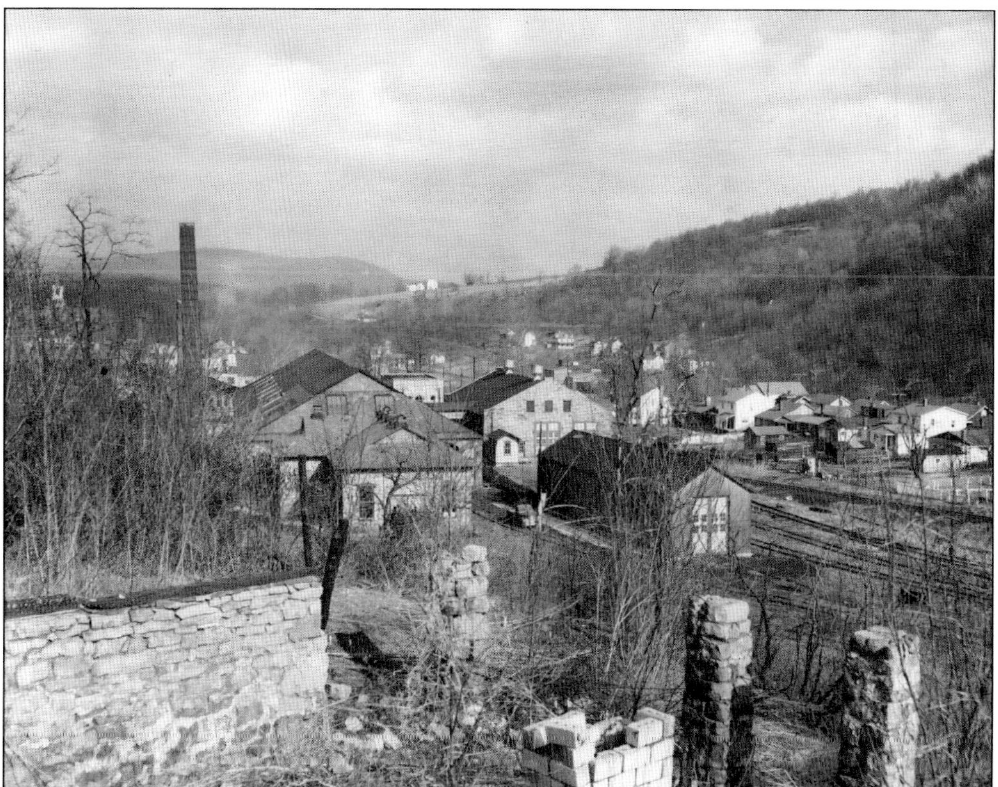

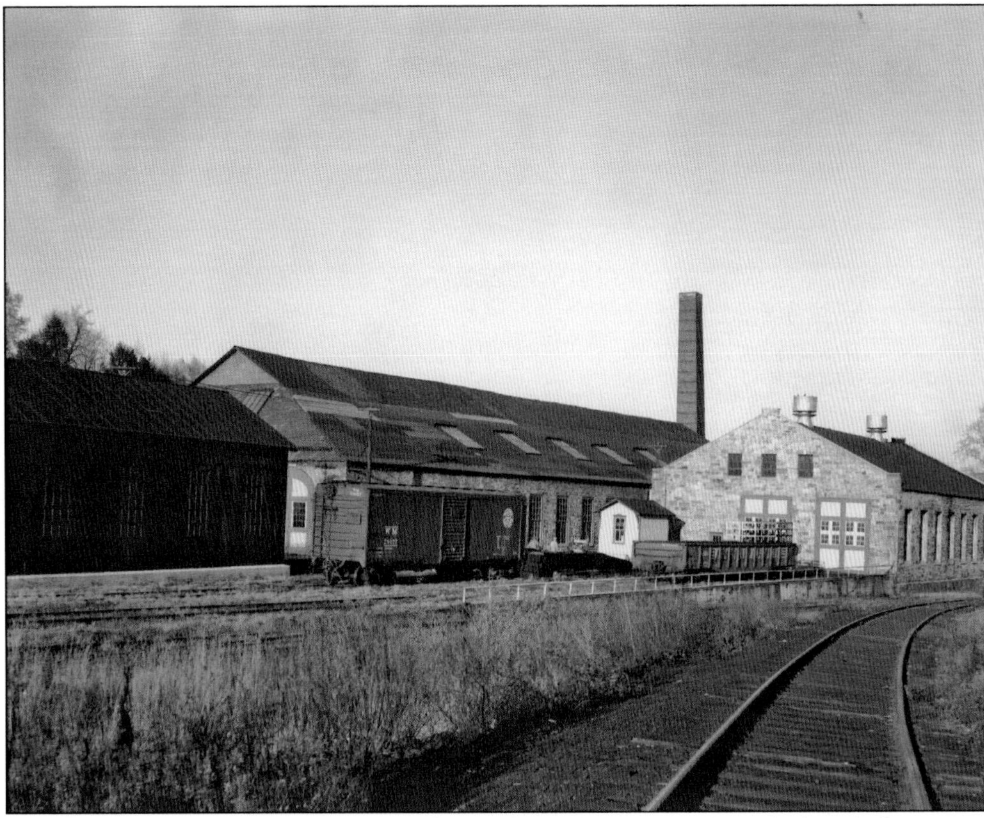

Silence had settled over the Cumberland and Pennsylvania Railroad yard at Mount Savage in this photograph from around 1955. The local brickyard provided a reason for occasional rail service to Mount Savage, but the town would never again witness the 2-8-0 Consolidation locomotives pulling coal hoppers or red passenger coaches through the town.

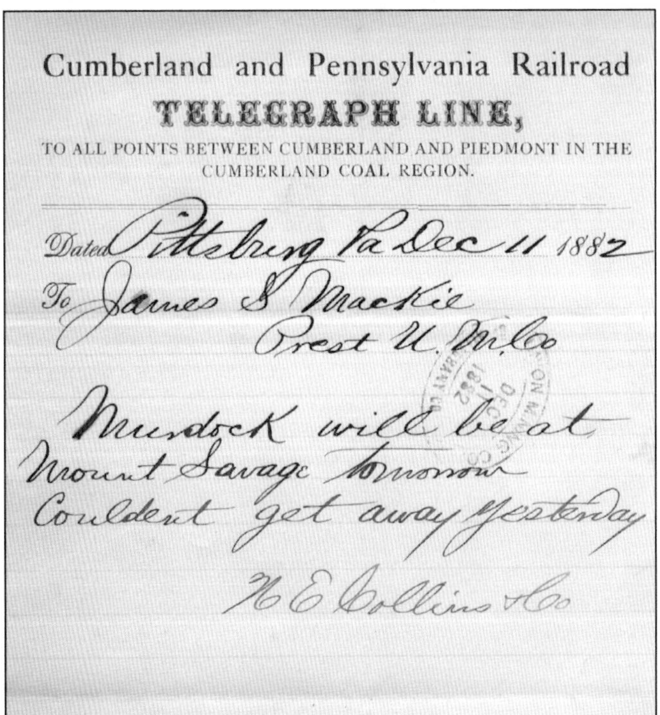

Cumberland and Pennsylvania Railroad

TELEGRAPH LINE,

TO ALL POINTS BETWEEN CUMBERLAND AND PIEDMONT IN THE CUMBERLAND COAL REGION.

Dated Pittsburg Pa Dec 11 1882

To James S Mackie
Prest U.M.Co

Murdock will be at
Mount Savage tomorrow
Couldent get away yesterday

W E Collins & Co

A December 11, 1882, Cumberland and Pennsylvania Railroad telegraph message informed James Mackie that "Murdock will be at Mount Savage tomorrow, couldn't get away yesterday. Signed W. E. Collins."

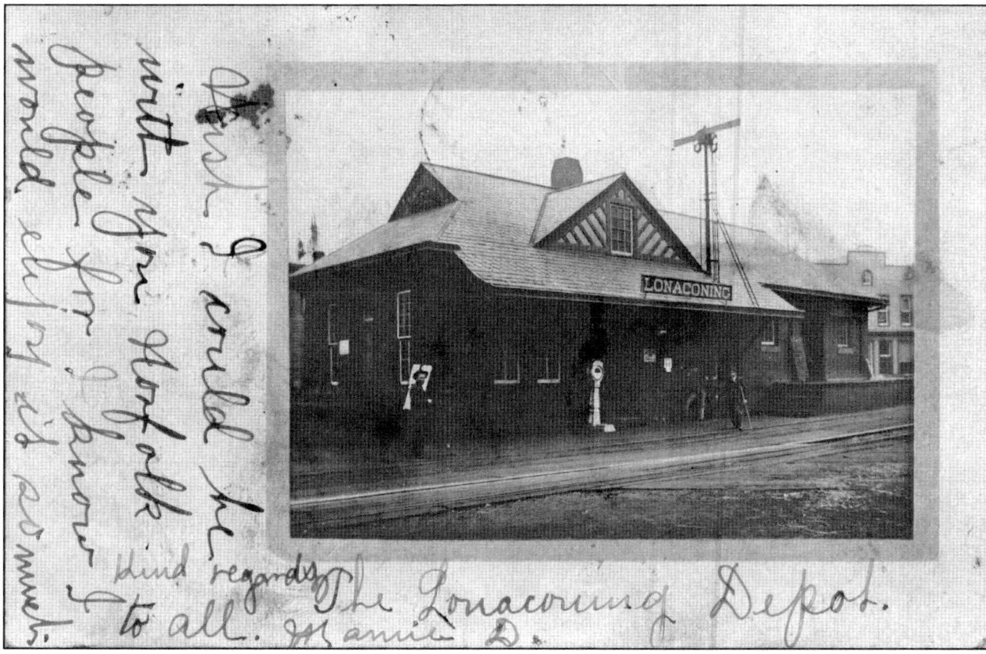

Passengers and merchants awaited the arrival of the afternoon train in this July 29, 1905, photograph of the Lonaconing station. The Cumberland and Pennsylvania Railroad station in Lonaconing housed a passenger ticket office, waiting room, and freight section.

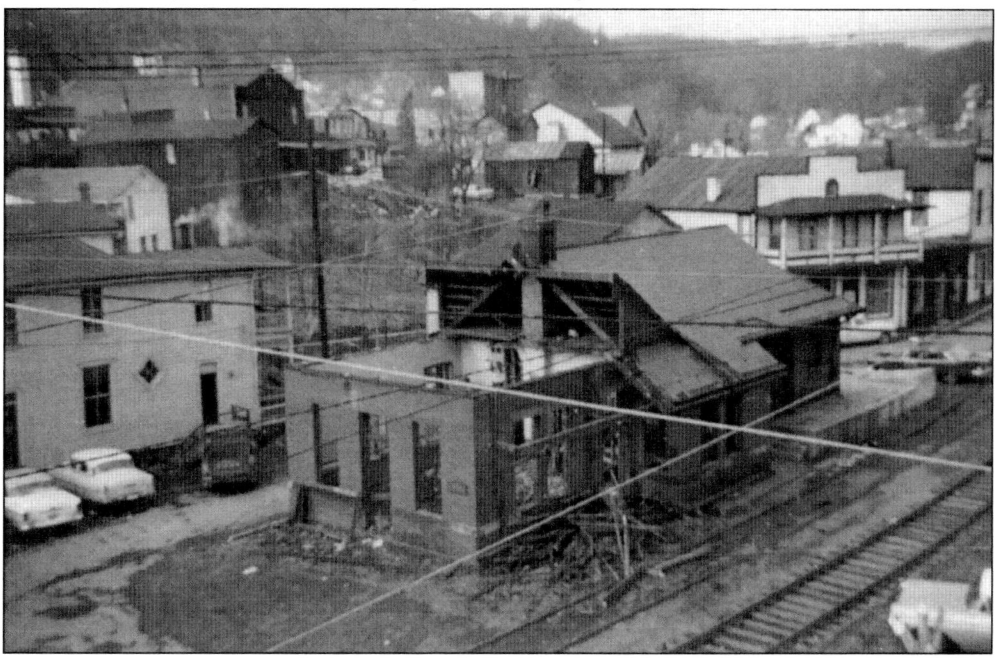

As the Cumberland and Pennsylvania Railroad faded into the past, its physical reminders began to fall to the wrecking ball, including the facility in Lonaconing, which is shown in this photograph. Smaller depots and related structures in Barton and Midland were razed, moved, or sold to individuals. Only the railroad's depots in Frostburg and Piedmont remain intact. This photograph was taken around 1959. (Courtesy of Trenent Brothers, Lonaconing.)

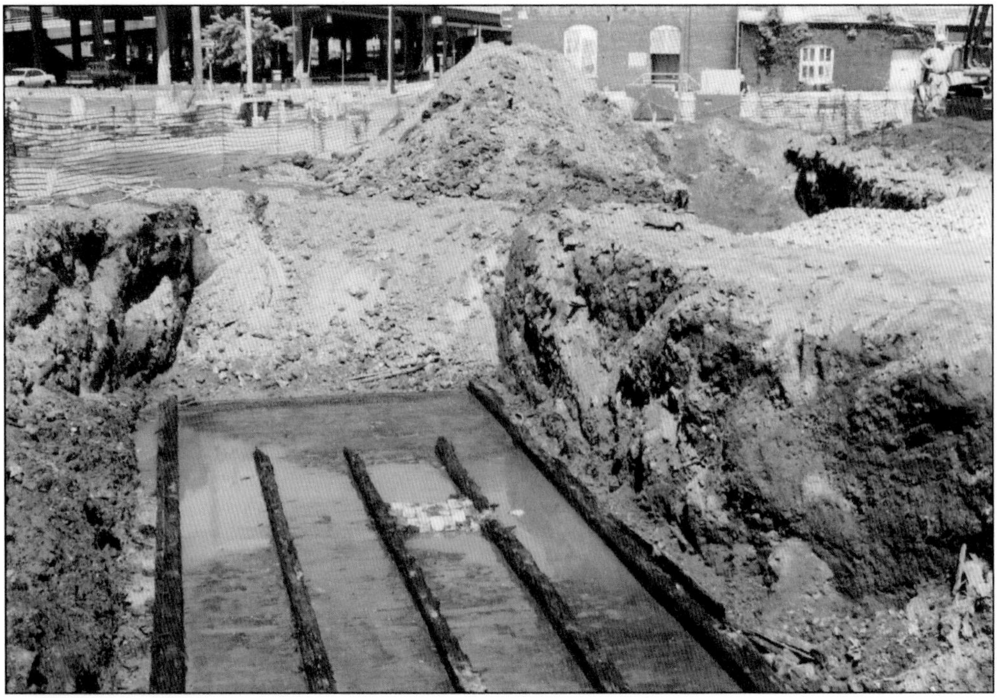

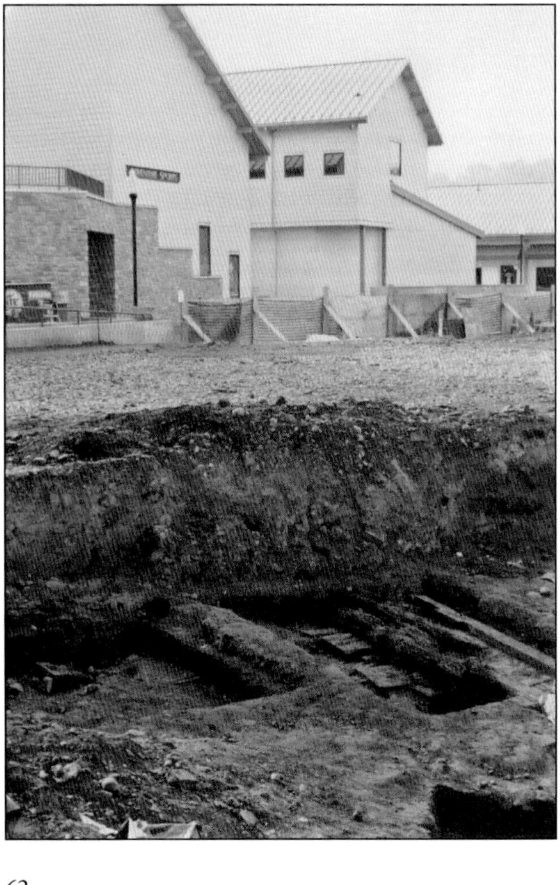

Excavation work for the purpose of developing Canal Place created unexpected excitement. Sections of canal boats were uncovered and subsequently documented by the archeological firm of John Milner Associates, Inc., before being reburied. The boat shown in this photograph was referred to as No. 11. This photograph is from 2002.

Excavations continued at Canal Place during the summer of 2003. A marine railway, used to pull canal boats from the water for repairs, was uncovered.

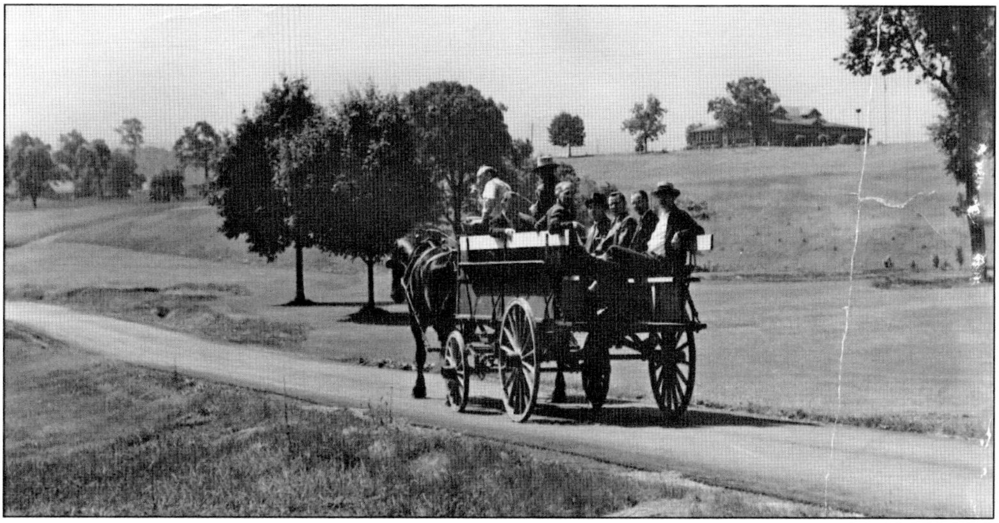

Gasoline rationing during World War II limited travel by automobile and caused an occasional increase in use of more traditional modes of transportation. When captured by the photographer, the horse and wagon shown in this photograph had just turned from Country Club Road to the entrance of the Cumberland Country Club.

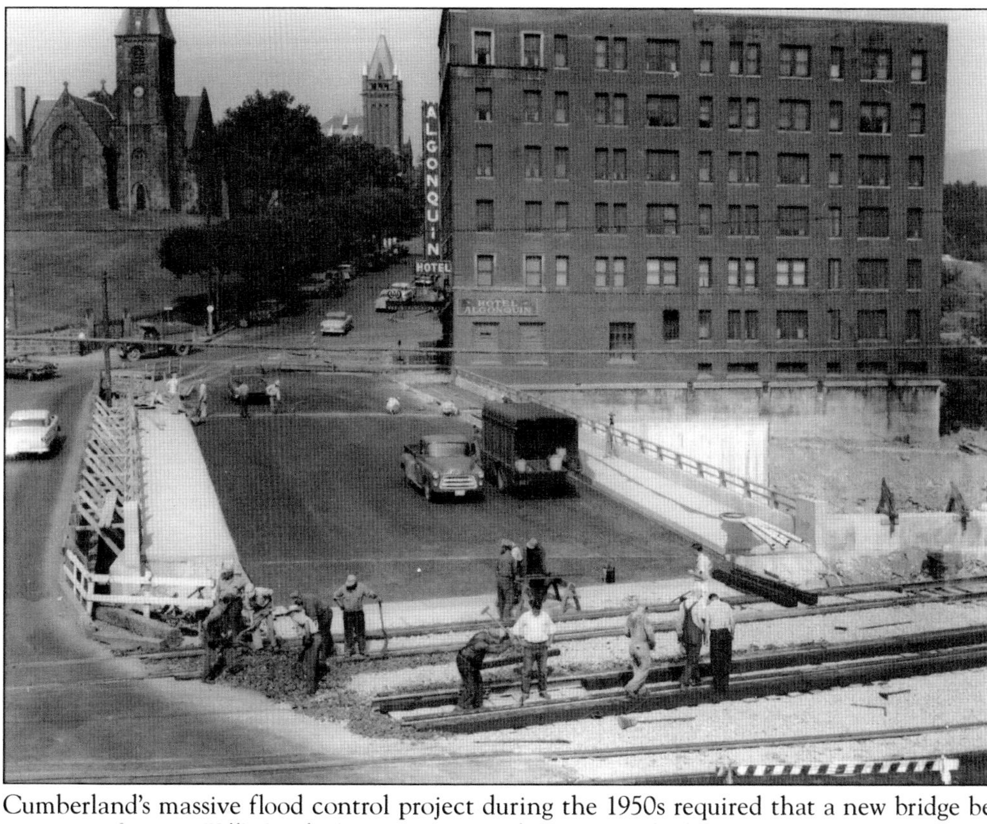

Cumberland's massive flood control project during the 1950s required that a new bridge be constructed across Will's Creek. A temporary wooden structure built to accommodate light traffic opened in July 1957 and remained in service until June 1958 when the new bridge opened. The project was completed by Hazelwood Construction Company.

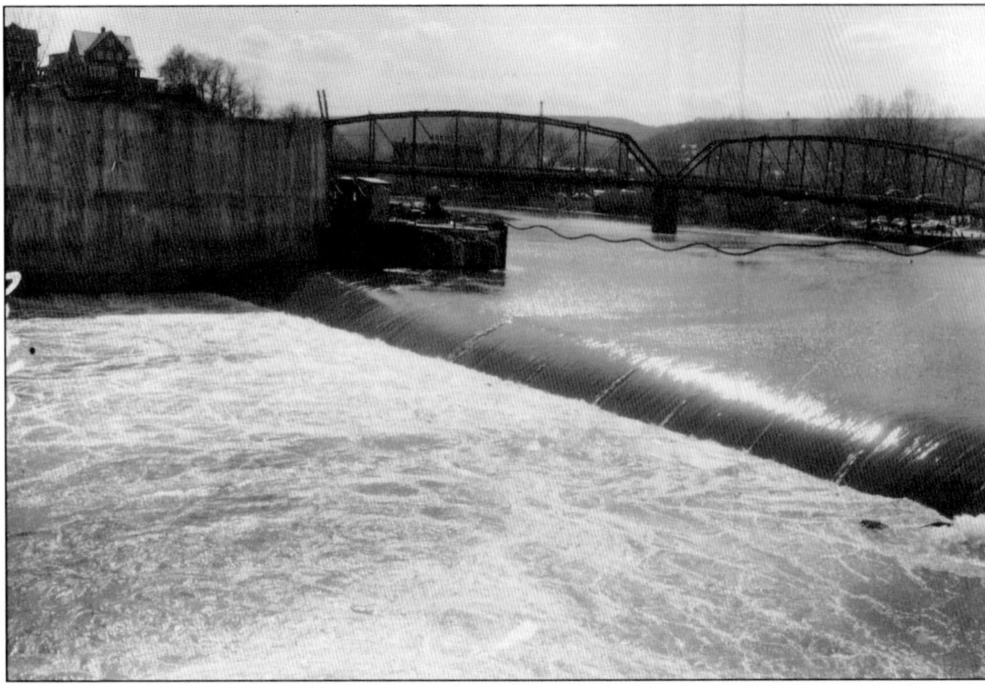

The old Johnson Street Bridge from Cumberland to Ridgeley was still being used when this photograph was taken around 1953. Evidence of construction work on the Ridgeley side of the Potomac River suggested that the new Blue Bridge was under construction.

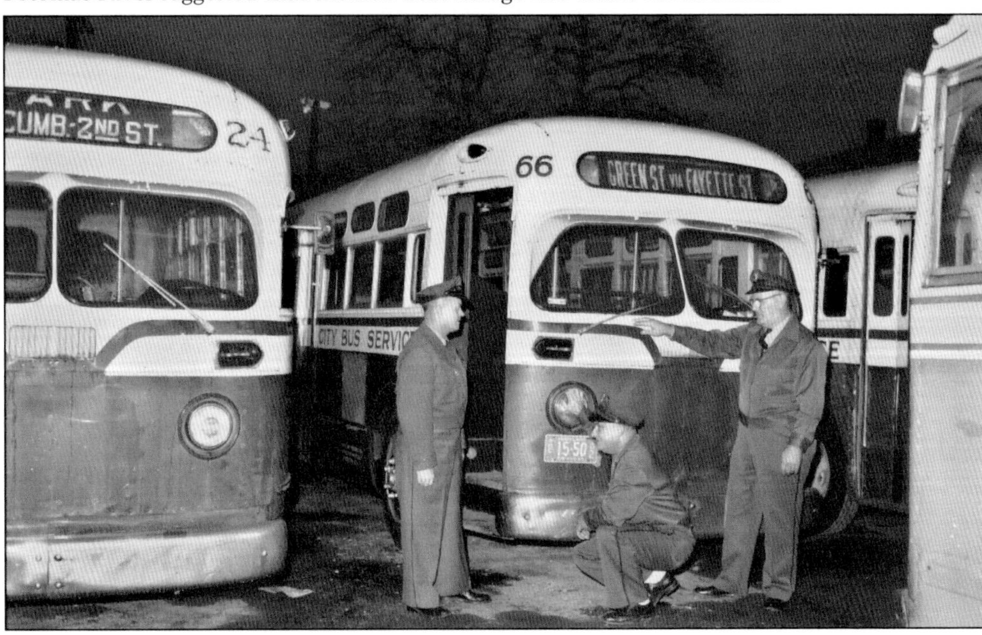

Apparently, Queen City Bus Lines drivers were discussing the condition of their buses. The red and cream painted buses provided regularly scheduled service from 1958 to 1974. Declining ridership in the 1960s meant less revenue for servicing the aging fleet. County officials responded to the need for public transportation by creating the Allegany County Transit Authority and taking over Queen City Bus Lines in 1974.

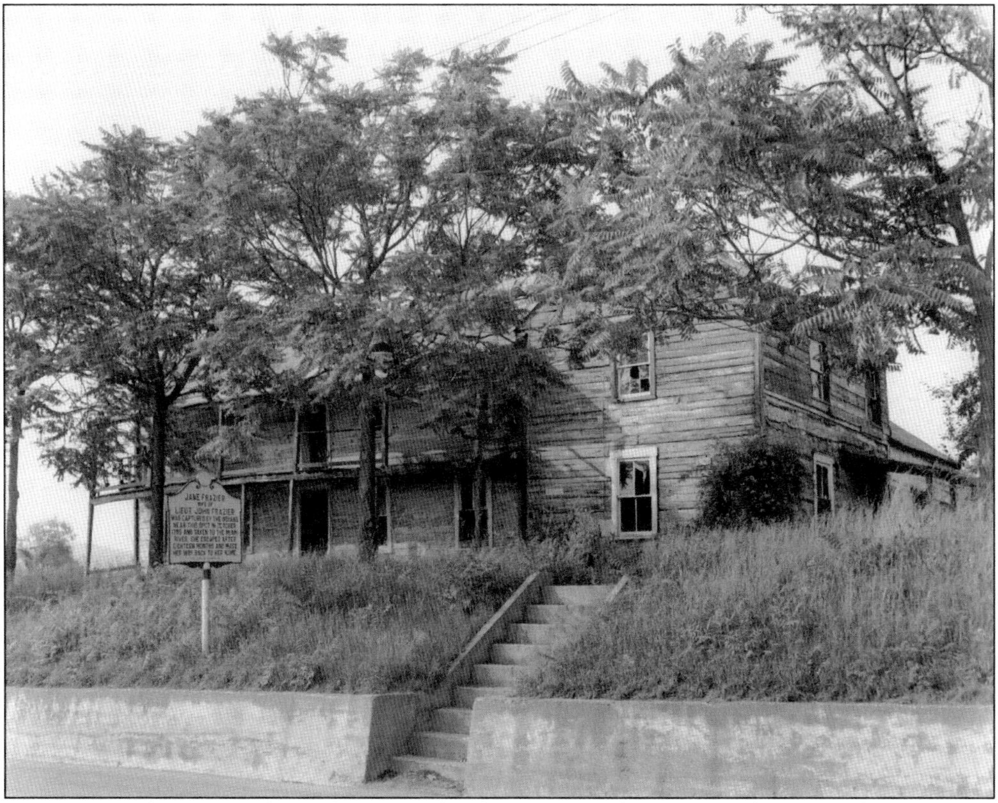

Jane Frazier's house was located on Maryland Route 51, Oldtown Road. Frazier's house was of historical interest following the publication of Ruby Frazier Frey's book titled *Red Morning*, which told the story of her capture and escape from Native Americans. Frazier's log house was built in 1754 and razed for the purpose of enhancing Route 51 near White Oaks Shopping Center.

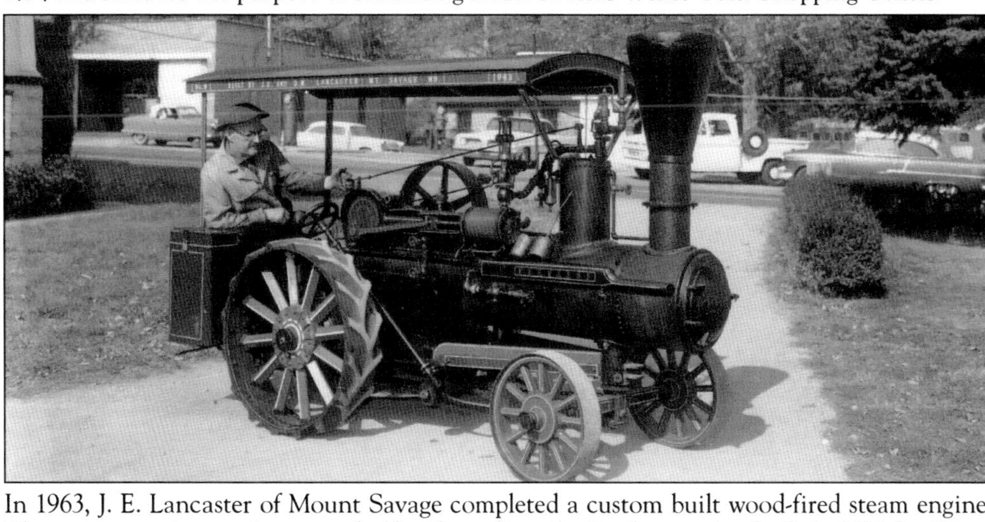

In 1963, J. E. Lancaster of Mount Savage completed a custom built wood-fired steam engine. The steam traction engine was a half scale replica of a Peerless engine built in 1898 by Geiser Manufacturing Company in Waynesboro, Pennsylvania. Lancaster was assisted in the two-year project by his nephew, David Lancaster. Lancaster was a skilled machinist at the Kelly-Springfield Tire Company.

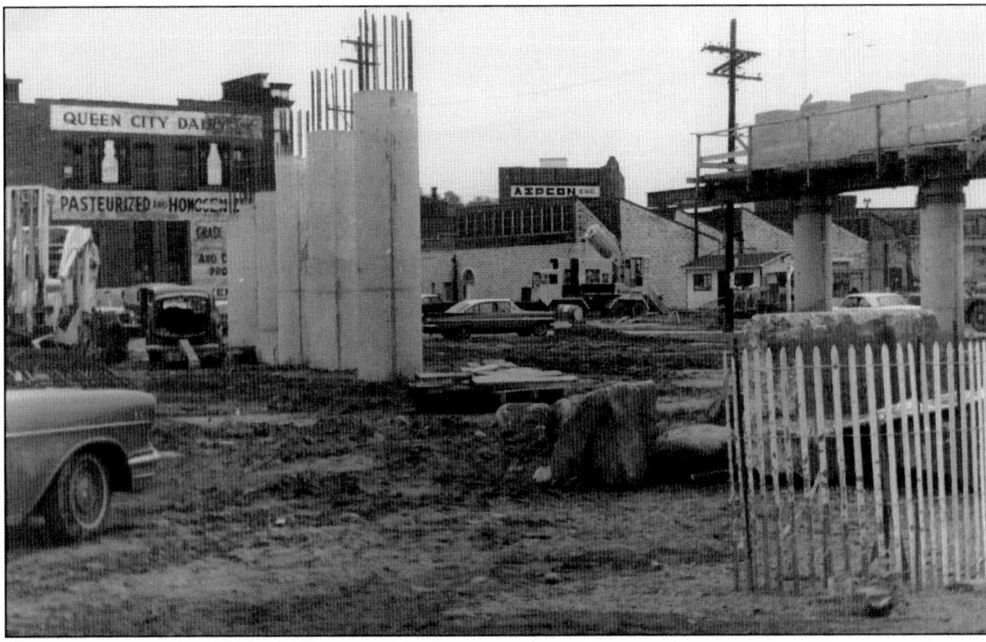

The city of Cumberland's crosstown bridge was designed to facilitate U.S. Route 40 traffic through Cumberland. The bridge begins at the east end of Cumberland and ends on the west side near South Lee Street. The Queen City Dairy building and sections of the Footer Dye building can be viewed in the background.

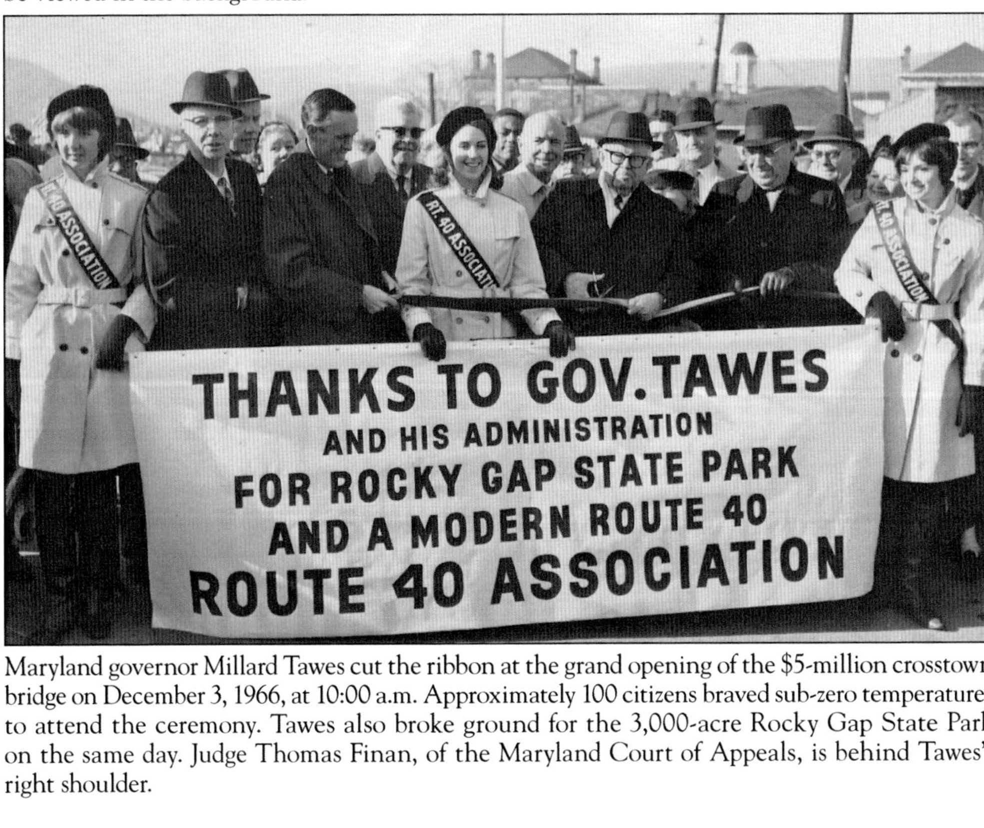

Maryland governor Millard Tawes cut the ribbon at the grand opening of the $5-million crosstown bridge on December 3, 1966, at 10:00 a.m. Approximately 100 citizens braved sub-zero temperatures to attend the ceremony. Tawes also broke ground for the 3,000-acre Rocky Gap State Park on the same day. Judge Thomas Finan, of the Maryland Court of Appeals, is behind Tawes's right shoulder.

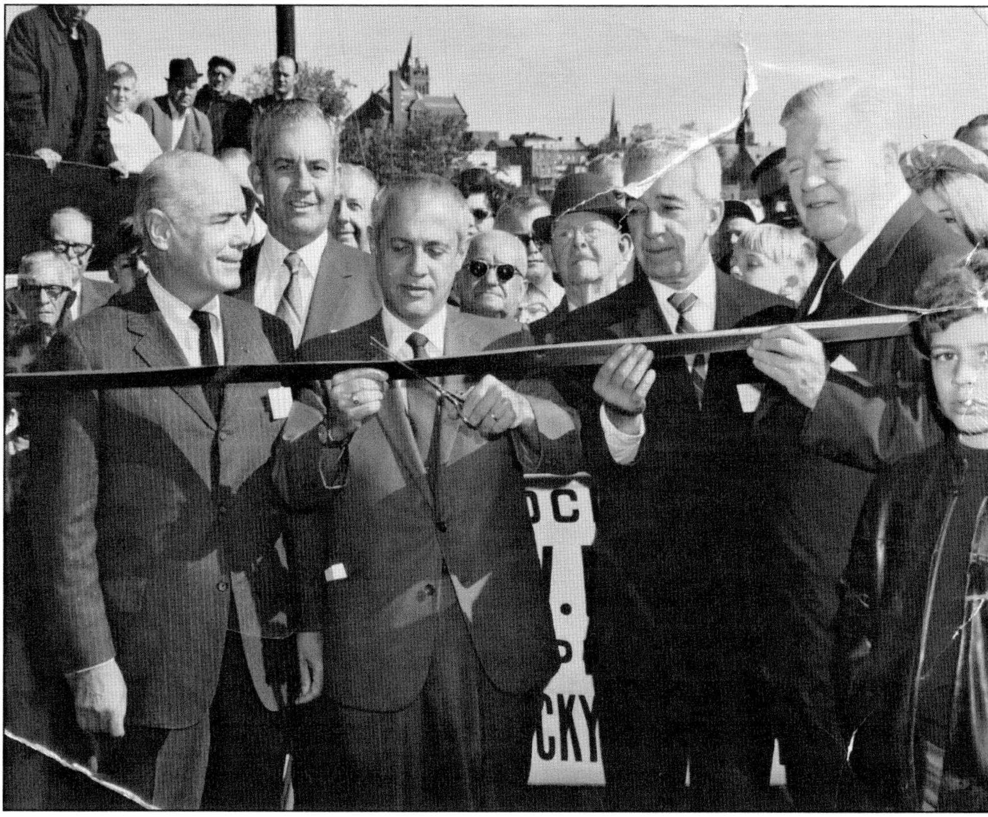

On October 29, 1969, Maryland governor Marvin Mandel officially opened a 5-mile stretch of the National Freeway from Lee Street to LaVale. Judge Thomas B. Finan, first row, left, was master of ceremonies. J. Glenn Beall, of the U.S. House of Representatives, is in the second row between Finan and Mandel. John McMullen, far right, holds the ribbon.

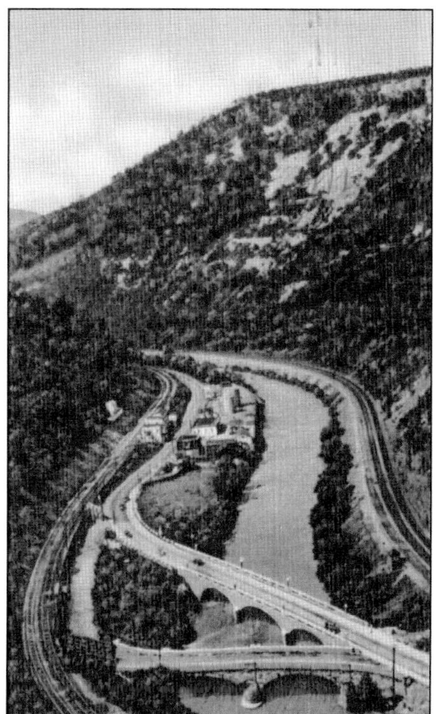

This postcard depicts the Cumberland Narrows in 1940. The Narrows has been a primary transportation artery for decades. There have been five railroad operations, a trolley car company, and motorized vehicles transporting people and goods through the water gap. In this view, the old U.S. Route 40 bridge remained standing but was not in use.

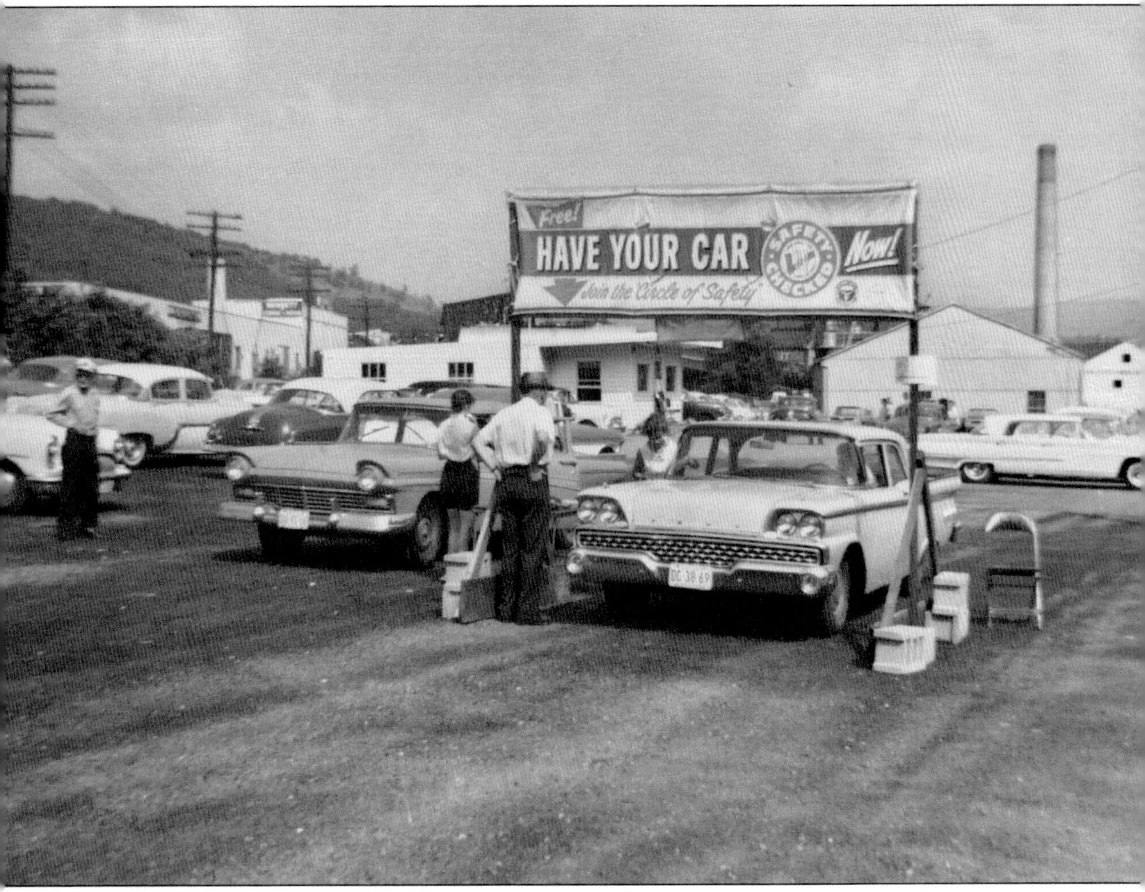

Motorists were offered the opportunity to have their vehicles inspected at a location near the southern end of the Cumberland Narrows. The Southern States Cooperative store is visible in the background in this c. 1960 photograph.

Four

Industry, Commerce, and Manufacturing

Allegany County's historical status as a manufacturing and commercial center can be attributed to natural resources, superior transportation facilities, and entrepreneurship.

Commercial development of western Maryland coalfields was initially hindered by a lack of affordable transportation—shipment by wagons was costly and river transport was unreliable and dangerous. Coal mining markets remained mostly local, and the commodity was conveniently shipped and sold by the bushel. The Baltimore and Ohio Railroad's arrival in 1842 made coal mining a major commercial enterprise. Bulk shipment reduced costs and offered incentives for further development of natural resources.

West Virginia Pulp and Paper Company benefitted from rail service. The company's manufacturing facility at Luke was strategically located along the Baltimore and Ohio Railroad line and in the midst of natural resources that were vital to its success—the North Branch of the Potomac River and vast timberlands.

In 1839, the George's Creek Coal and Iron Company in Lonaconing built an iron furnace that required the labor of 38 furnace hands and 220 miners. Mount Savage was also transformed into an industrial site when iron furnaces and a rolling mill were constructed in 1837. The first iron rails manufactured in the United States rolled off the mill in 1844.

As iron ore deposits diminished, clay mines proved to be profitable. The Union Mining Company located in Mount Savage extracted clay for the purpose of brick making when it began production in 1861. Andrew Ramsey, a Scottish immigrant, also worked with local entrepreneurs to establish a brick factory in 1895.

Entrepreneurship and skilled artisans enabled Allegany County to be a leading manufacturer of glassware. Hundreds of skilled workers commanded high wages for decades in a variety of glass factories located throughout the county.

Advantages to locating factories in Allegany County were also noted in the 20th century by officials of the Celanese Corporation, the Kelly Springfield Tire Company, and Pittsburgh Plate Glass Company.

Allegany County's industrial prosperity attracted a variety of merchants. Main Street in Frostburg and Baltimore Street in Cumberland hosted the greatest number of stores, although smaller towns also had Main Street merchandisers. In recent decades, those shopping districts have been affected by suburban shopping centers and regional malls.

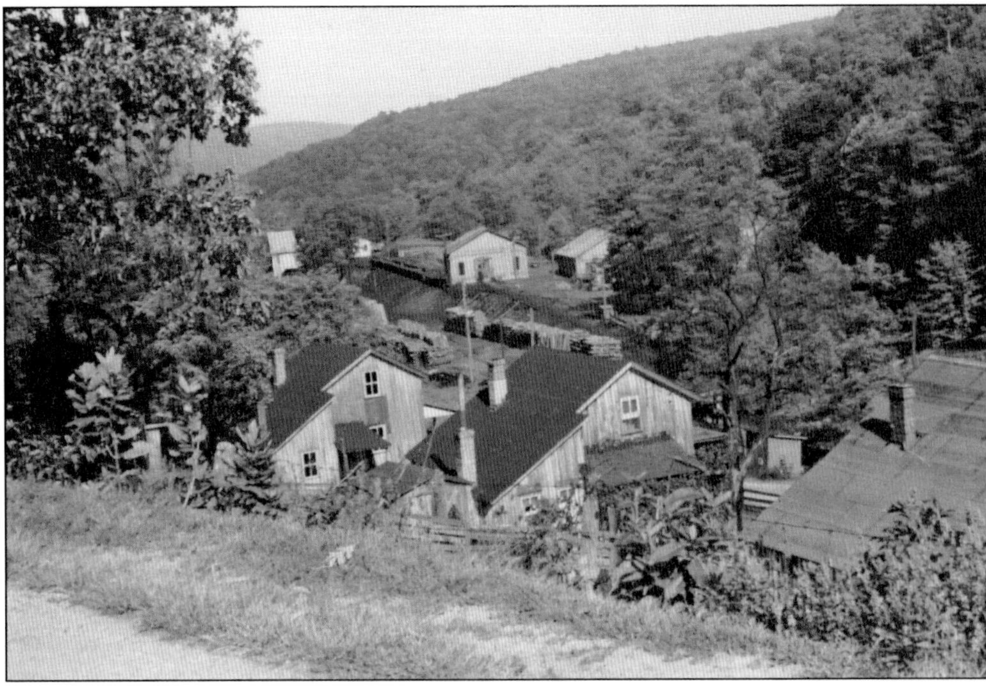

This photograph was inscribed "Hoffman Mines." The community of Hoffman Hollow (pronounced locally as *Huff-men*) hosted one of the oldest coal mining operations in the region. The mine's peak production year was 1917 when 447,252 tons of coal was transported from the site. Construction of Interstate 68 cut through the mine, but many houses from the community remained unaffected by the highway project.

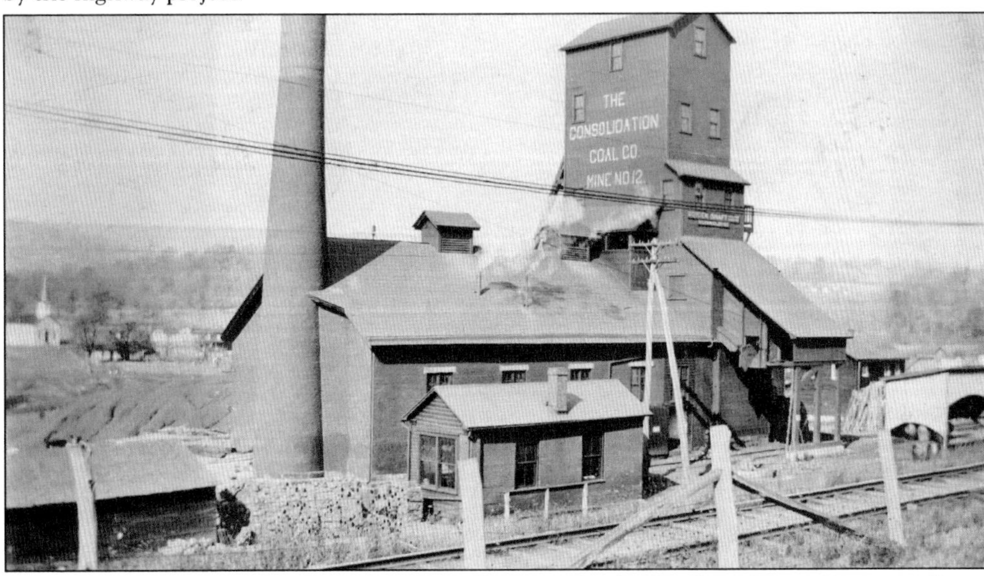

The Borden Shaft mine was originally opened in 1859 by the Borden Mining Company. It was an unusual operation because of its vertical shaft. Consolidation Coal Company later leased the site—after Borden ceased production in 1890—for the purpose of drawing off water, which had entered adjacent mines. Coal production subsequently resumed at Borden Shaft under the name of Consolidation Coal Company Mine No. 12. The mine closed in 1937.

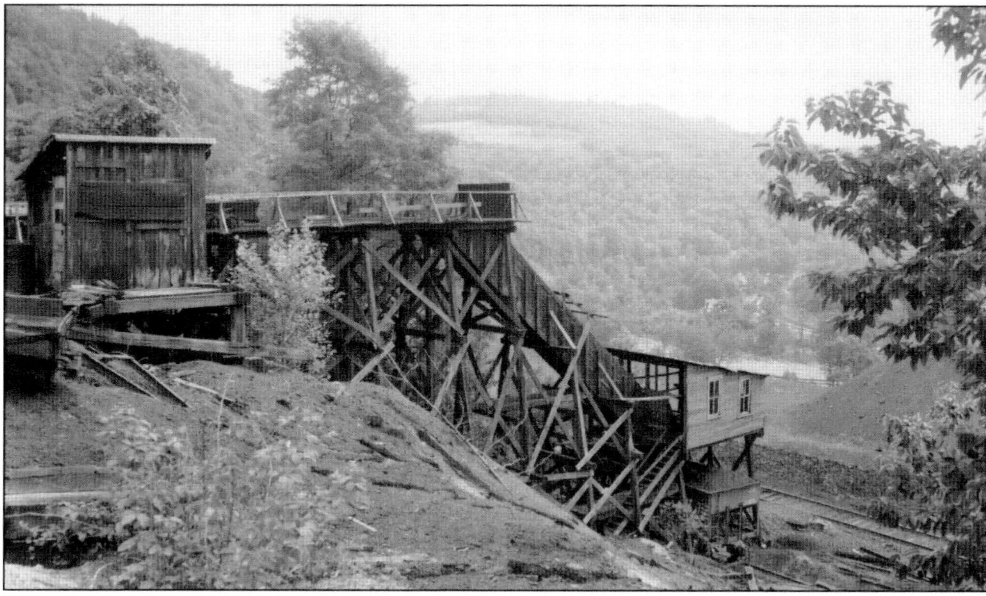

The tipple in this photograph was likely located in the community of Franklin, north of Westernport along Maryland Route 36. There were several mines located at Franklin that operated under different ownership, including Tacoma, Washington, Roberts, Barton Georges Creek Nos. 1 and 2, Cross No. 1, Daily Coal Company, and Westernport Coal Company. The date of this photograph is unknown.

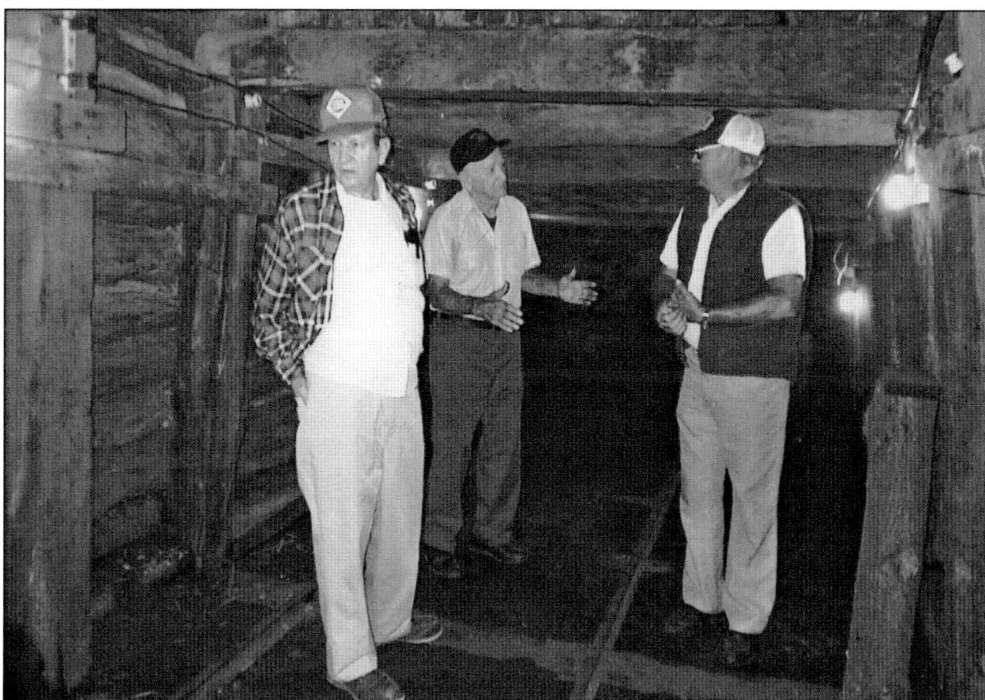

From left to right, retired coal miners Edwin Eckhart, James Phillips, and Jack Ayers discuss a Little Vein coal mine located in Potomac Hollow in Barton. Little Vein coal seams were typically less than 43 inches in height, and Big Vein seams ranged from 5 to 15 feet in height.

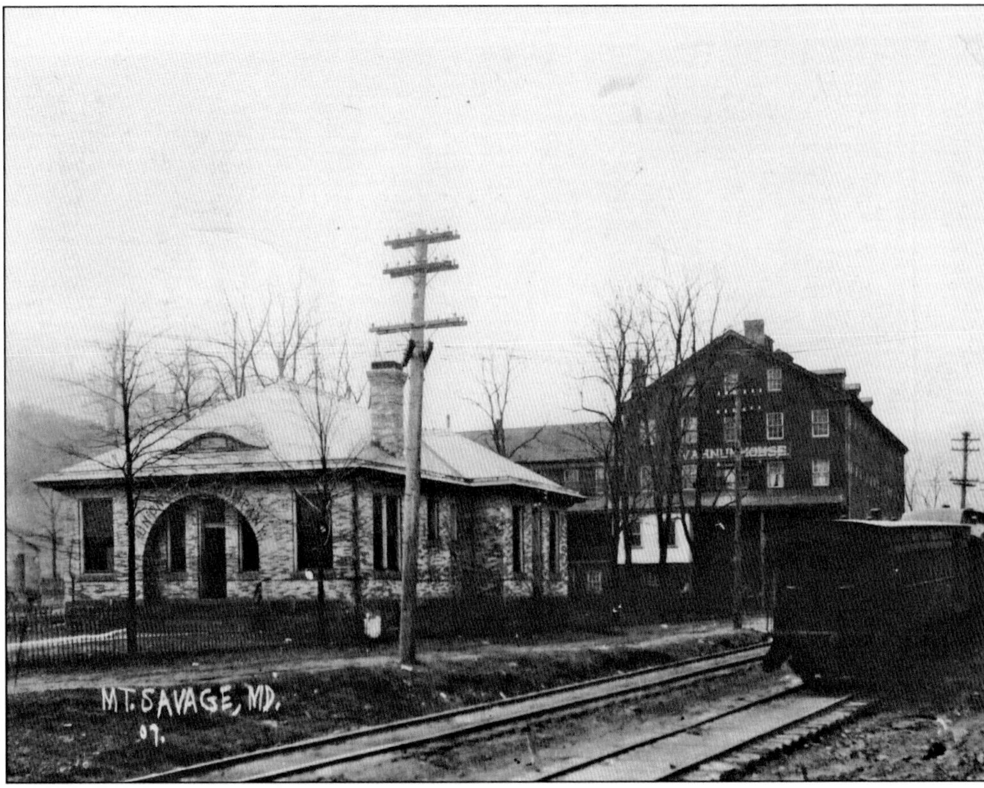

The Union Mining Company constructed a brick office building early in the 20th century. The company specialized in brick manufacturing but also conducted coal mining operations. The Varnum House, located adjacent to the Union Mining Company building, served as a boardinghouse and commercial center for the town. It was built around 1870. (Photograph courtesy of Cora Carter.)

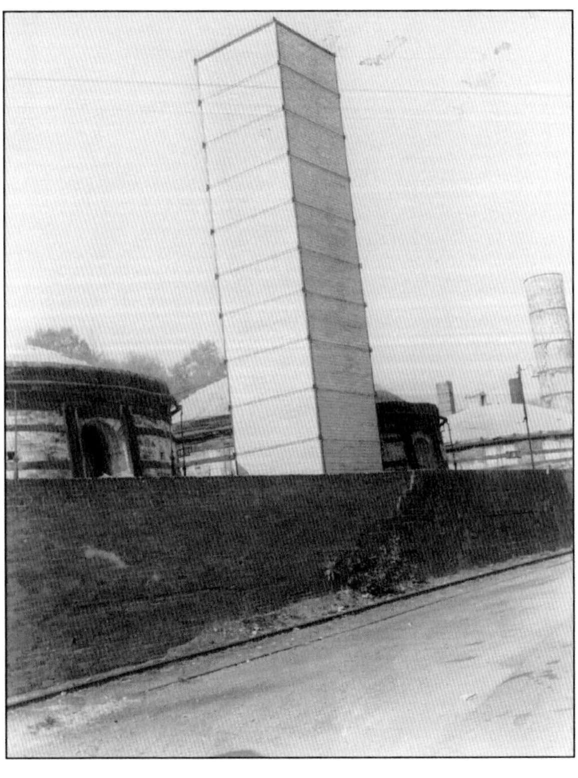

A small section of the Mount Savage brickyard during the 1960s is depicted in this photograph. The plant complex spanned both sides of Maryland Route 36 in Mount Savage and produced flue tile, house brick, and other specialty bricks. The operation originally included a plane, tram, and motorized wheelhouse located on Big Savage Mountain. In the 1950s and 1960s, the plant was called the Mount Savage Refractory.

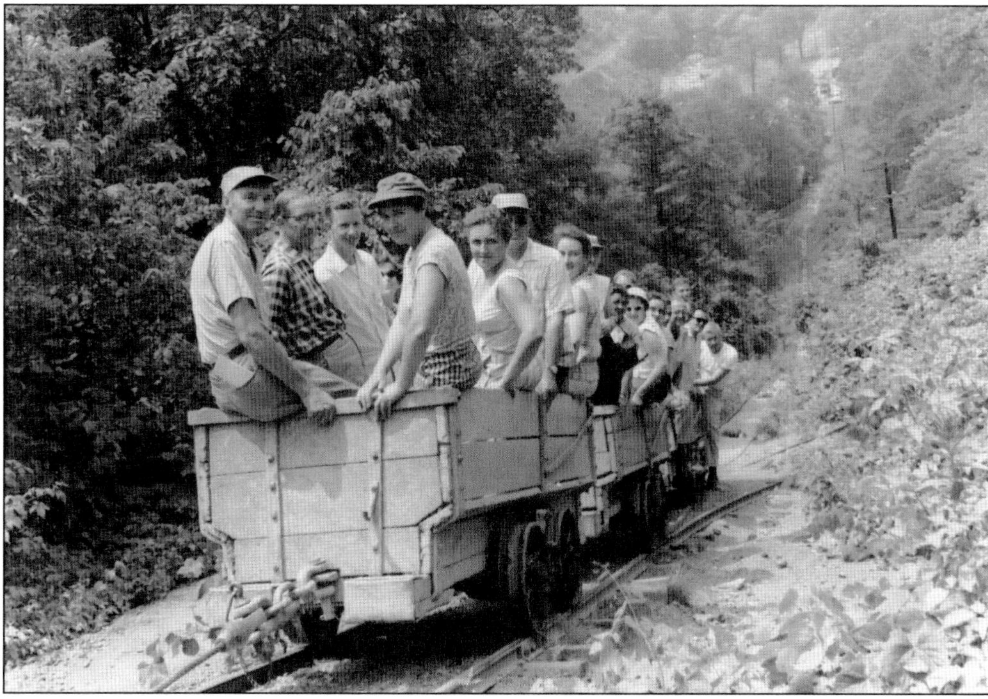

Residents were apparently enjoying a visit to the clay mine located near the intersection of Maryland Routes 36 and 47 in Barrellville. The uphill ride concluded at a motorized wheelhouse approximately 800 yards from Route 36. The tram system was to facilitate the extraction of clay. Route 36 and Jennings's Run are visible in the background. This photograph is from around 1960.

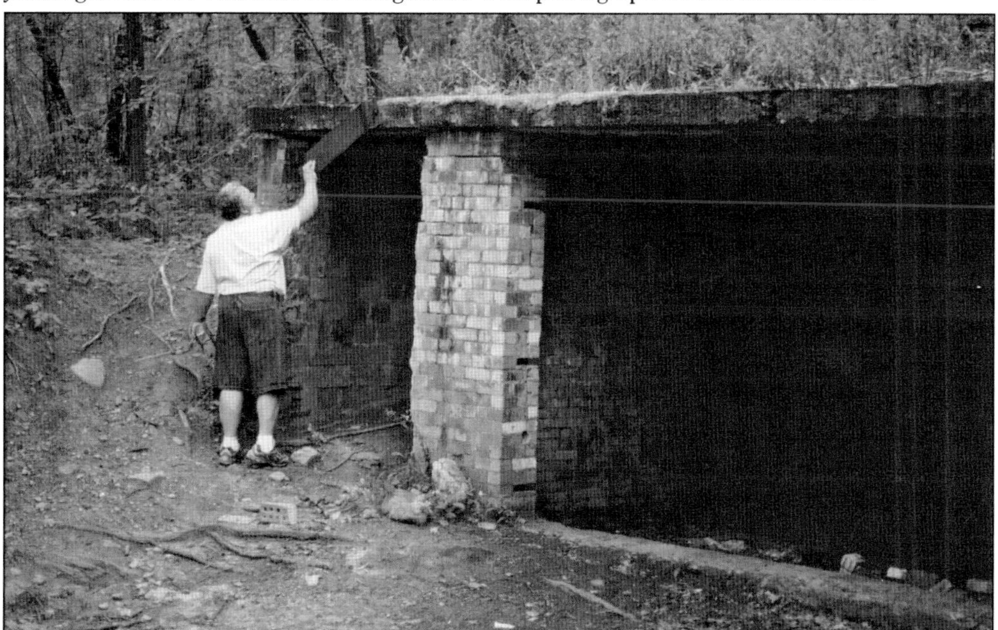

Allegany County resident Jay Walters examines the brick and concrete wheelhouse building located on Big Savage Mountain above the town of Mount Savage. The exterior wall is inscribed with the date "1918." A plane descends from the motorized wheelhouse to the town of Mount Savage.

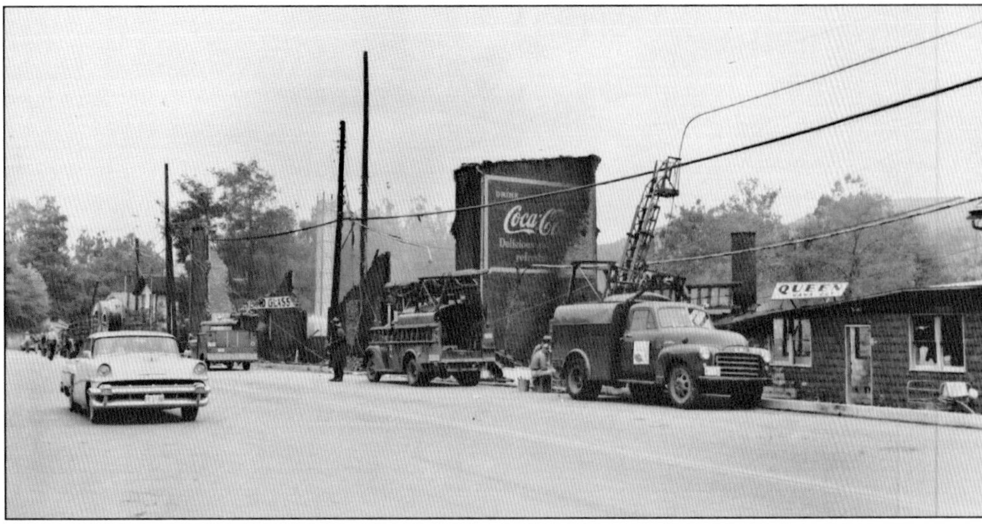

The Cumberland Glass Company organized in 1932 after equipment was installed in a warehouse formerly owned by the Clark Distilling Company, located along U.S. Route 40 in LaVale. A fire destroyed the business in September 1956 and the Cumberland Glass Company relocated to Mount Savage. The Queen City Glass Company, located in the building next door to Cumberland Glass Company, was also destroyed in the blaze.

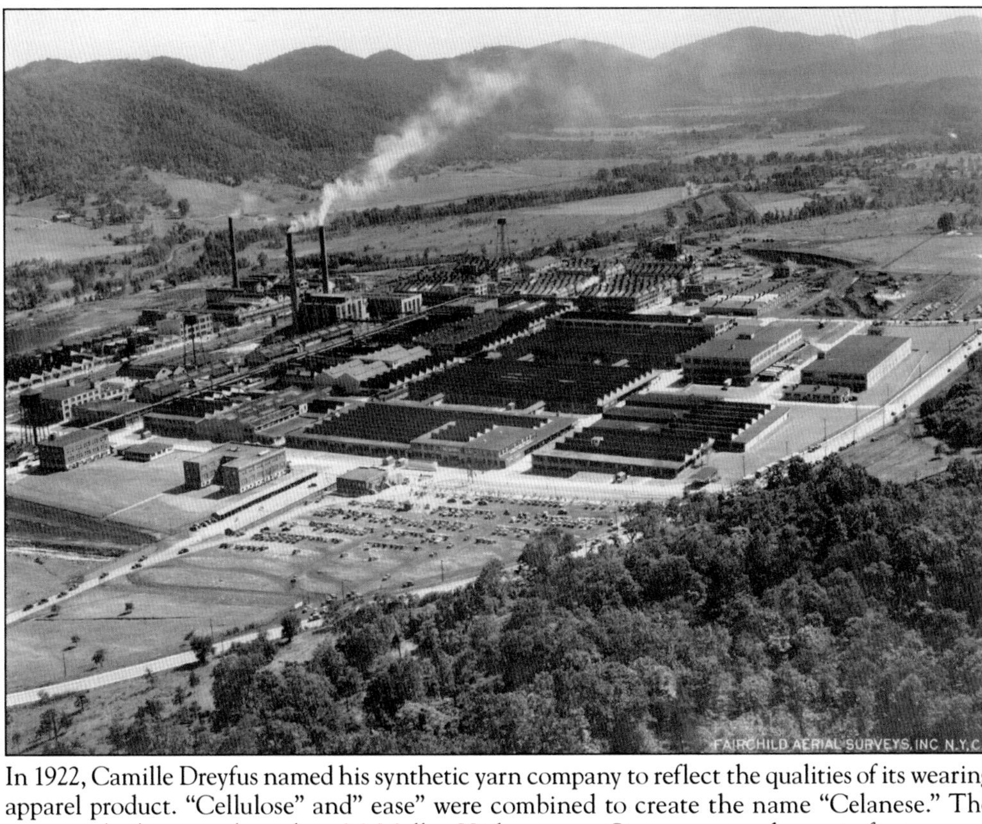

In 1922, Camille Dreyfus named his synthetic yarn company to reflect the qualities of its wearing apparel product. "Cellulose" and" ease" were combined to create the name "Celanese." The company built a new plant along McMullen Highway near Cresaptown and spun its first yarn on Christmas Day 1924. Later a large swimming pool was built adjacent to the factory.

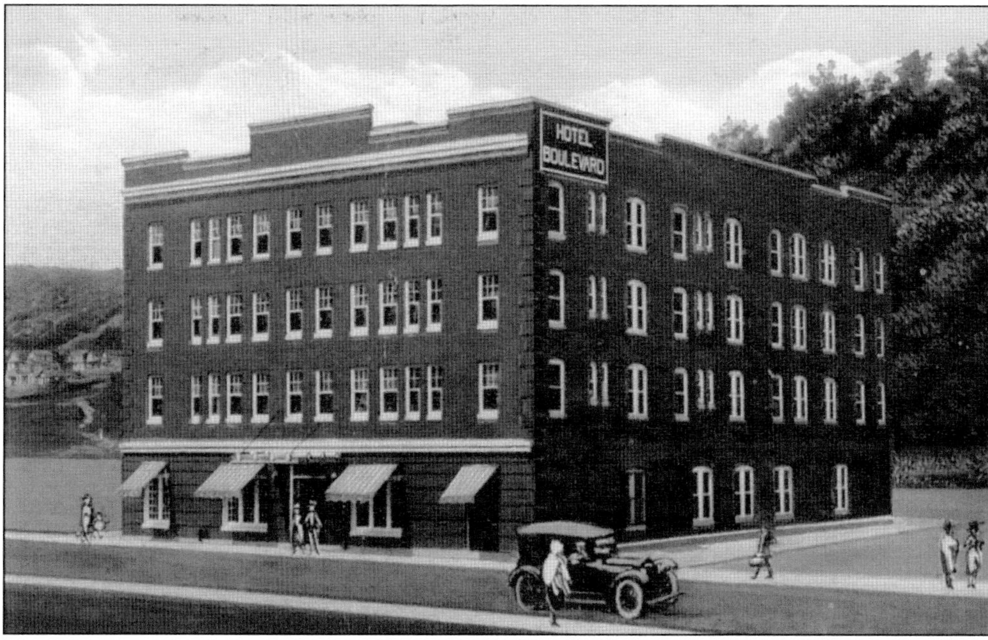

Hotel Boulevard was built along Kelly Springfield Boulevard in 1919. Upon opening, the hotel advertised furnished accommodations for $20 per month. A bowling alley and billiards room rounded out the amenities. The original owners counted on business generated by the Kelly Springfield Tire Company's plant located nearby. This postcard is dated 1930.

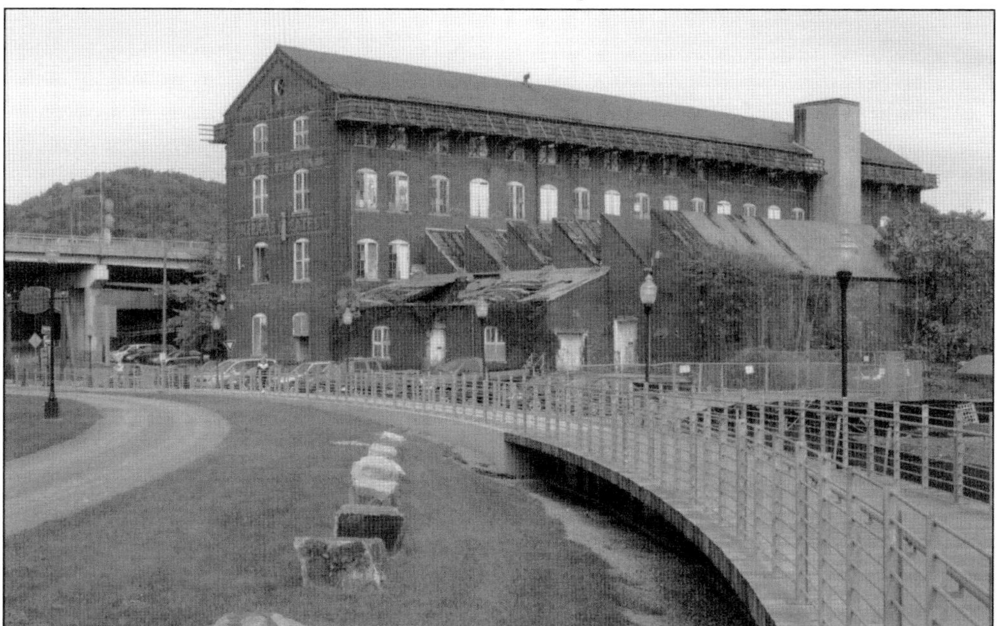

Thomas Footer emigrated from England and later established a massive dye works facility at Wineow Street. Footer's closed in 1937 and sections of the complex were subsequently used by other businesses. Only one section of the original complex remains, shown here. A trestle walk was added in recent years to enhance Canal Place and create a trail connection to the Chesapeake and Ohio Canal towpath. The sawtooth structure was torn down in 2009.

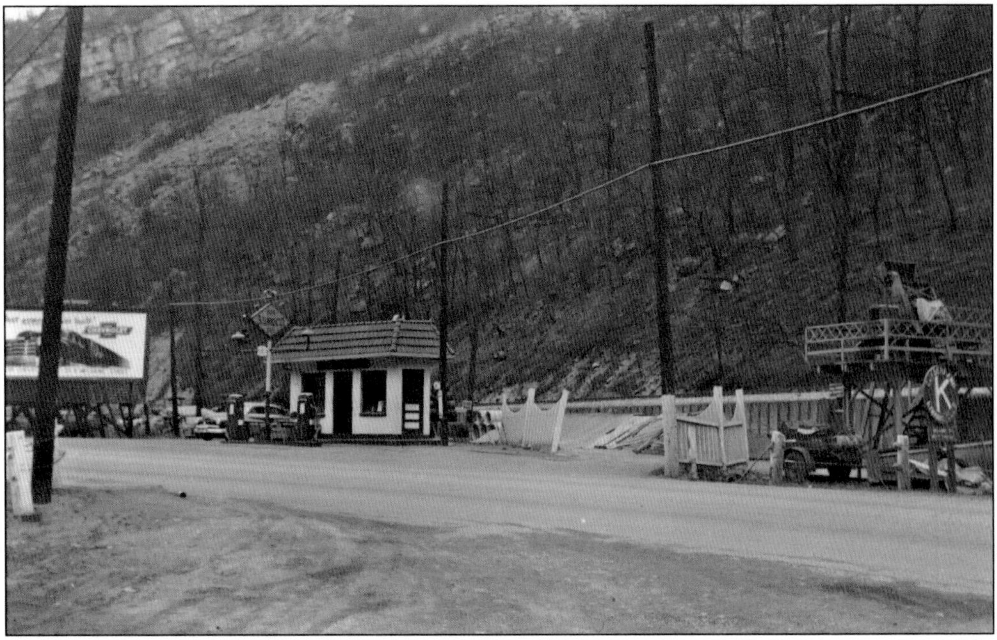

This *c.* 1950 photograph shows a Sunoco Service Station and surrounding area near the Will's Creek Bridge in the Cumberland Narrows.

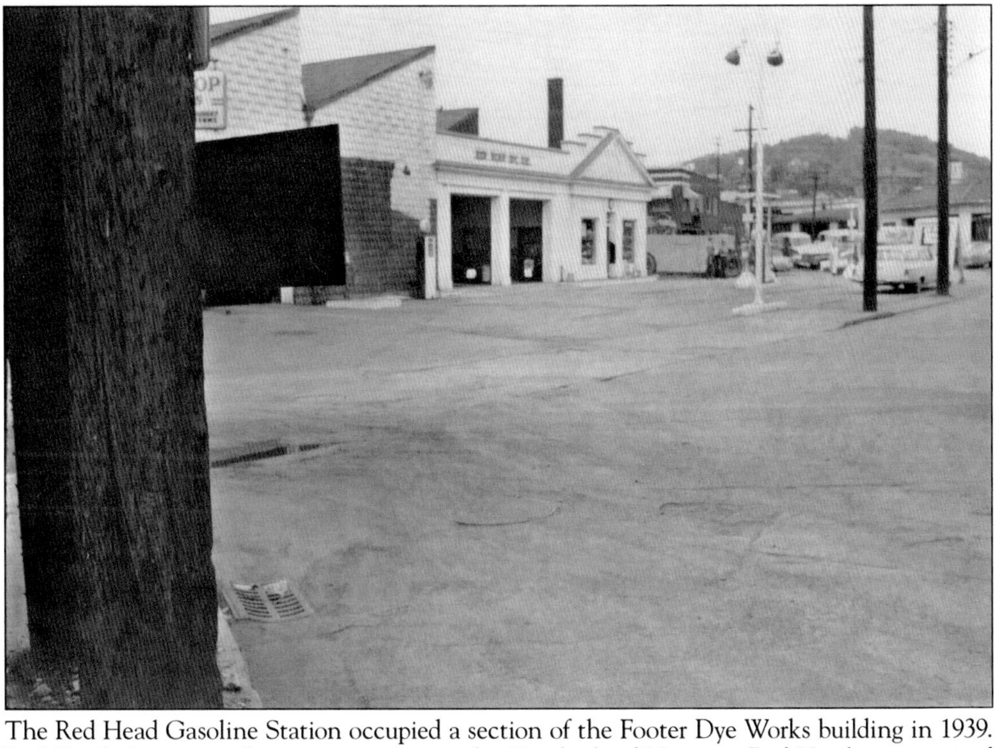

The Red Head Gasoline Station occupied a section of the Footer Dye Works building in 1939. Red Head also operated a service station in the Cumberland Narrows. Red Head was acquired by Ashland Oil Company in the 1970s, and the brand faded away. The section of the Footer building housing Red Head Gasoline Station was razed in 2009.

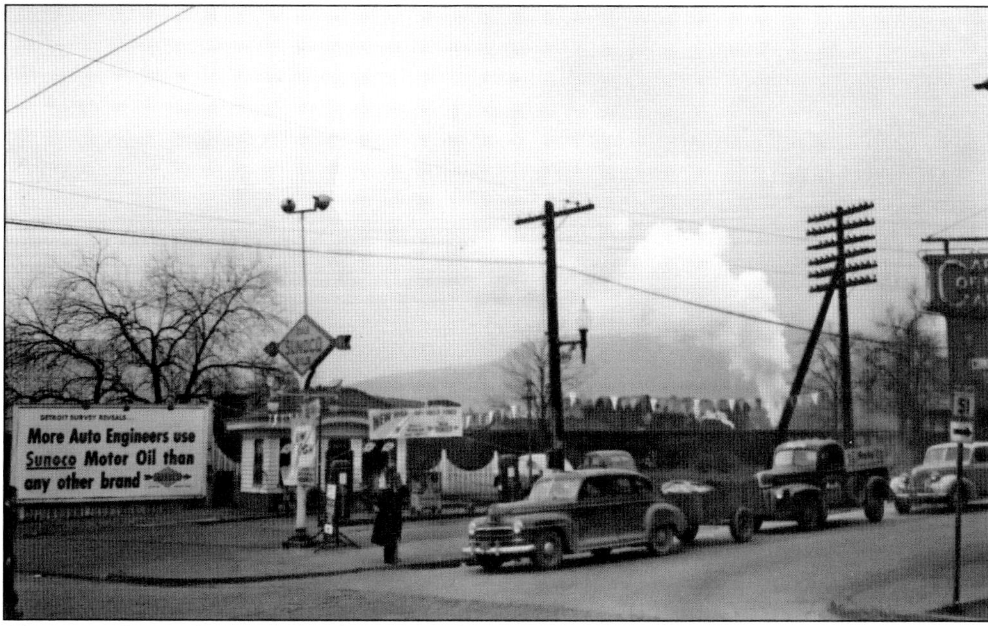

The general area shown in this late-1940s photograph has been developed in recent years. The Sunoco Gasoline Service Station was located on the corner of what is today the U.S. Postal Service property at the intersection of Park and Williams Streets.

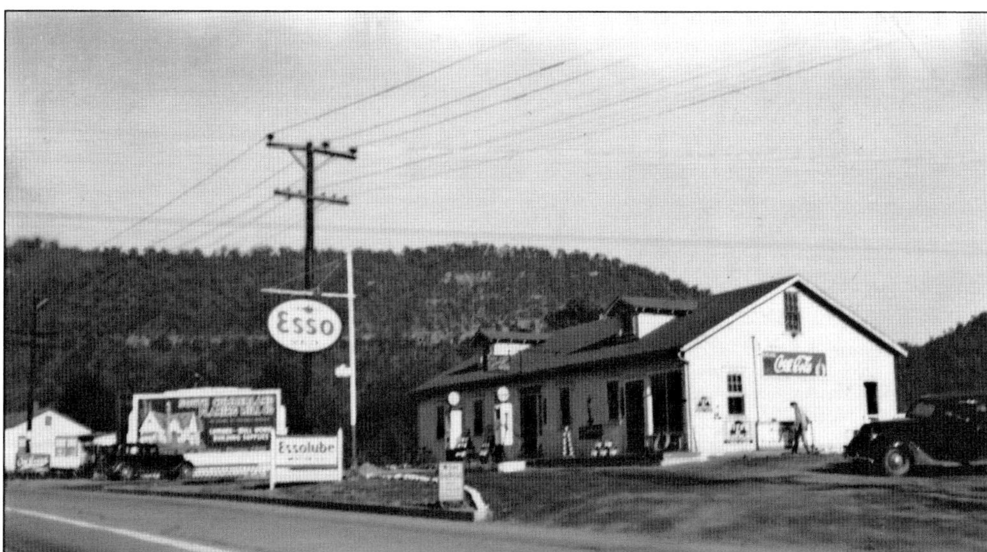

The Esso Service Station was located along U.S. Route 220 at Moss Street near the entrance to the Allegany County Fairgrounds. The billboard sign stated, "South Cumberland Planing Mill Company. Lumber. Mill work. Building supplies. When in a hurry phone 2918." During the 1950s and 1960s, the building served as Twigg's Fairgo Tavern and in more recent times as Shooters.

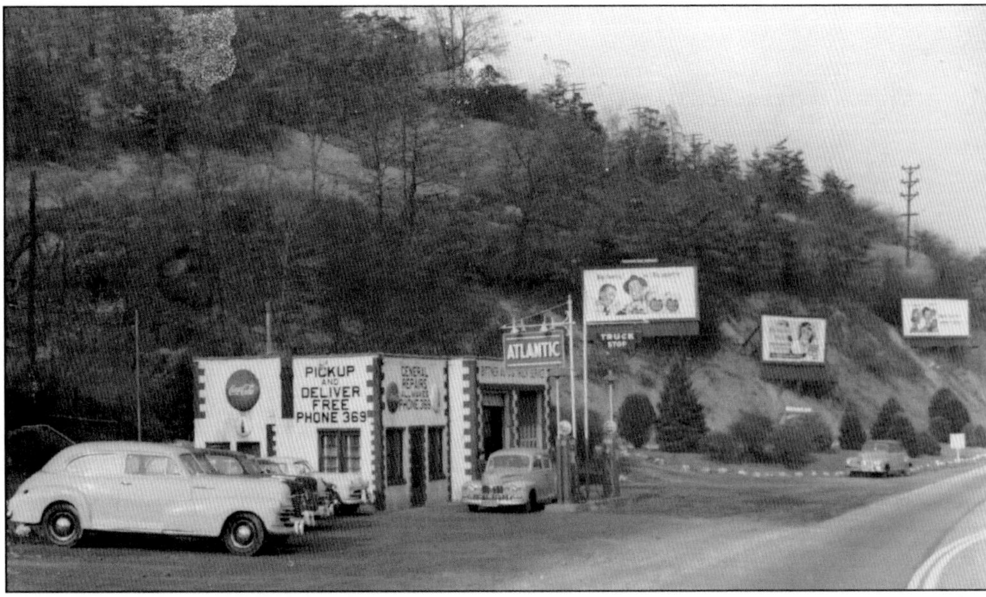

Central Repairs on U.S. Route 220, also called McMullen Highway, occupied a small building at the base of Dingle Hill, not far from the entrance of today's Upper Potomac Industrial Park. Over the years, the location was home to several small businesses, most recently Nature's Art. The Circle Inn, a well-known bar and nightclub, was located behind the service station. This photograph is from sometime around 1955.

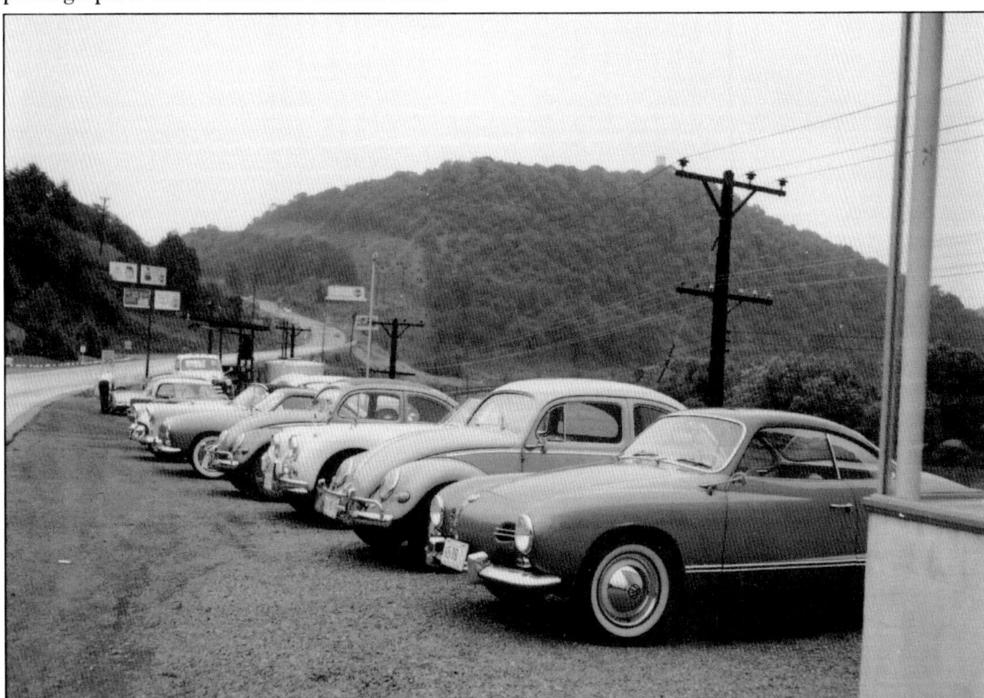

A used car dealership operated directly across from Central Repairs Service Station at the base of Dingle Hill. The location also hosted a Sinclair Service Station for a brief period of time. The only visible reminder of the businesses is a partially exposed, rusty bulk storage tank.

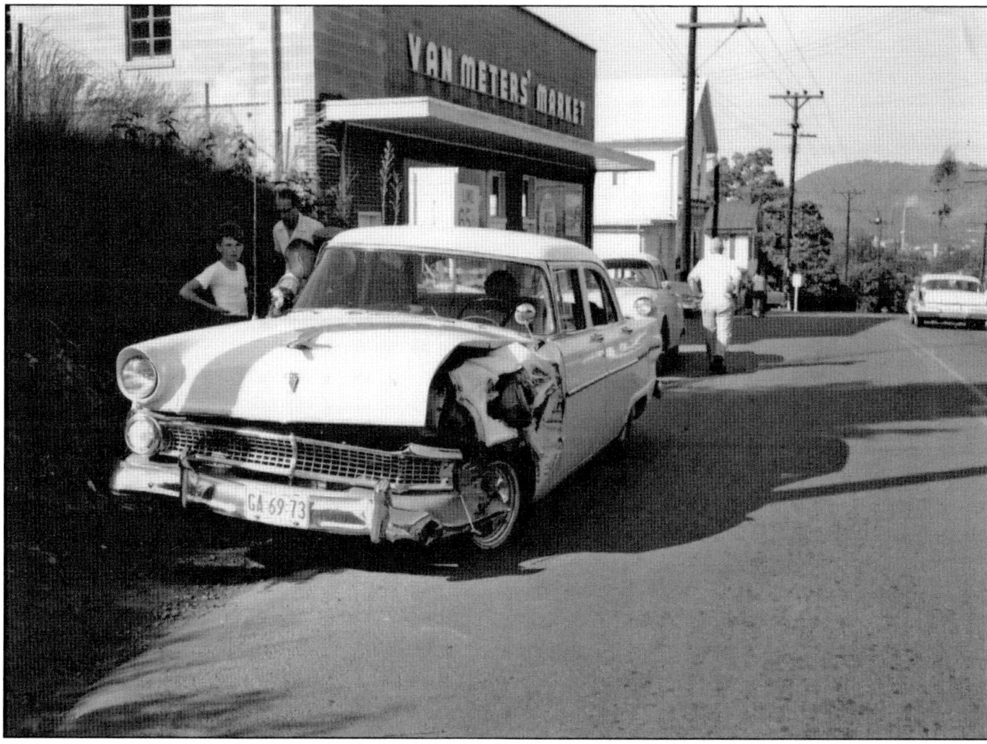

This photographer was documenting an automobile accident near the intersection of Winchester Road and U.S. Route 220 in Cresaptown. Van Meter's Market, shown on the left, was a family-owned, full-service market. The former Cresaptown Post Office is visible in the background.

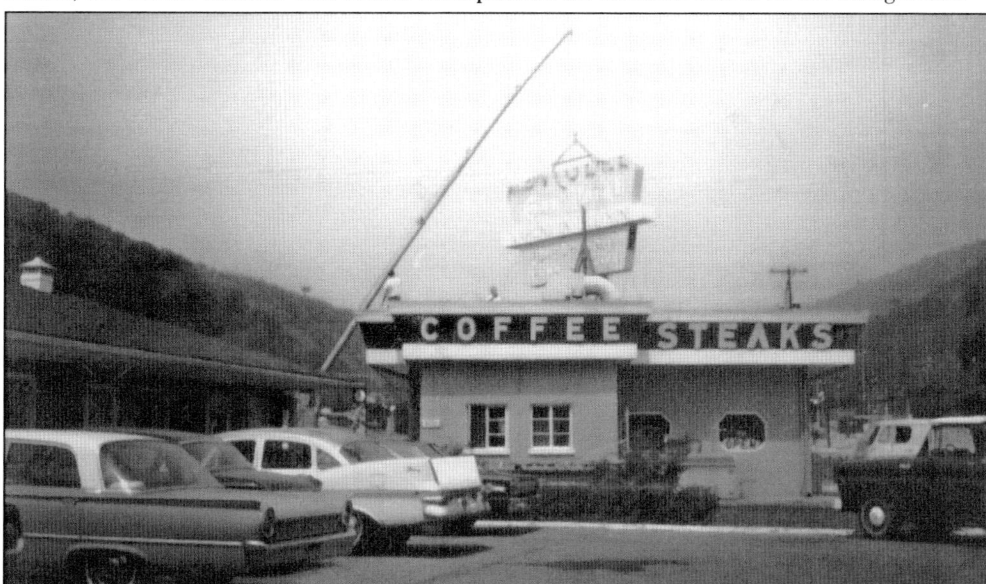

Henry Gehauf built a small hot dog and custard stand in 1949 near the intersection of Route 40 and Winchester Road. An eight-room motel was added in 1954, shown at left in this photograph taken around 1967. Henry's son, David, continued the business and oversaw Gehauf's Restaurant, Henny's Grill and Bar, and the Braddock Motor Inn. (Courtesy Dave Gehauf.)

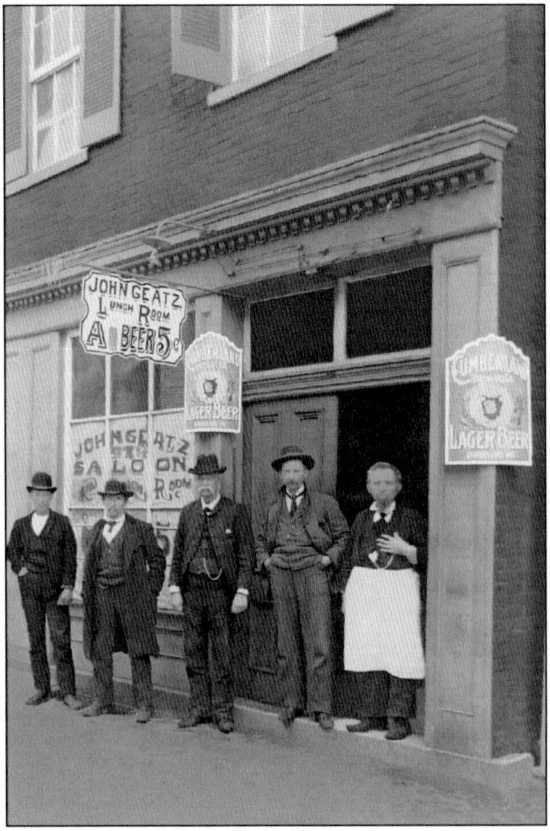

Maryland's oldest continuously owned family business had its origins in Johannes Gotz's emigration from Bavaria, Germany, in 1860. After settling in Cumberland, Gotz—whose last name later changed to Geatz—opened a saloon and restaurant business on Baltimore Street around 1880. In 1905, the Geatz restaurant moved to 206 Paca Street where it has remained. The fifth-generation business is currently under the ownership of John "J. P." and Brenda Geatz. (Courtesy J. P. and Brenda Geatz.)

In 1954, Edward Mason opened a root beer stand along two-lane U.S. Route 40, now Interstate 68. In 1955, the business was enlarged to accommodate indoor seating and curb service as seen in this photograph. The owner later changed the business's name to Snackologist Ed's. In 1967, Snackologist Ed's became Mason's Barn, a full-service restaurant furnished with antique farm implements. Mason also served as a Maryland state senator from 1971 to 1983.

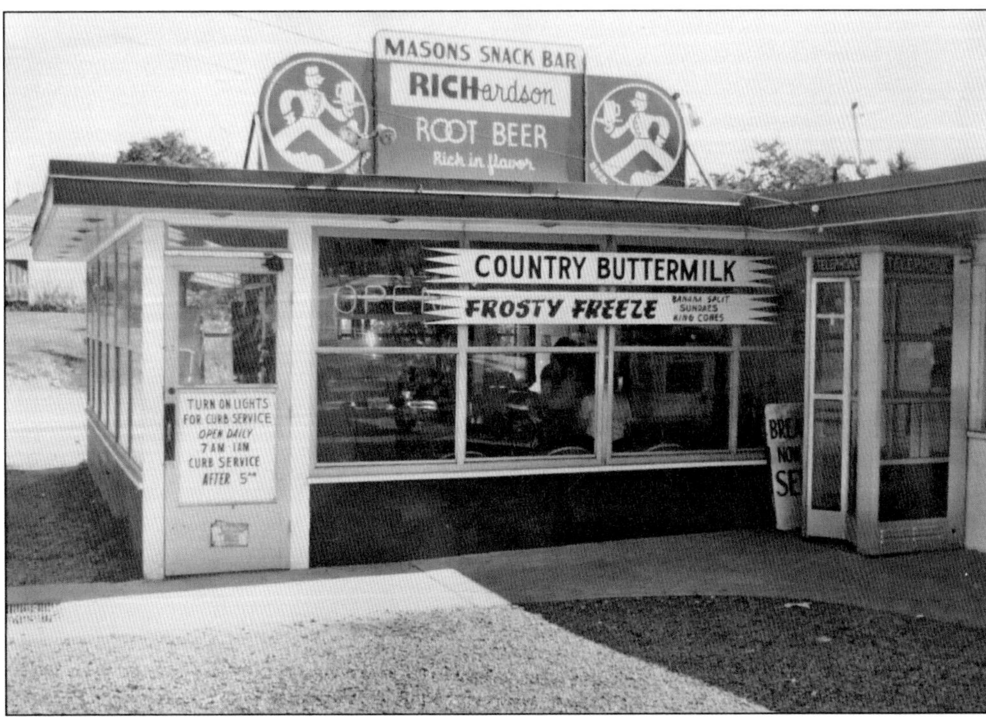

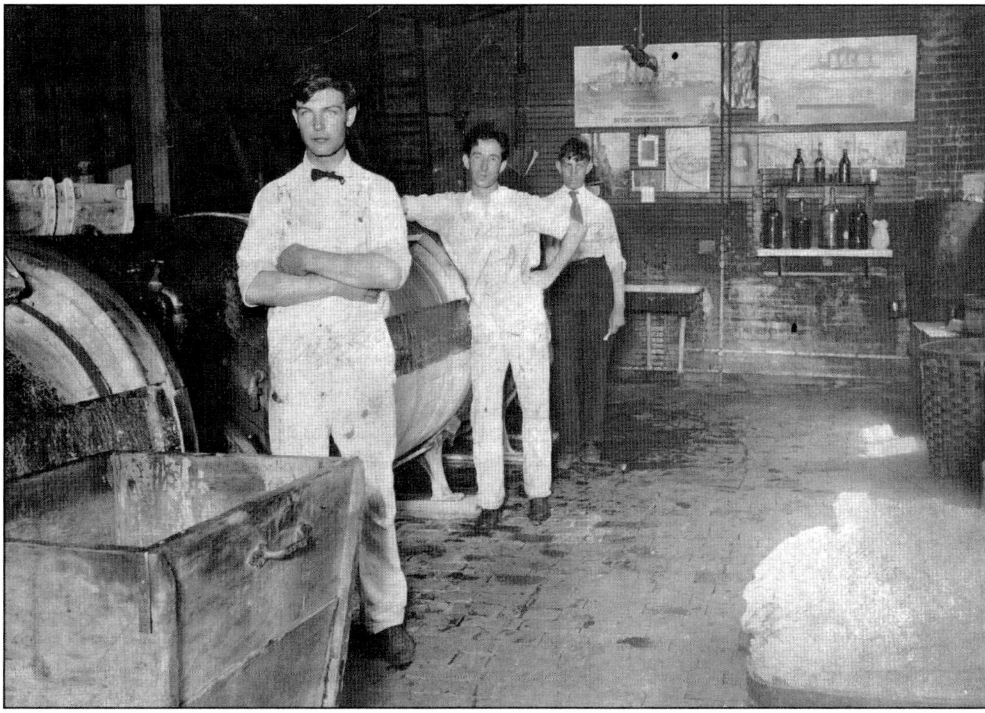

"Cumberland, MD, W. Pugh" was inscribed on the back of this photograph, which appears to be a picture of a small flour mill. This photograph may have been taken in the Wilson and Pugh Hardware store located at 26 George Street in downtown Cumberland.

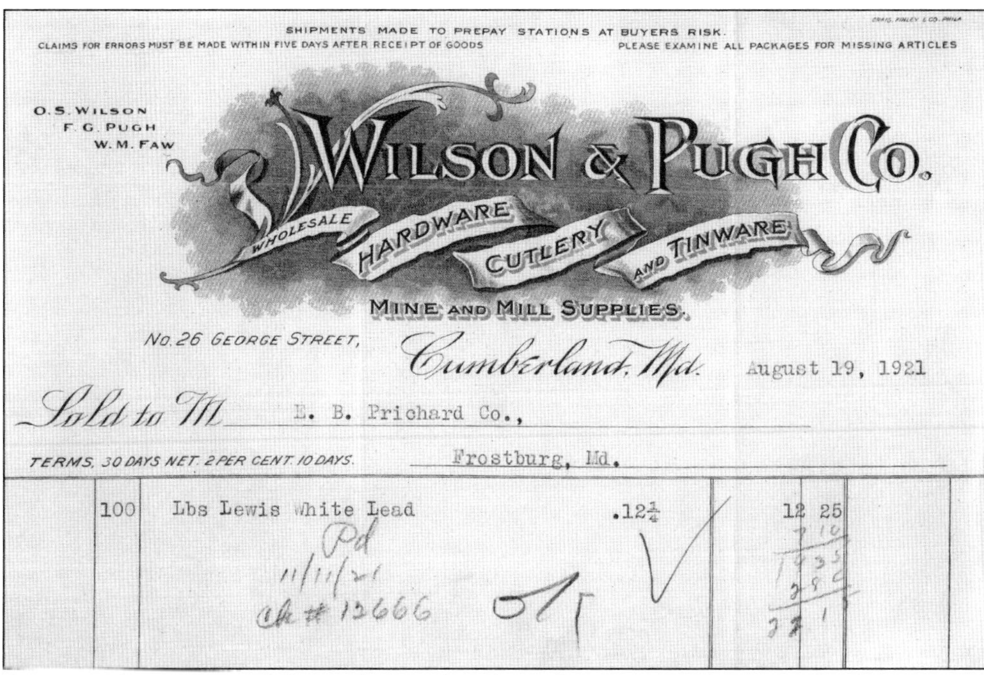

SHIPMENTS MADE TO PREPAY STATIONS AT BUYERS RISK.
CLAIMS FOR ERRORS MUST BE MADE WITHIN FIVE DAYS AFTER RECEIPT OF GOODS
PLEASE EXAMINE ALL PACKAGES FOR MISSING ARTICLES

O. S. WILSON
F. G. PUGH
W. M. FAW

WILSON & PUGH CO.
WHOLESALE HARDWARE CUTLERY AND TINWARE
MINE AND MILL SUPPLIES.

No. 26 GEORGE STREET, Cumberland, Md. August 19, 1921

Sold to M E. B. Prichard Co.,

TERMS, 30 DAYS NET. 2 PER CENT. 10 DAYS. Frostburg, Md.

100	Lbs Lewis White Lead	.12¼	12 25

Pd
11/11/21
Ck # 12666

An original invoice stated that Wilson and Pugh Hardware provided E. B. Prichard Company of Frostburg with 100 pounds of white lead according to this invoice dated August 19, 1921.

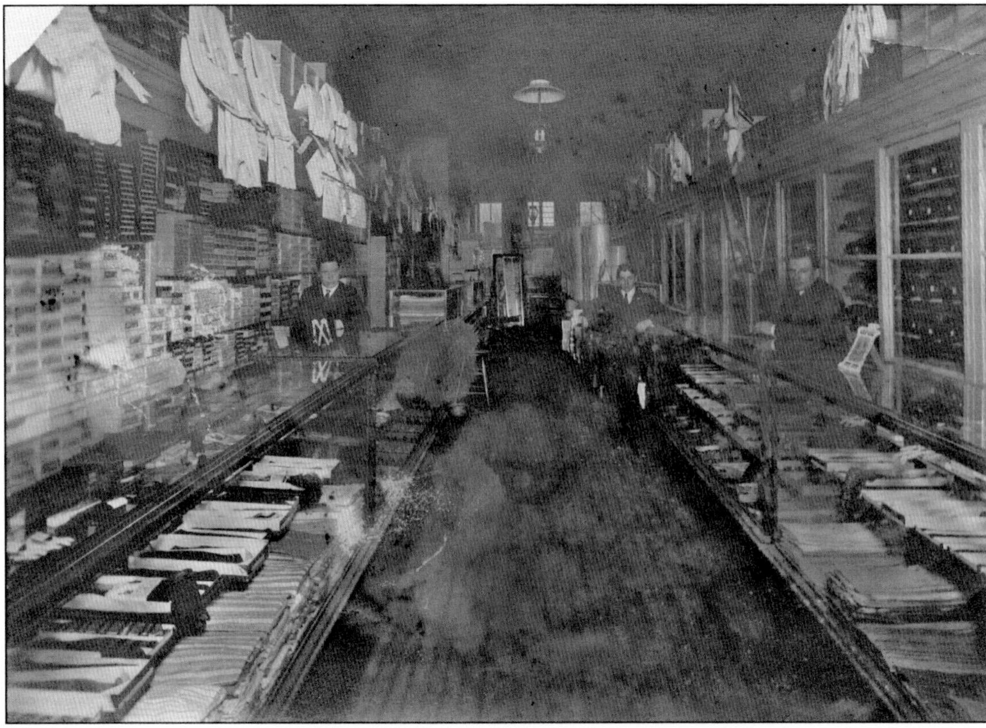

Two Gross brothers' stores operated under the direction of family members. The largest store operated on Baltimore Street and was a major retailing establishment. This interior view of the much smaller and lesser-known dry goods and clothing store was taken on North Centre Street.

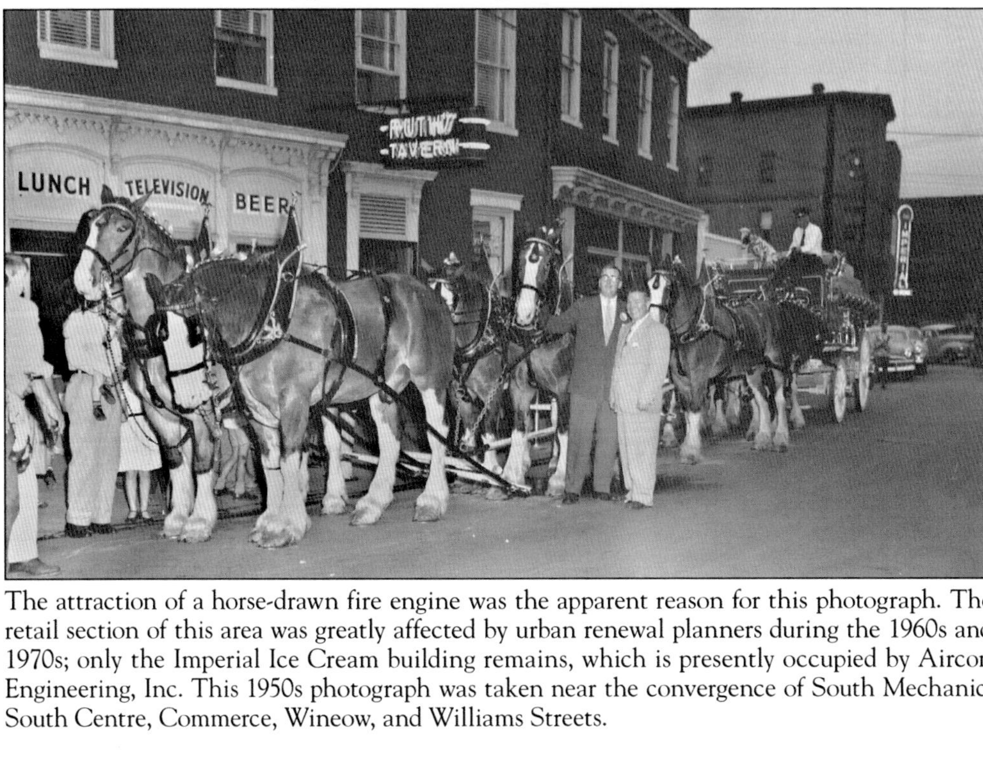

The attraction of a horse-drawn fire engine was the apparent reason for this photograph. The retail section of this area was greatly affected by urban renewal planners during the 1960s and 1970s; only the Imperial Ice Cream building remains, which is presently occupied by Aircon Engineering, Inc. This 1950s photograph was taken near the convergence of South Mechanic, South Centre, Commerce, Wineow, and Williams Streets.

Planning for the downtown Cumberland pedestrian mall began in 1975. Construction started at 10:00 a.m. on May 15, 1978, when barricades were erected across Baltimore Street, thereby ending the movement of vehicles on the thoroughfare for the first time. This photograph was taken on Baltimore Street midway between Mechanic and Liberty Streets.

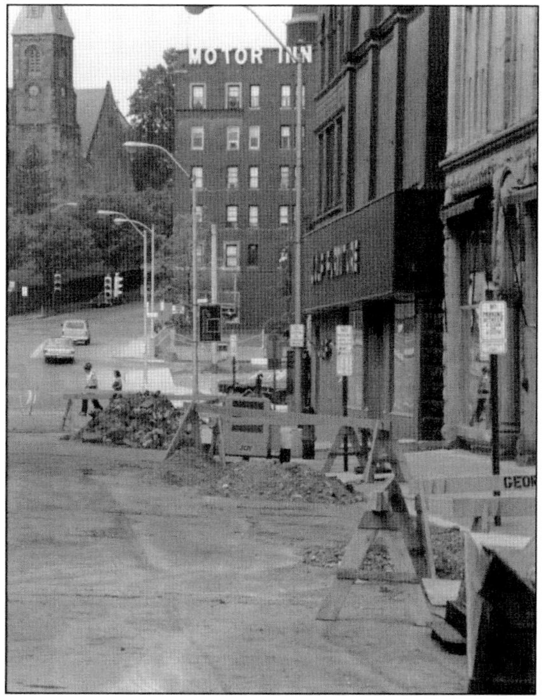

Looking east on Baltimore Street at the beginning of mall construction reveals the locally owned businesses of Cumberland Cloak and Suite, Shinnamon's Shoe Store, the Manhattan men's clothing store, Morton's Jewelry, and Burton's. Merchants believed the pedestrian mall would stem the flight of retail business from downtown to suburban shopping centers that opened in the 1960s. The pending Country Club Mall opened in 1981.

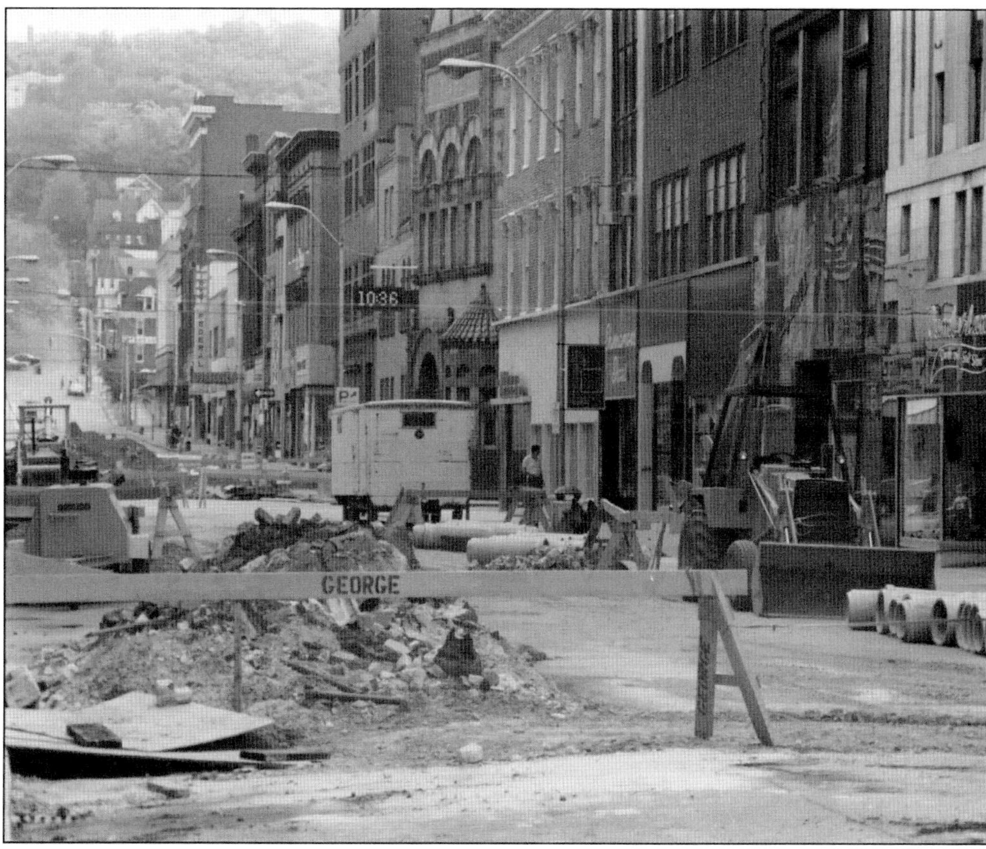

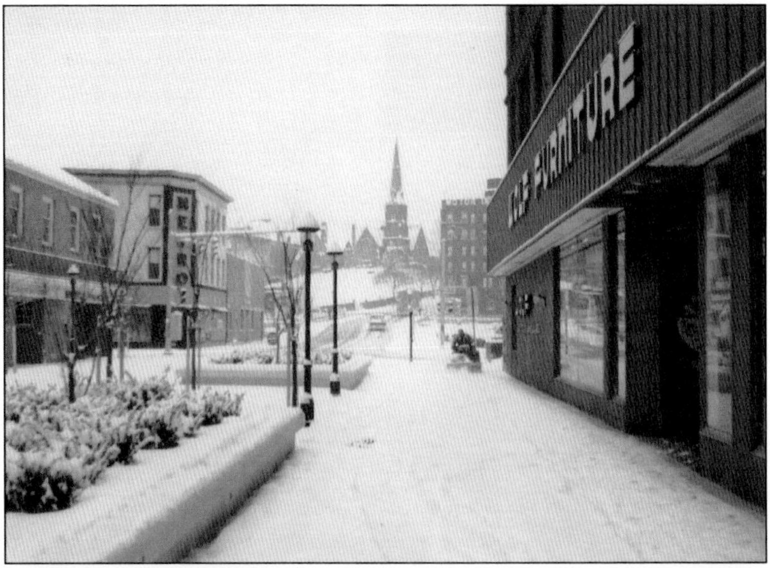

From this view of the western end of the Cumberland pedestrian mall, Metro Clothes is on the south side and Wolf's Furniture store is on the north side. Metro Clothes closed in 1984.

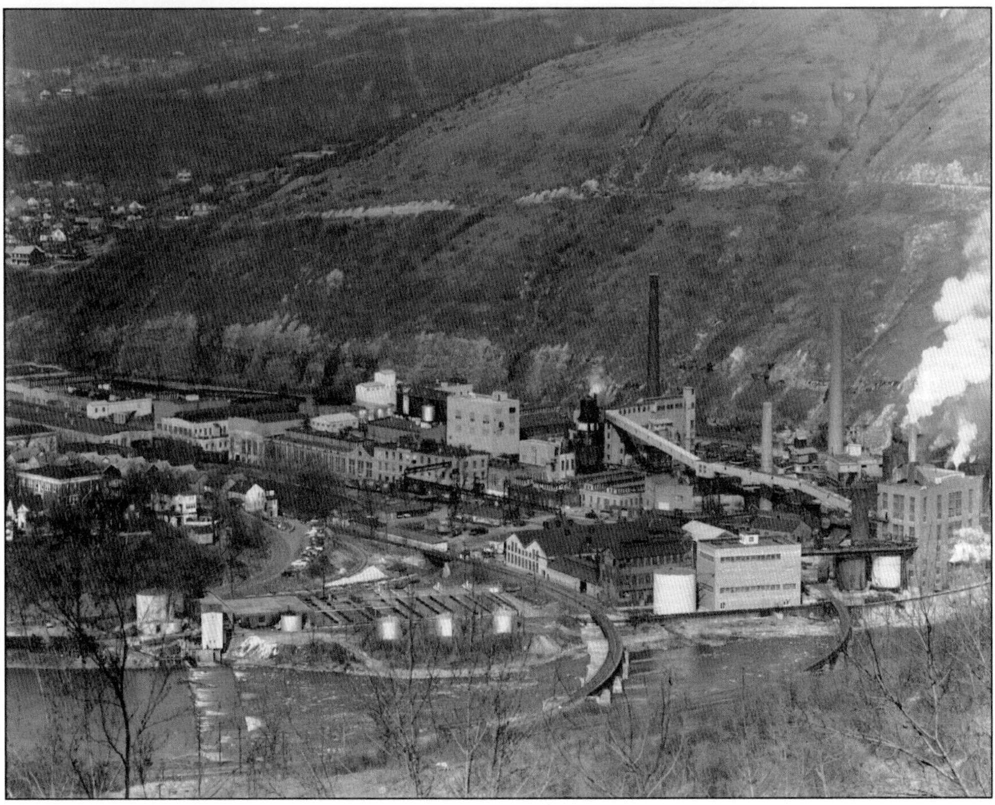

In 1888, the Piedmont Pulp and Paper Company of Allegany County was founded by William Luke along the North Branch of the Potomac River. The company later became known as West Virginia Pulp and Paper Company and then in 1969 became Westvaco Corporation. In 2005, the Luke plant became part of NewPage Corporation, the largest manufacturer of paper in the United States. NewPage remains one of Allegany County's major employers. This photograph is dated 1954.

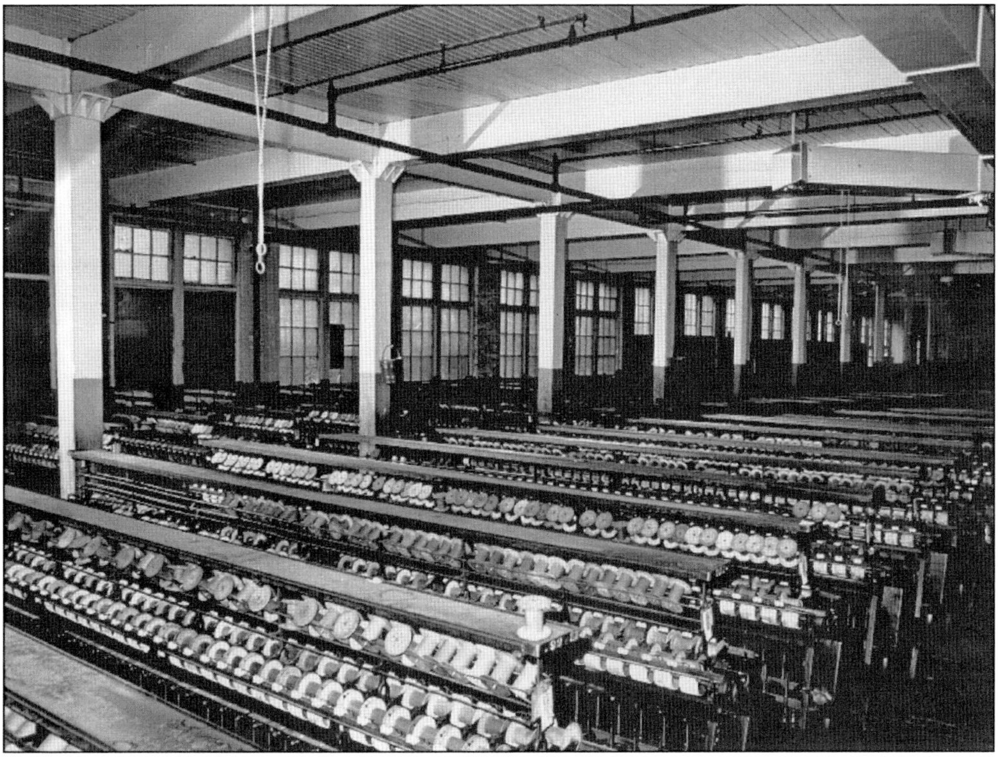

The Klotz Throwing Company, commonly called the Lonaconing Silk Mill, began production in 1907. Raw silk was imported from Asia for the purpose of "throwing"—a cleaning, doubling, and twisting process of silk fibers. Records show that silk threads were shipped from Lonaconing to many eastern states and Havana, Cuba. The Lonaconing mill closed in 1957 and remains essentially intact. This view shows a section of the first floor.

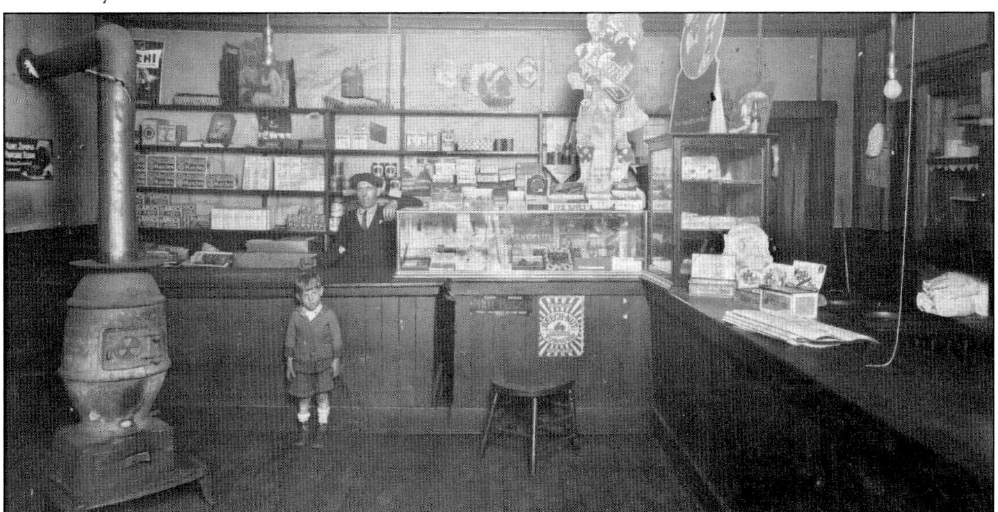

Allegany County residents conducted daily business with store owners like John Kirk, who operated a small general store on Main Street in Barton. Kirk is standing behind the counter with his son, David, in front. In later years, the Kirk family opened a confectionery business across the street from the original store. This photograph was taken around 1926. (Courtesy Jeff Kirk.)

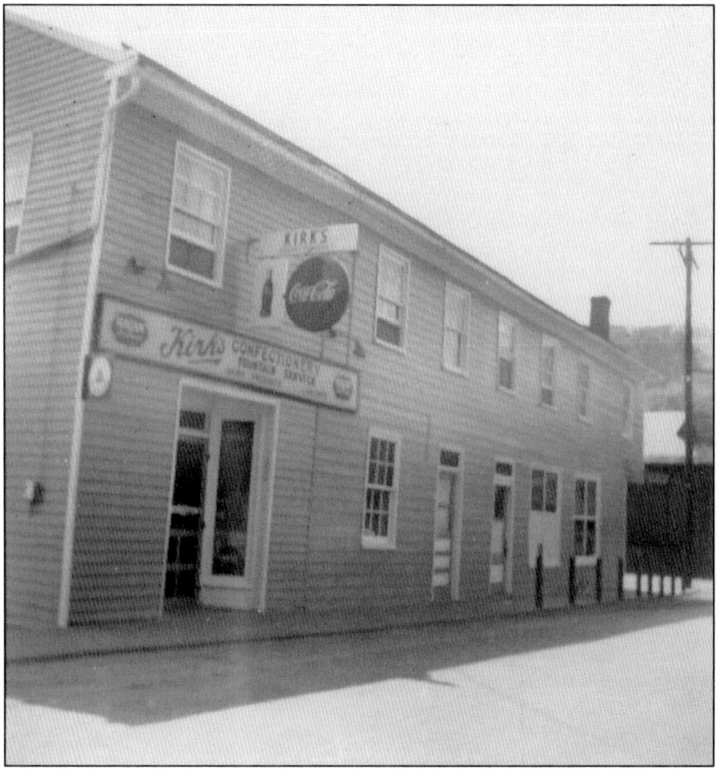

John, Maude, and their son, David, operated Kirk's Confectionery on Main Street in Barton. The store opened in the 1940s and continued business through the 1950s. The store featured a jukebox, soda fountain, and limited menu that attracted teenagers. (Courtesy Jeff Kirk.)

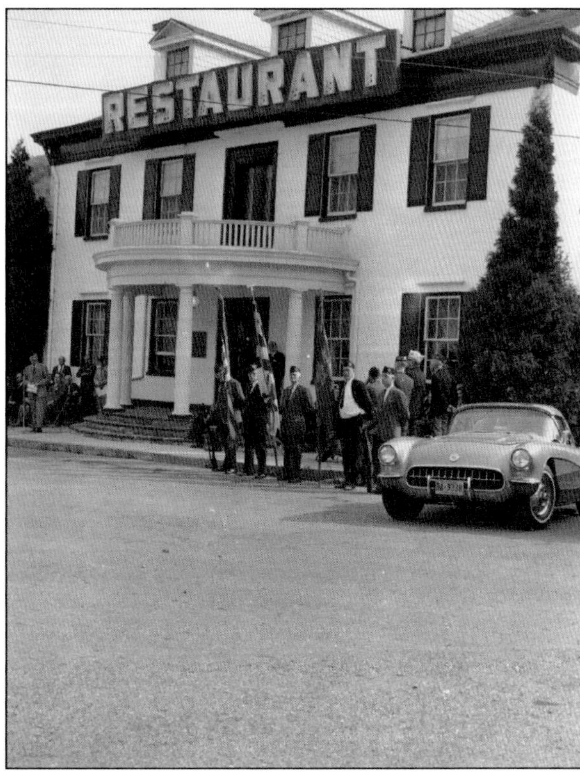

In 1958, a military veterans group conducted a ceremony at the historic Clarysville Inn. It was constructed in 1807 and served travelers along Braddock's Road, later called U.S. Route 40. The Union army leased the property from Rebecca Clary in 1862 for the purpose of establishing a convalescent Civil War hospital. The inn was destroyed by fire in March 1999.

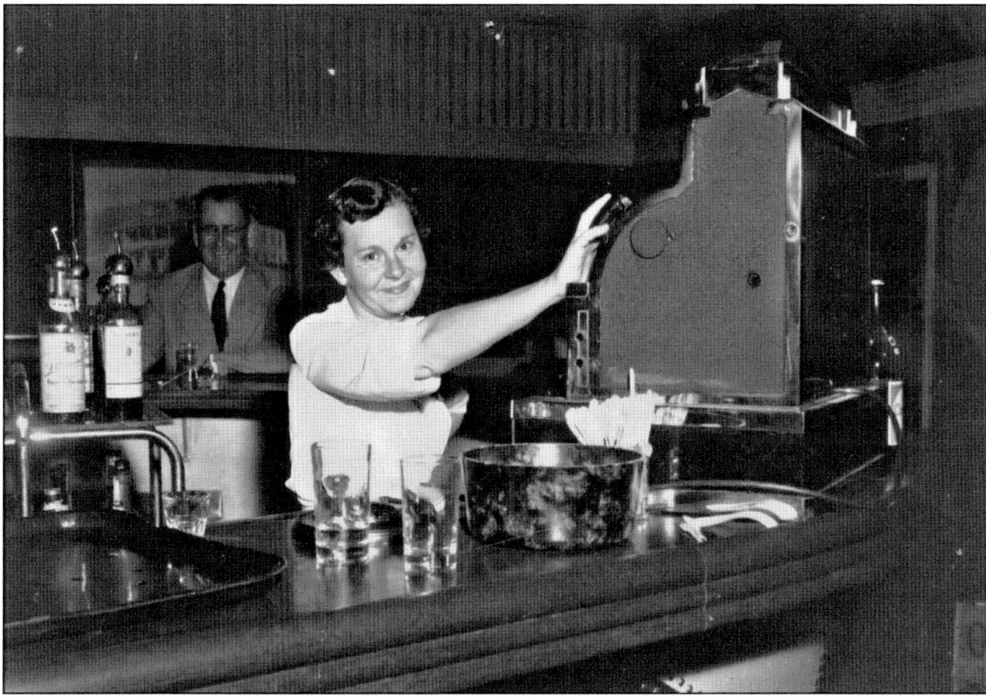

The Clarysville Inn offered a bar and lounge area that also hosted traveling entertainers during the 1950s and 1960s. LaRue Broderick, shown in this photograph, tended bar at the Clarysville Lounge during the 1950s.

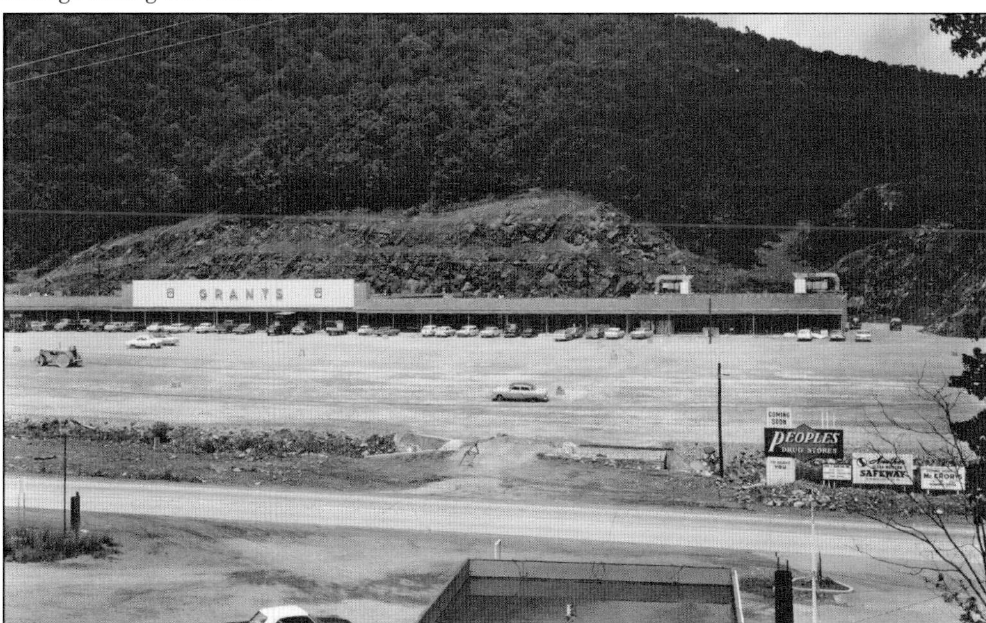

The LaVale Plaza Shopping Center was nearing completion when this photograph was taken in 1961. The anchor stores were McCrory's on the east end, Grant's in the center, and Safeway on the west end. Building of the shopping center required road improvements in the area. The two-lane U.S. Route 40 was widened to accommodate increased traffic flow to the shopping center.

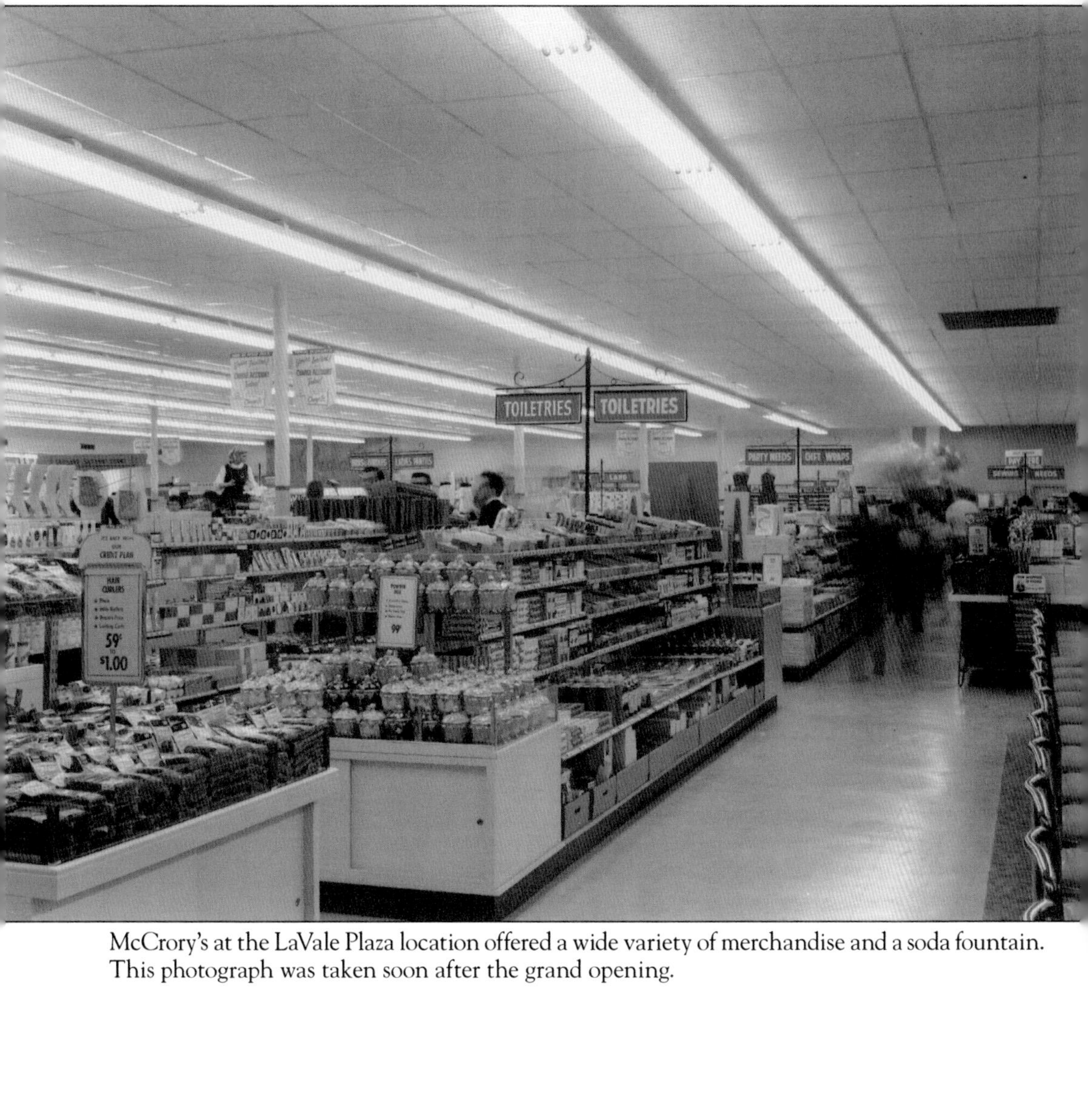

McCrory's at the LaVale Plaza location offered a wide variety of merchandise and a soda fountain. This photograph was taken soon after the grand opening.

Five

Hometown Happenings

Allegany County's rural character helped to create a number of small towns that were nearly self-sufficient in the 19th century. Travel between towns or to the cities of Frostburg and Cumberland was not taken for granted, as it is today. Many residents relied on rail and bus services for travel well into the 20th century.

The end of World War II brought many changes to towns. Increasing prosperity during the 1950s meant automobiles were affordable for most families, and travel became a routine event. Improved highway systems also increased travel options and tended to make residents less connected to goods and services offered by neighborhood merchants. Nevertheless the sense of community remained strong in Allegany County, and residents still proudly pointed to their origins.

Especially interesting was the evolution of Main Street communities. Main Street was where merchants, restaurants, bars, parades, and civic activities could be found; family-owned businesses dominated the retail and service sectors, and residents knew the owners as neighbors and friends. Main Street is also where some of the most notable changes have occurred over the last century. Examining old photographs illustrates how much Allegany County communities have changed.

The following photographs depict individuals, organizations, notable events, and landscapes from around Allegany County, serving, more or less, as a scrapbook of historic photographs that recalls different times.

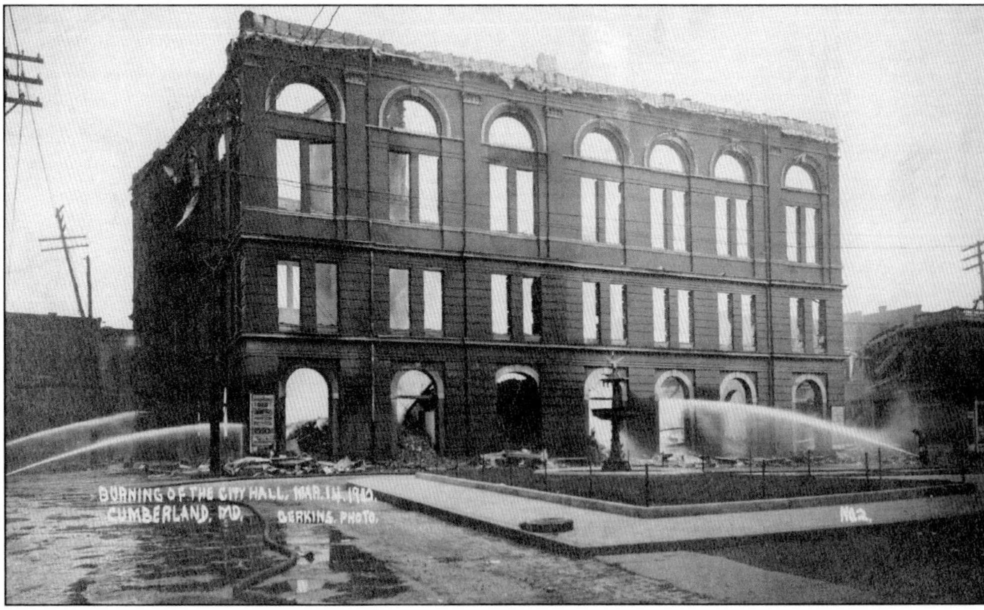

Cumberland City Hall was a multipurpose building begun in 1874 and completed in 1876. The first floor housed a public market with stalls leased to vendors, the second floor contained city offices, and the third floor was the academy of music. A fire destroyed the building. This photograph was taken March 14, 1910. (Courtesy Russell Livengood.)

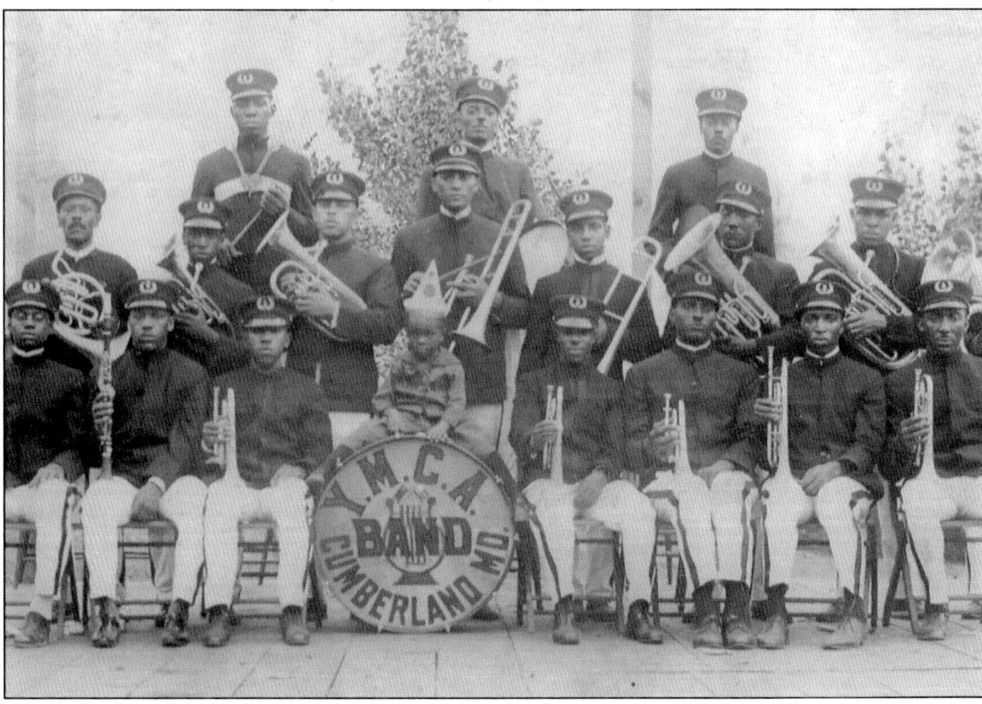

African Americans in the Cumberland community organized a YMCA band during the 1920s. The YMCA building was located on Independence Street in north Cumberland on a site that had previously served as Mary Hoye School, the first public school for African Americans in Allegany County. (Courtesy Greg Powell.)

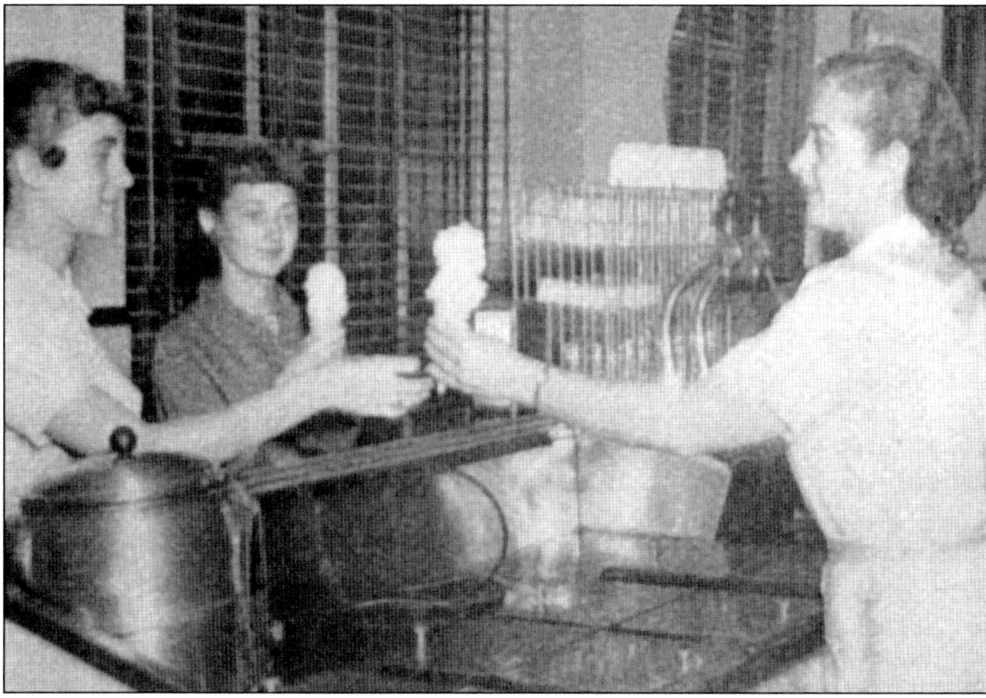

A favorite place for residents to enjoy ice cream treats was Queen City Dairy located on South Mechanic Street in Cumberland. White House Cherry ice cream was perhaps the most popular flavor. Inside the dairy were a few booths and tables for customers' seating. This photograph was taken in 1960. (Courtesy Opessan Log.)

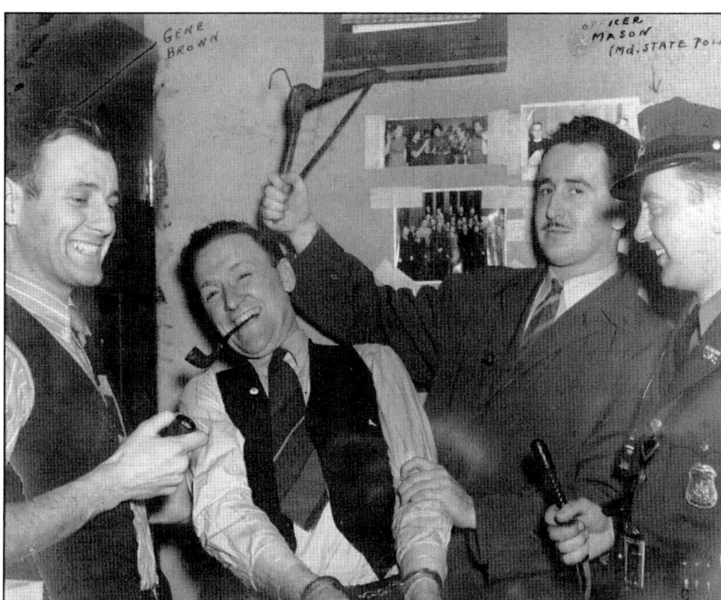

Cumberland Times-News employees enjoyed a prank for the photographer's benefit in December 1940. From left to right are Gene Brown, Clarence "Jiggs" Burns, unidentified, and Maryland state trooper Mason. Brown and Burns served in many capacities over the years at the Cumberland newspaper.

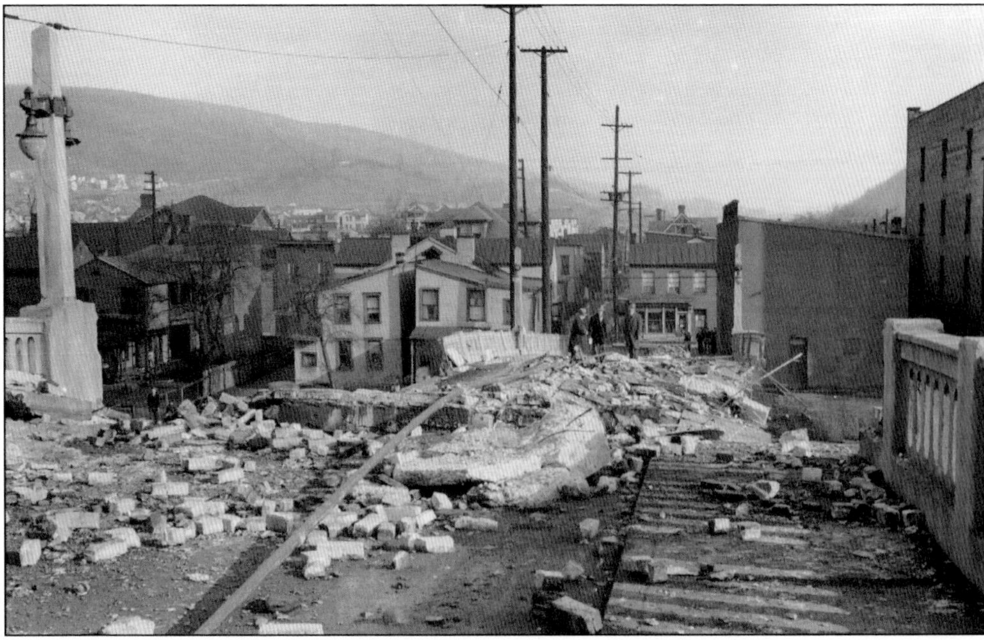

The Valley Street Bridge was constructed in 1916 at a cost of $27,000 by Vang Construction Company. On February 12, 1945, 2- and 4-inch gas mains exploded under the bridge floor, causing substantial damage to the structure. Two 14-year-old boys were seriously injured in the blast.

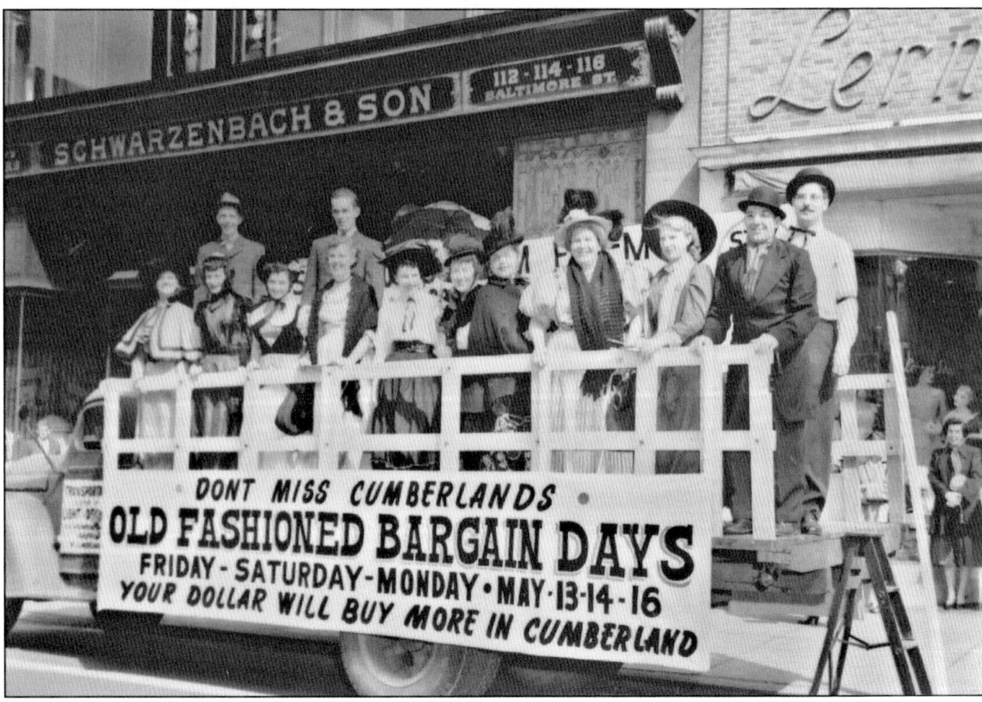

Cumberland's Retail Business Association promoted Old Fashioned Bargain Days in 1956. Cumberlanders were encouraged to dress in 1890s attire when attending special events, including outdoor concerts at Constitution Park. Prizes were awarded for best outfits. The theme continued for several years and proved to be successful in attracting shoppers to the downtown area.

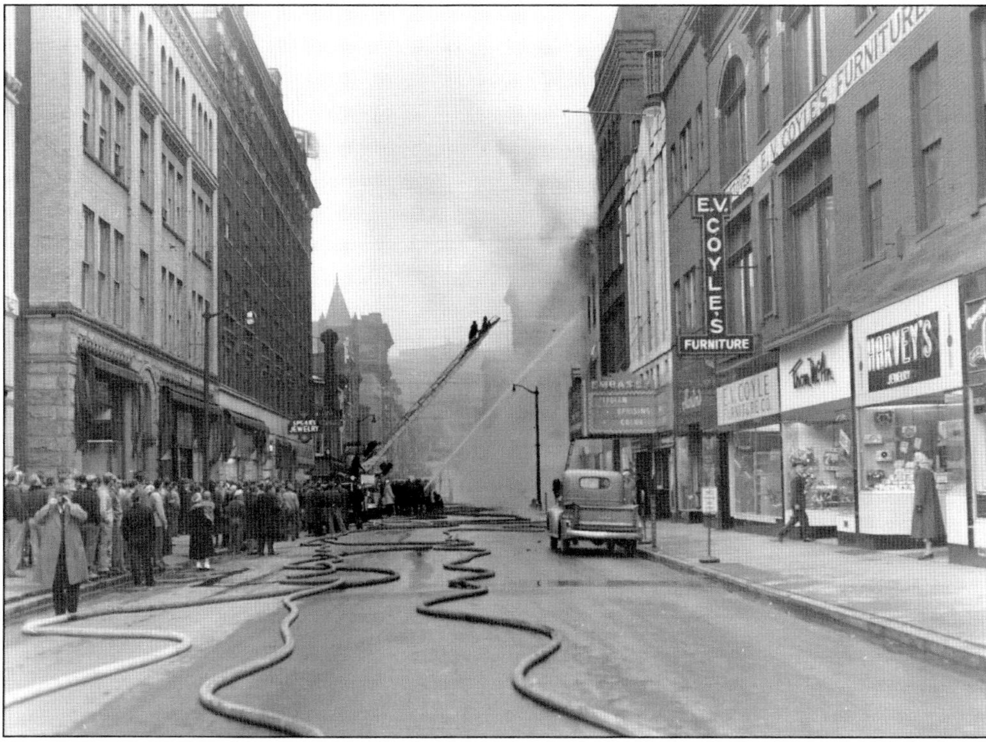

City of Cumberland firefighters and several volunteer companies fought a major blaze on Baltimore Street in February 1952. The fire started on the third floor of the Potomac Edison building and caused an estimated $200,000 in damages. This photograph also reveals many family-owned businesses that once dominated the downtown district, including the Embassy Theatre, E. V. Coyle Furniture, Cumberland Cloak and Suit, and Spear's Jewelry Store. (Courtesy Jeff Kirk.)

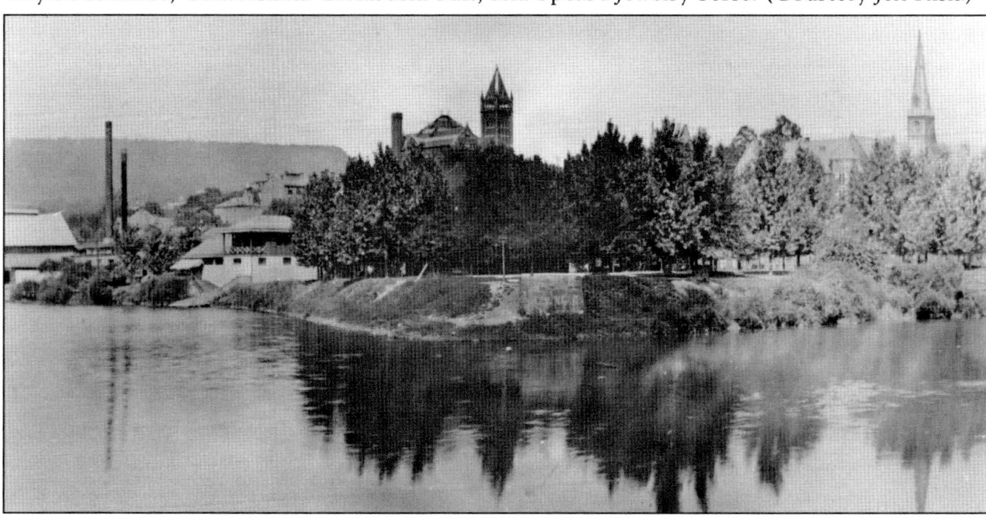

This photograph, taken from a small boat, predated Cumberland's flood control project and the new Blue Bridge to Ridgeley. The smokestacks to the left were part of the Cumberland waterworks plant. Also observed along the waterfront is a ramp for the purpose of launching and boarding small boats. The Allegany County Court House on Washington Street is clearly visible in the center background.

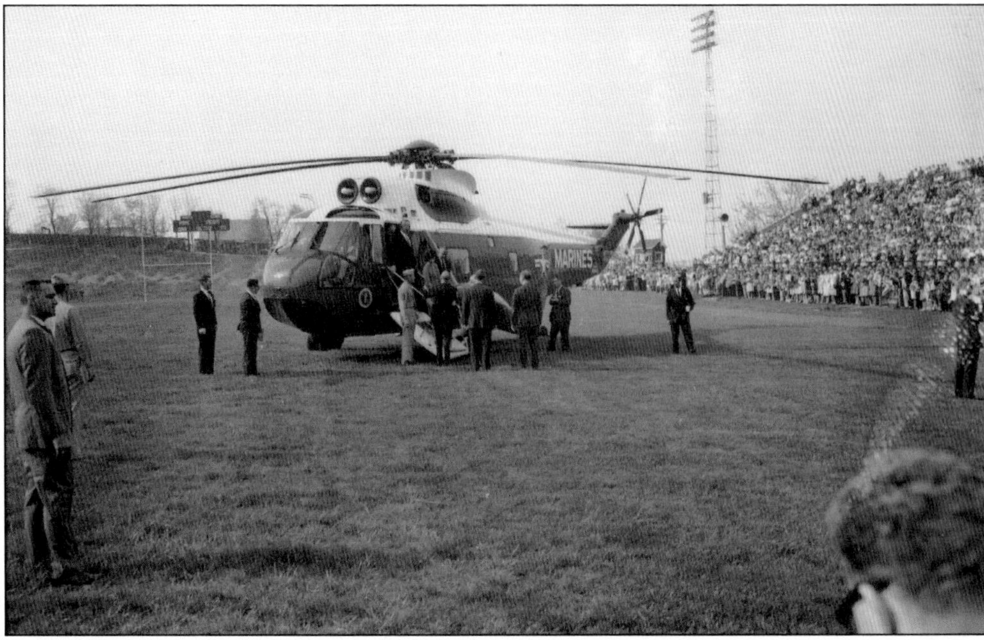

Lyndon Johnson visited Allegany County on two occasions. His first visit was October 7, 1960, as a vice presidential candidate on the Democratic ticket. Johnson's second visit in May 1964 was in the role of president of the United States. The primary purpose of that visit was to promote his War on Poverty program. After landing in a U.S. Marine Corps helicopter at Greenway Avenue Stadium, the president spoke to the capacity crowd from a podium that was built specifically for this occasion. A motorcade transported him from the stadium through city streets, where he received an enthusiastic reception. At city hall, another capacity crowd provided a tumultuous welcome as the motorcade arrived. Part of the capacity crowd was filled with students who were dismissed from classes to take part in the historic moment.

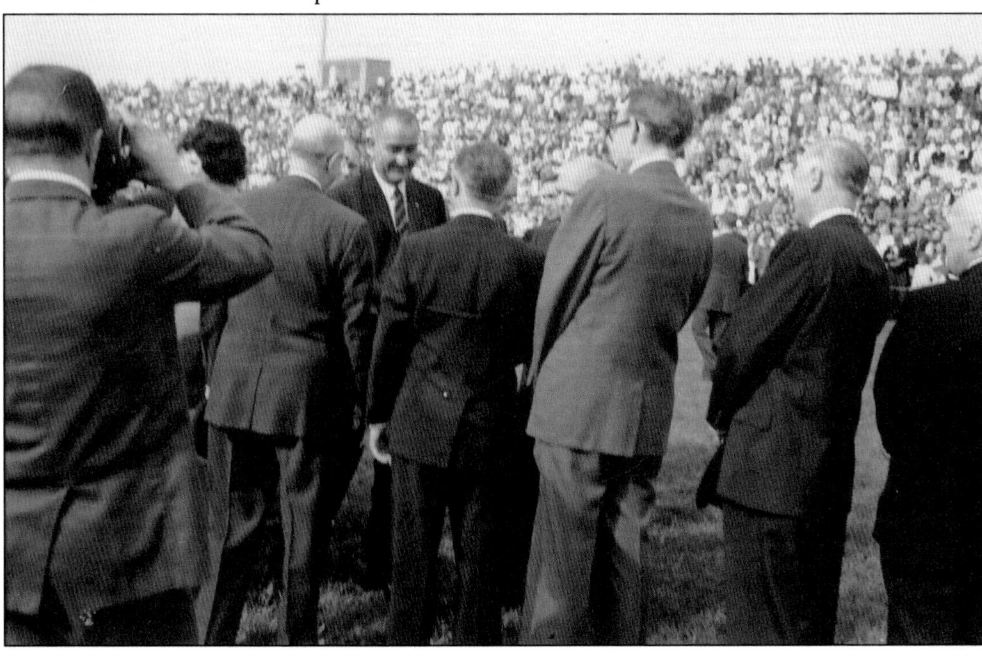

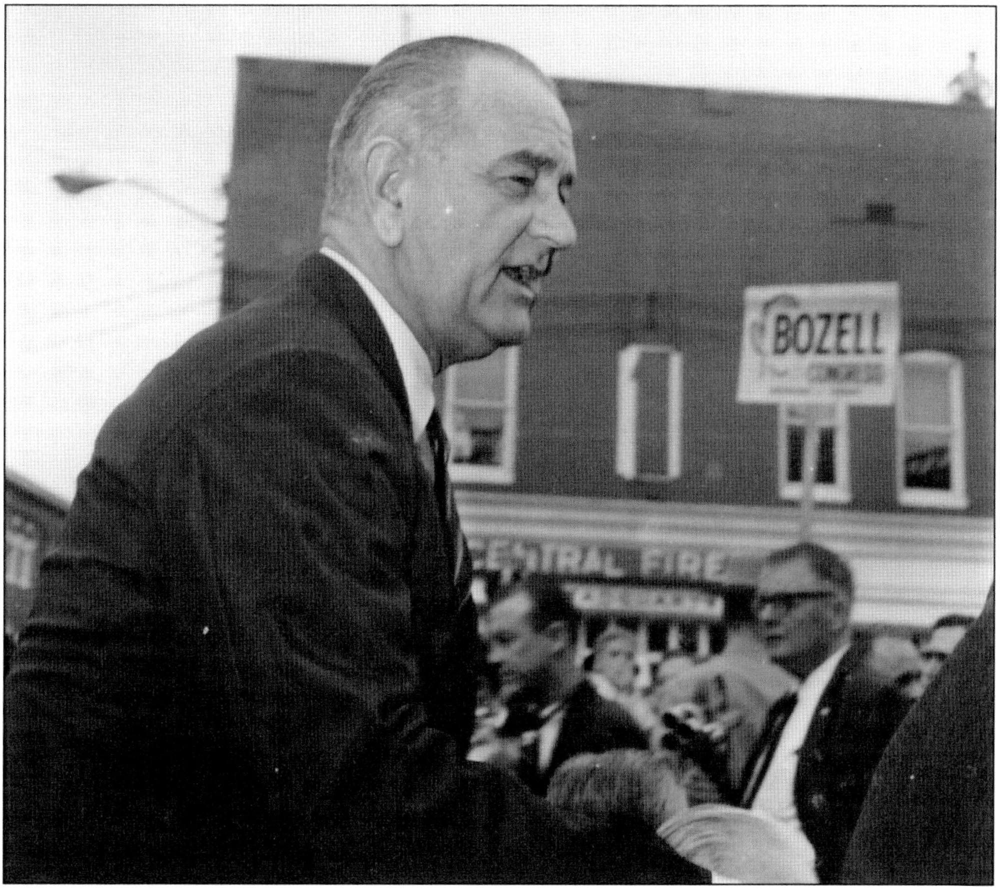

Pres. Lyndon Johnson's remarks at City Plaza defined the nature of the enemy that his War on Poverty program confronted. "Today the enemies that confront our people are more complex. They will not yield simply to guns or force. They take the form of disease and poor schools, of untrained men and unemployment, of exhausted mines and obsolete skills." Perhaps the most animated moment at City Hall Plaza was when the president asked, "We are going to provide a way out (of poverty), aren't we?" A tremendous "Yes" was shouted by the crowd. The presidential motorcade proceeded out of town by traveling south on Mechanic Street toward Greenway Avenue Stadium, where the U.S. Marine Corps helicopter awaited the president for a trip to Martinsburg. In this photograph, Johnson's daughter, Lynda Byrd, stands next to her father.

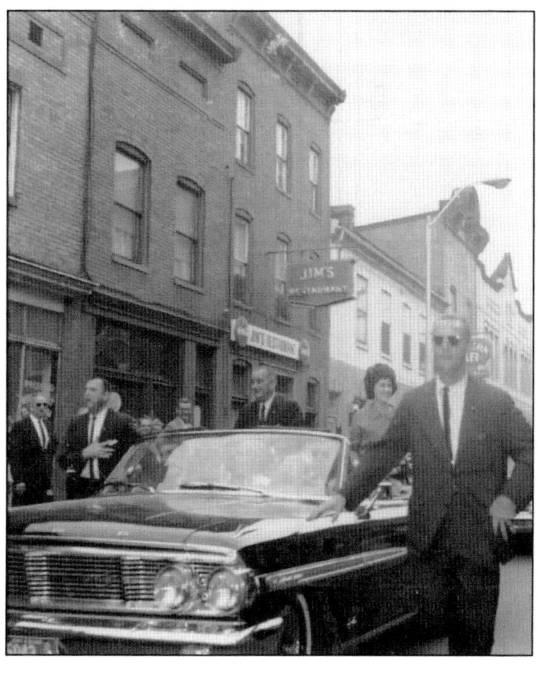

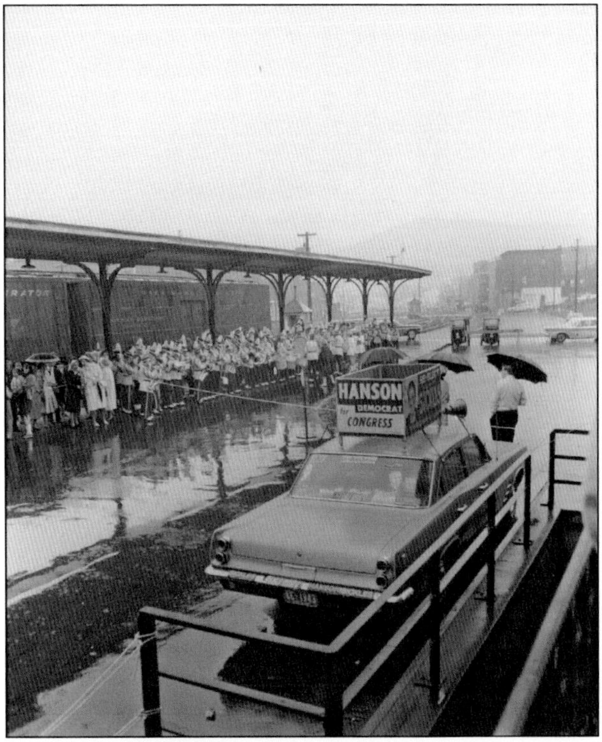

Maryland Democratic candidates in the 1964 election campaign organized an extended "Whistle Stop Special" tour on the Baltimore and Ohio Railroad. Joseph Tydings, candidate for the U.S. Senate, was accompanied on the tour by Rep. Carlton Sickles and Royce Hanson, Democratic candidate for the 6th Congressional District seat. The Allegany High School Band greeted the candidates at 3:00 p.m. on October 14, 1964.

Buildings along Bedford Street that housed United Television and Central Clothing Service are being demolished in this July 1957 photograph. The area was intended to become a parking lot under the ownership of George G. Holzshu. United Television was located at 128–130 North Centre Street.

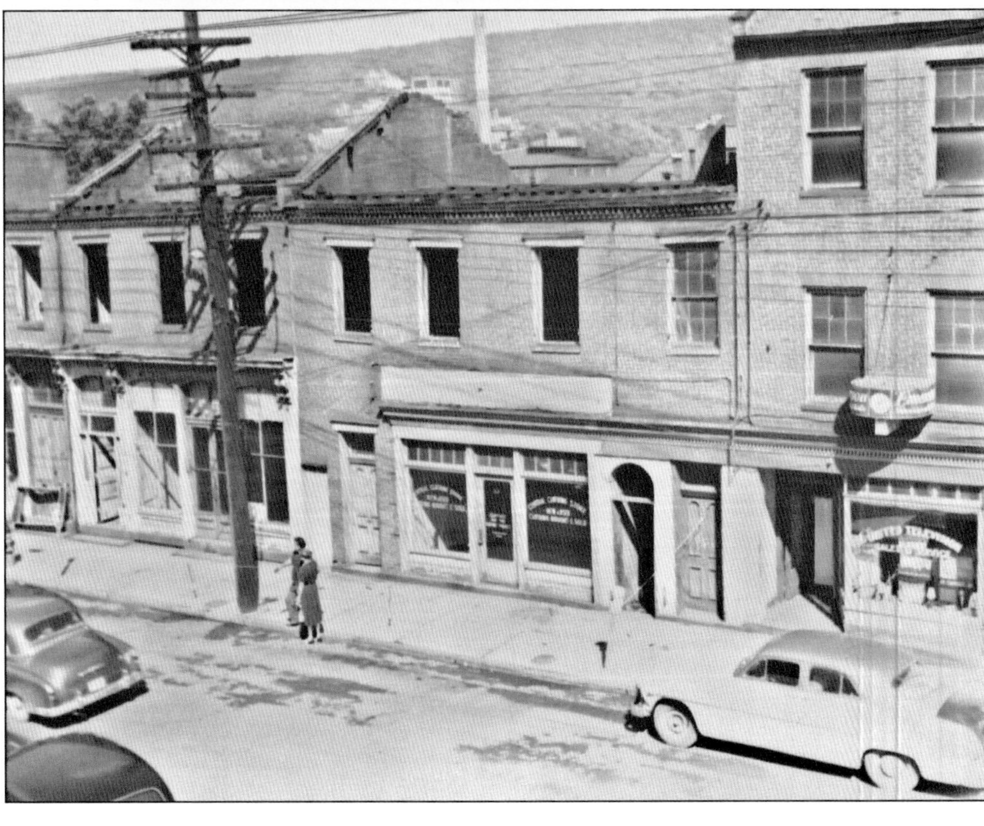

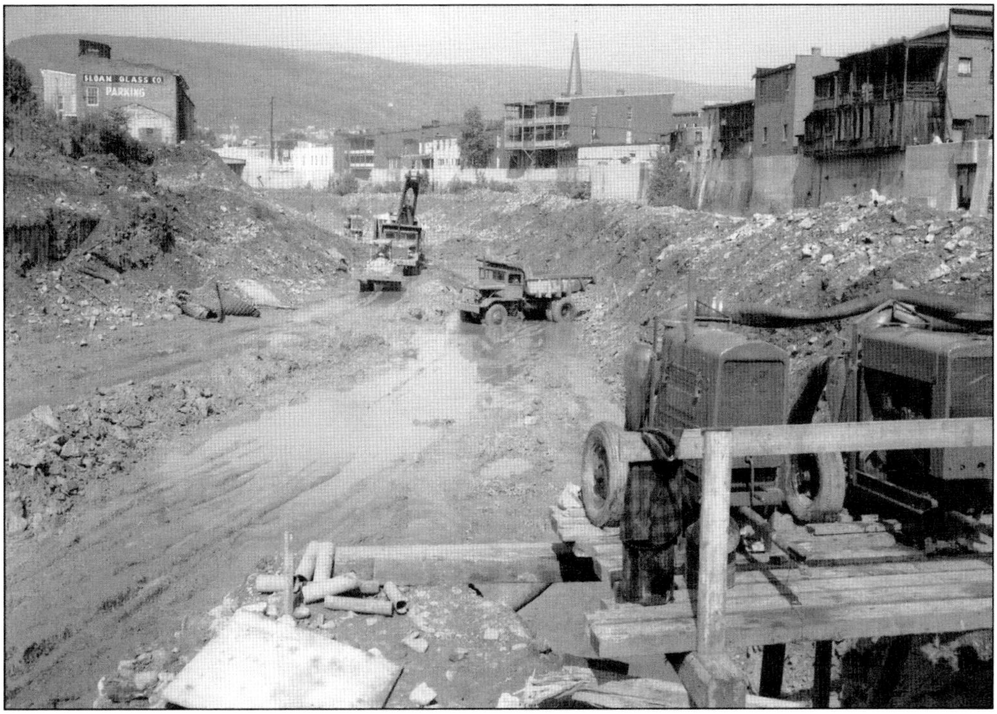

Work began on Cumberland's massive flood control project in 1949. Temporary dirt walls were created in the center of the creek where water was pumped from one side to the other so that construction could proceed in a dry environment. Sloan Glass Company and the Queen City Brewing Company are in the background.

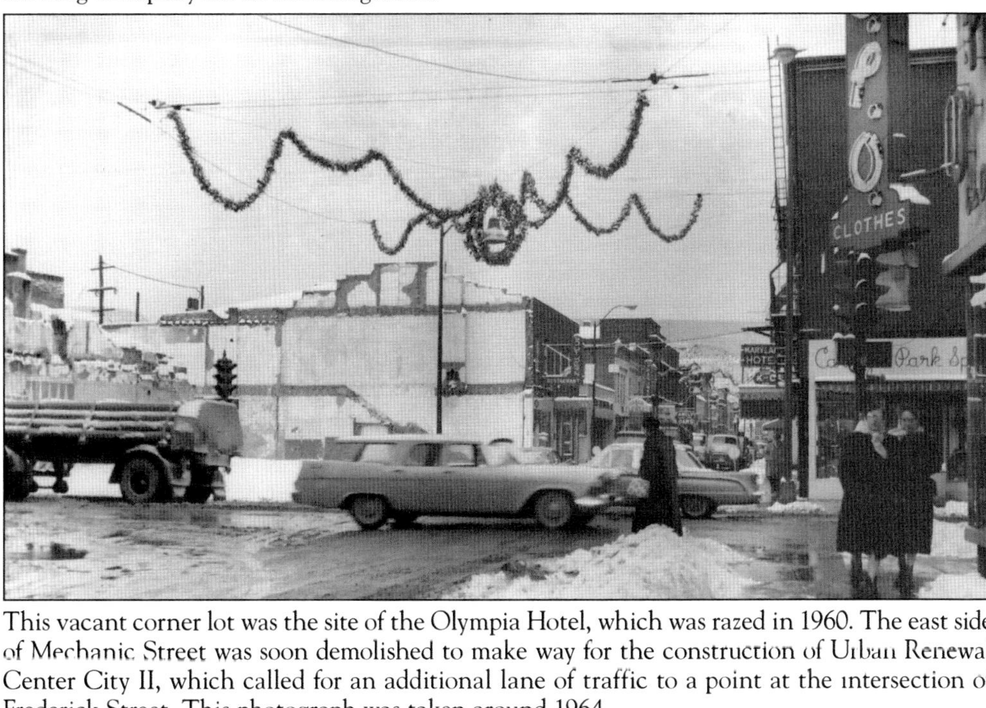

This vacant corner lot was the site of the Olympia Hotel, which was razed in 1960. The east side of Mechanic Street was soon demolished to make way for the construction of Urban Renewal Center City II, which called for an additional lane of traffic to a point at the intersection of Frederick Street. This photograph was taken around 1964.

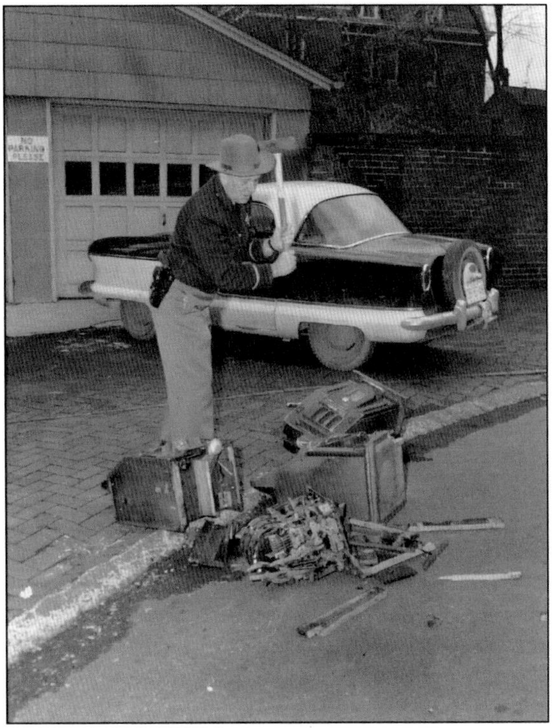

Taken around 1960, this photograph shows Allegany County sheriff's deputy George "Doggie" Harris destroying a slot machine behind the circuit court building at Prospect Square. During the early 1960s, the regulation of slot machines was a major political issue in the state of Maryland. Raids on business establishments operating the illegal gambling devices occurred throughout Allegany County.

This section of south Cumberland was significantly affected during the 1960s with the building of Fort Cumberland Homes (in the foreground), construction of a bridge over the Baltimore and Ohio Railroad tracks, and the opening of Industrial Boulevard. The Fort Cumberland complex was completed in 1960. The row of houses along the top ridge is on Browning Street.

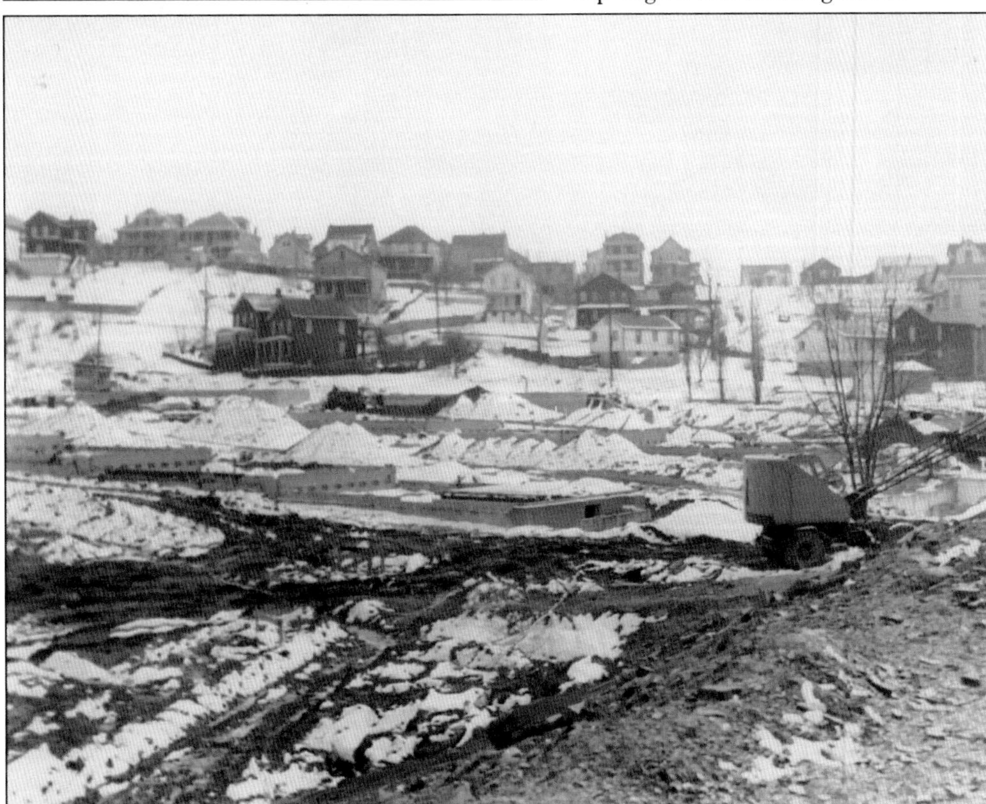

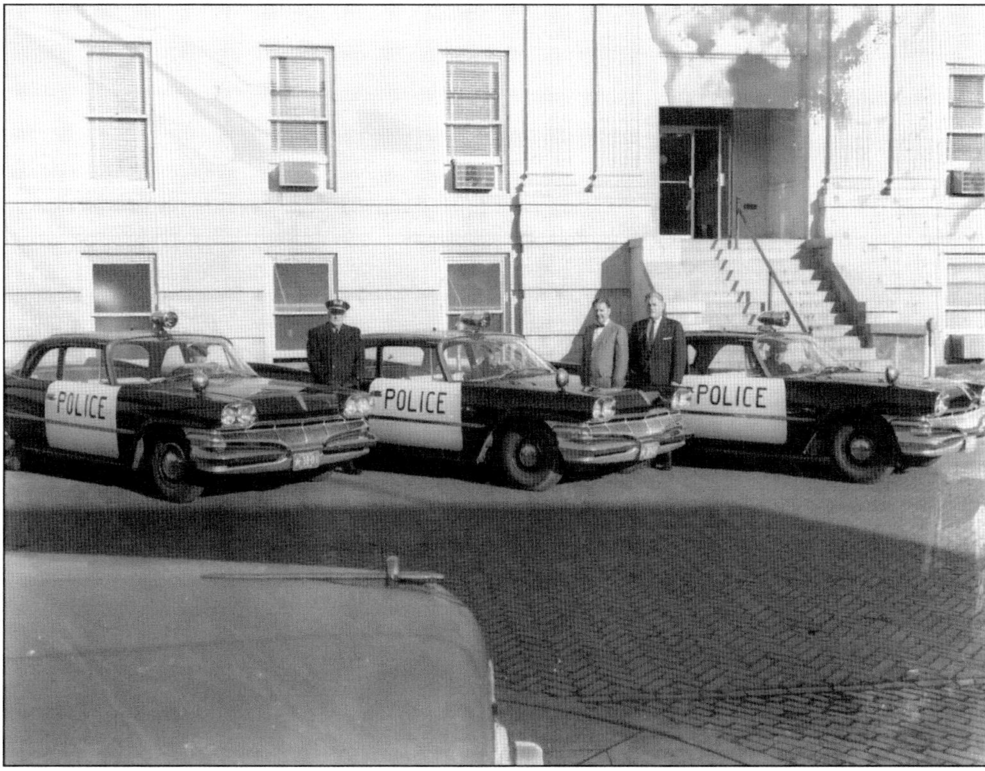

An officer of the city of Cumberland's police department poses with commissioner Phil Fleming, far right, and three police cruisers on the west side of city hall for this early-1960s photograph. During this time period, police cruisers were typically painted in two distinct colors. The section of Liberty Street shown here was once open to traffic.

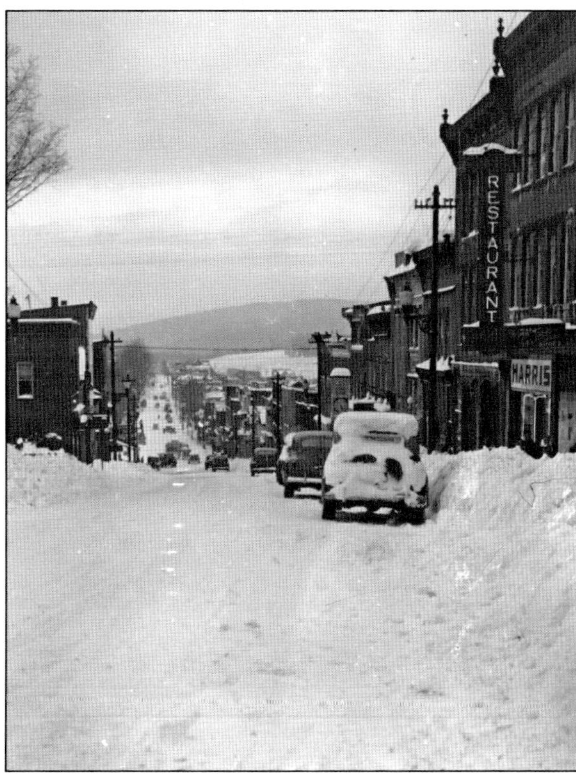

Frostburg residents have long been accustomed to heavy snowfalls. This view of Main Street, looking east in the 1940s, identifies many family-owned businesses of the post–World War II era.

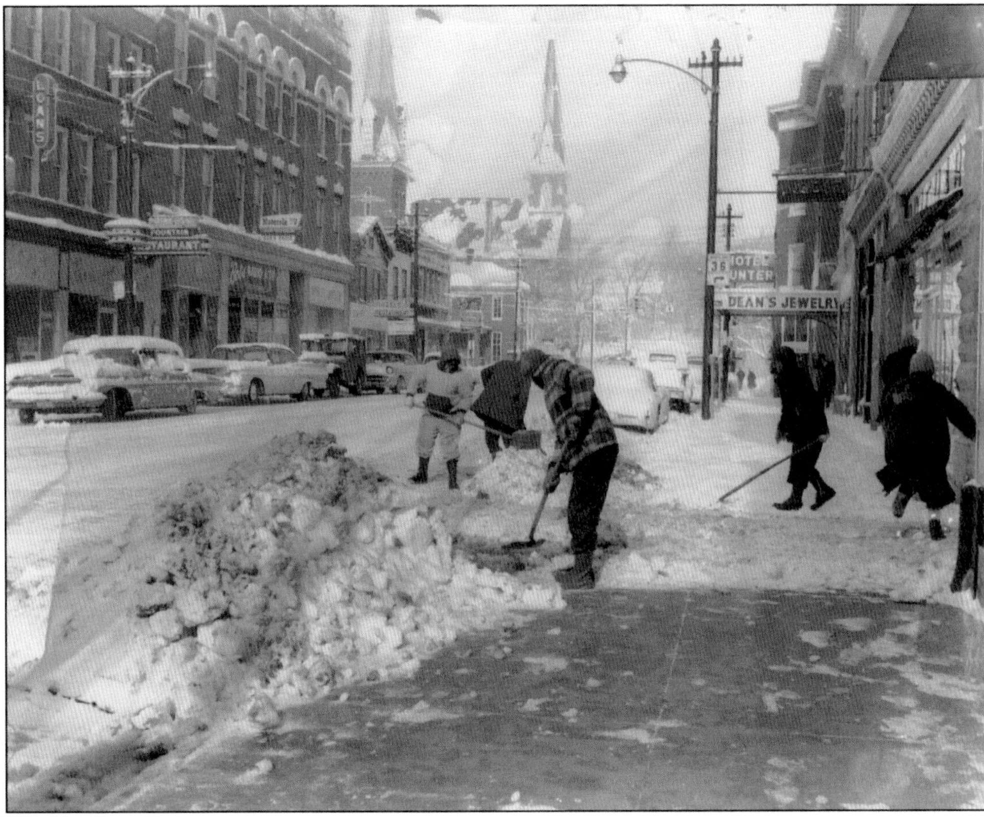

Here is a view of Main Street in Frostburg, looking west, around 1960.

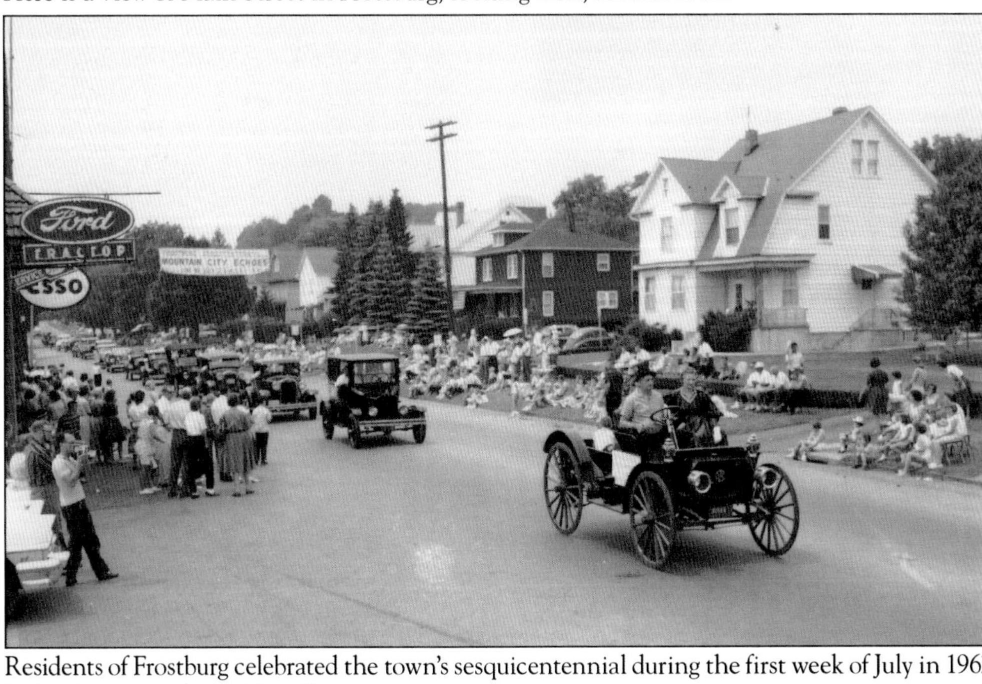

Residents of Frostburg celebrated the town's sesquicentennial during the first week of July in 1962 by having a parade on Main Street.

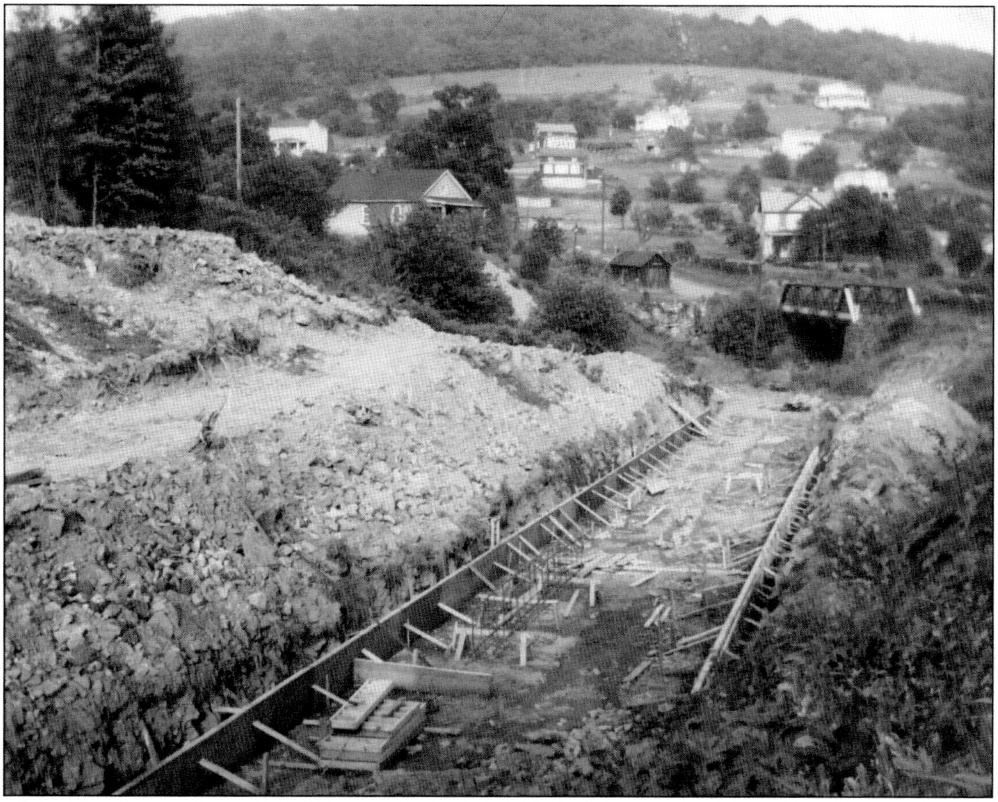

This photograph labeled "new cut into Frostburg" shows roadwork near U.S. Route 40 at Eckhart.

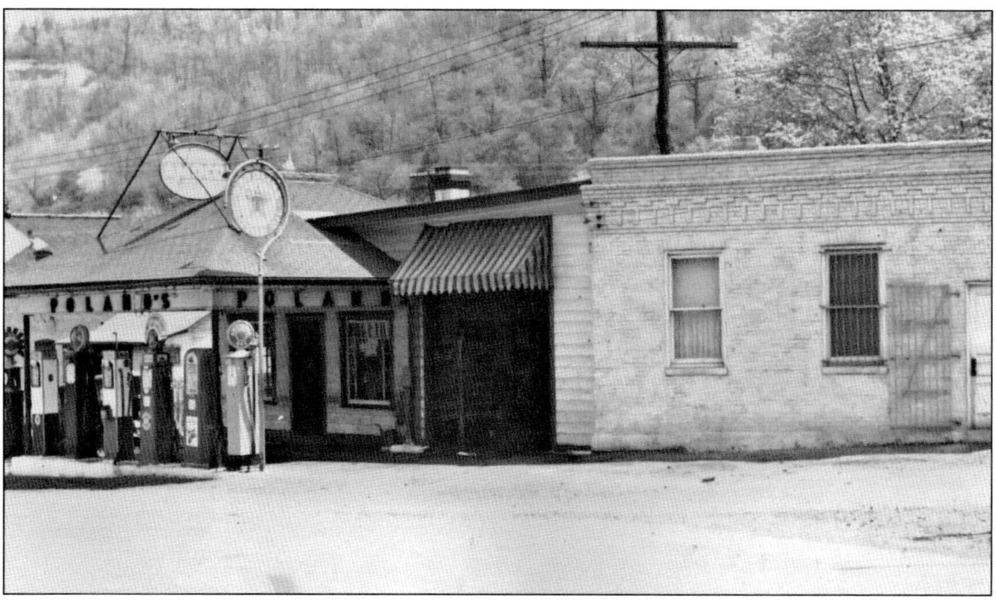

Harry and Johnny Poland's full-service gas station and garage provided Mount Savage customers with all the products of today's specialty stores, including hand washing vehicles. The Polands owned the station through the 1950s and later sold it to Richard "Dick" Beal in the 1960s.

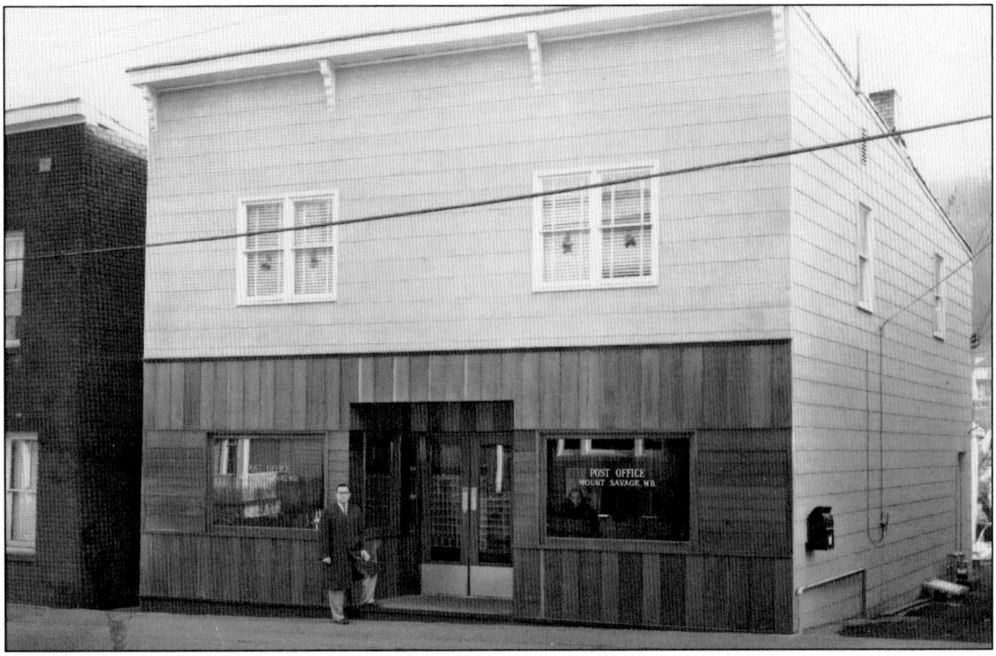

The Mount Savage Post Office, located along Maryland Route 36 in the center of the town, provided friendly conversation as well as postal services. The post office shown in this photograph was demolished, along with other buildings on the same side of the street in 2009. This photograph is from around 1960.

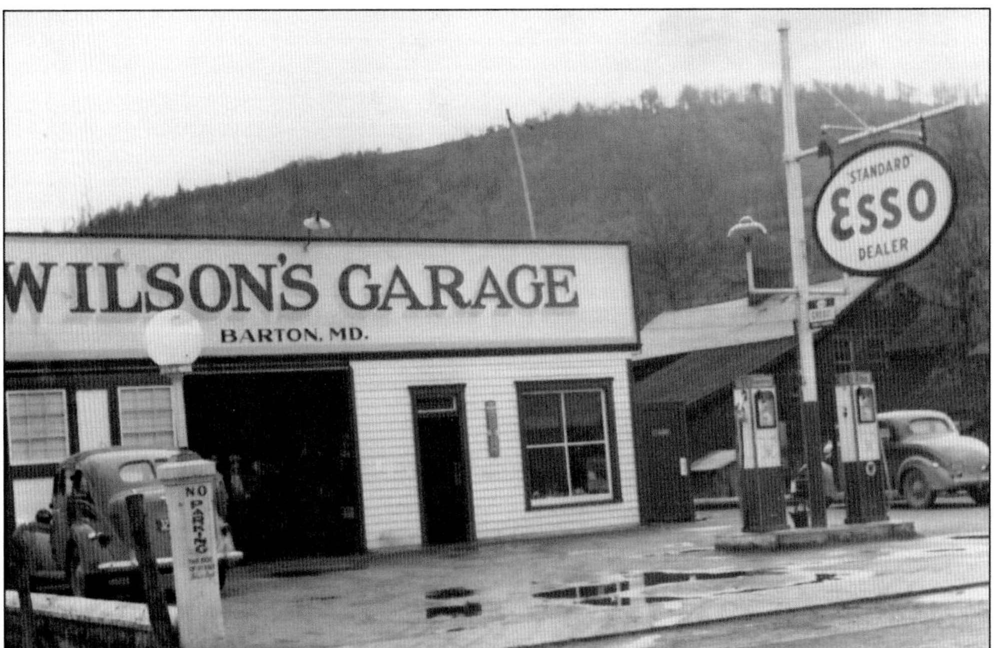

"Bink" Wilson's Garage, located in Barton, provided service and maintenance for local residents. Wilson later operated an automobile parts business in Cumberland. The garage is still in use, although not as a service station. It is pictured here around 1945.

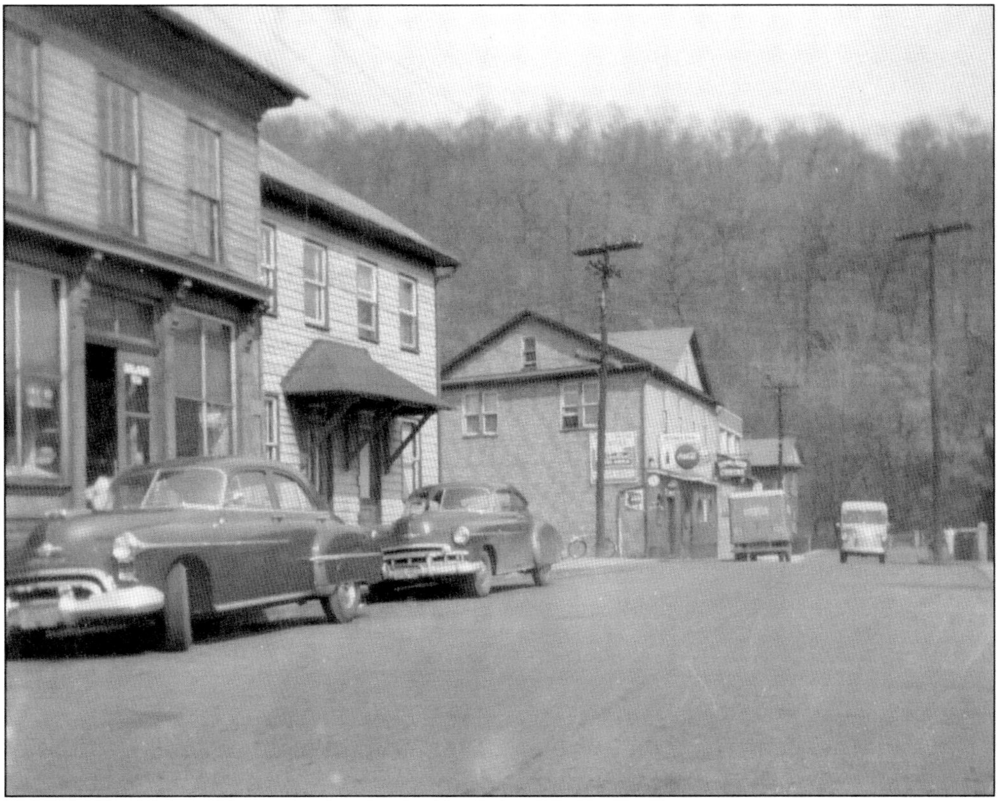

Ayer's Store occupied the first building in this view of Main Street in Barton. This photograph is from around 1955. (Courtesy Jeff Kirk.)

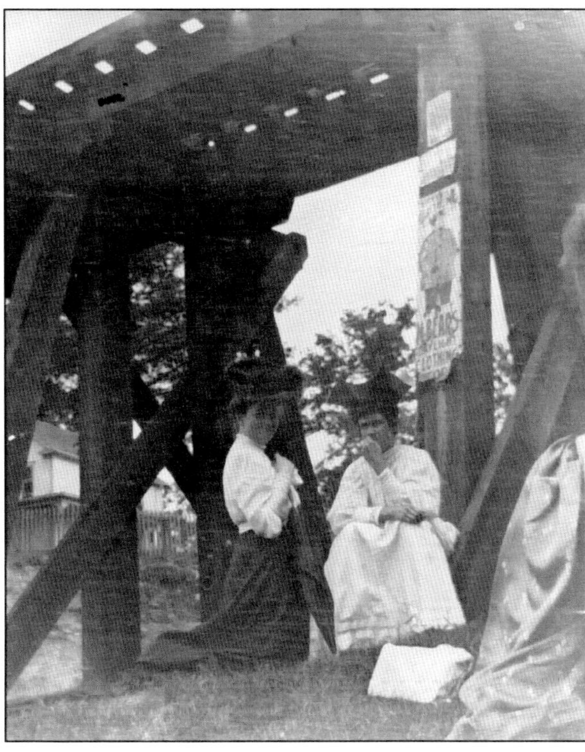

Two women attired in Victorian clothing enjoy a picnic lunch under a railroad trestle. The sign advertising Bear's Daylight Clothing suggests the location was along George's Creek. Moses Bear operated a successful clothing store in Lonaconing.

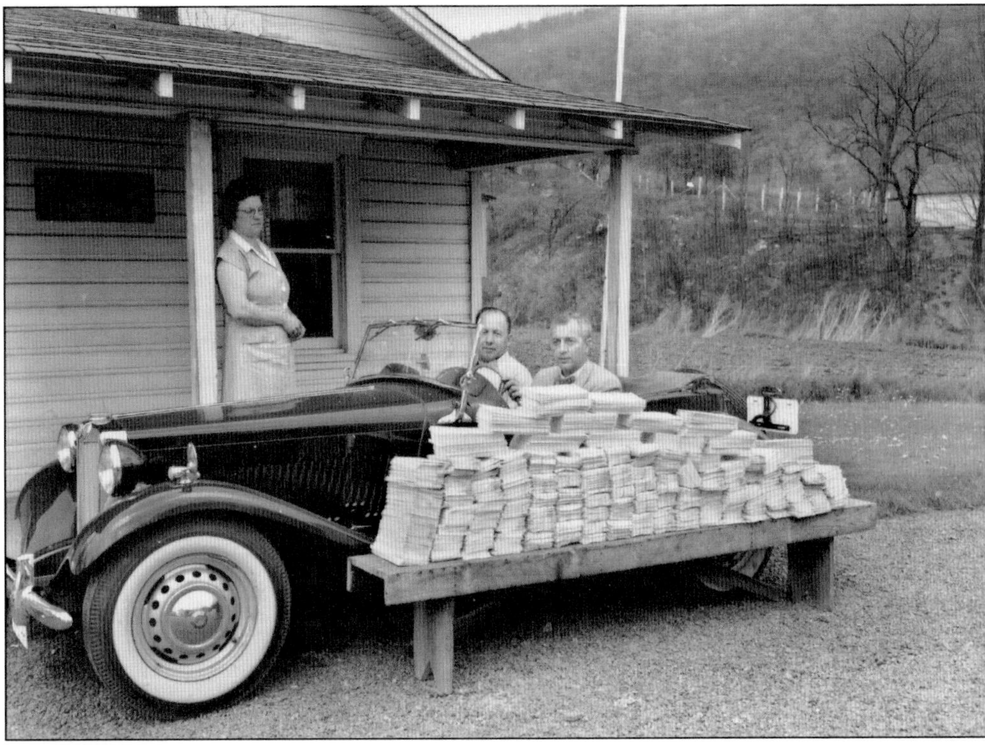

Dr. Benedict Skitarellic was photographed outside the Flintstone Post Office in the mid-1950s. Because of his involvement in the hill climb competitions at Breakneck Road, it could be speculated that he was preparing to mail fliers advertising the event.

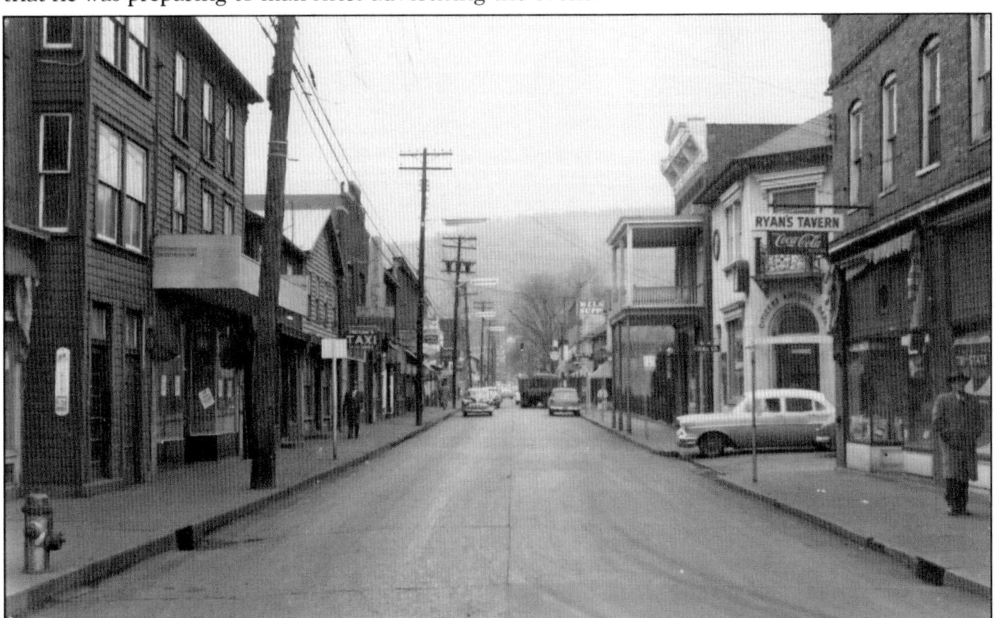

This view of Main Street in Westernport, Maryland, around 1960 offers a glimpse of locally owned businesses, including Ryan's Tavern, the Citizens National Bank—which was built in 1901—Trenum's Taxi Stand, and the Potomac Club.

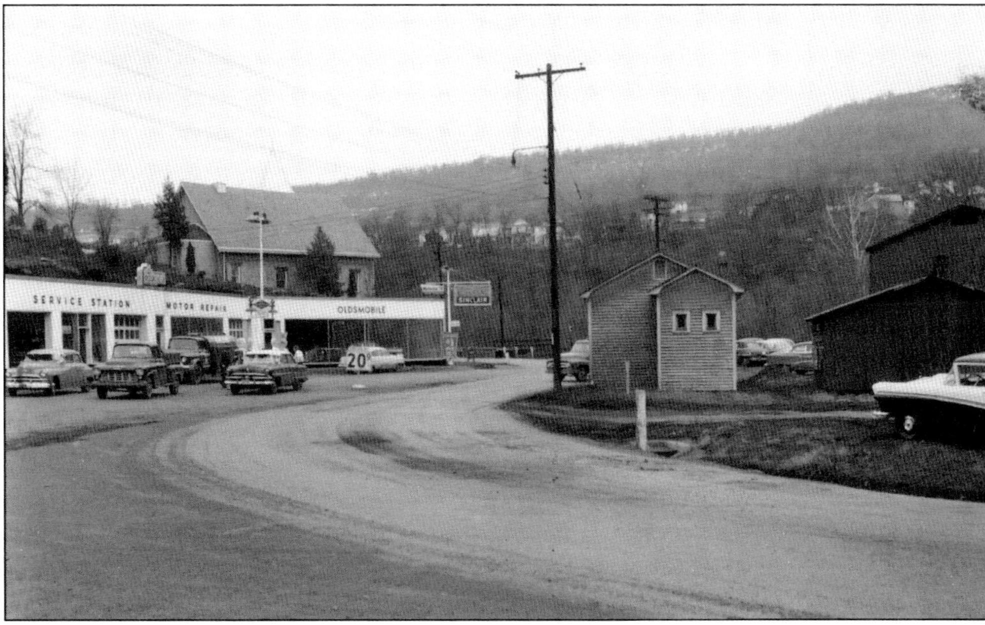

This section of Westernport is still referred to as "Jake's Elbow." Jake's Service Station and an automobile dealership operated at the site in the 1930s and remained in business during the 1950s, as shown in the photograph.

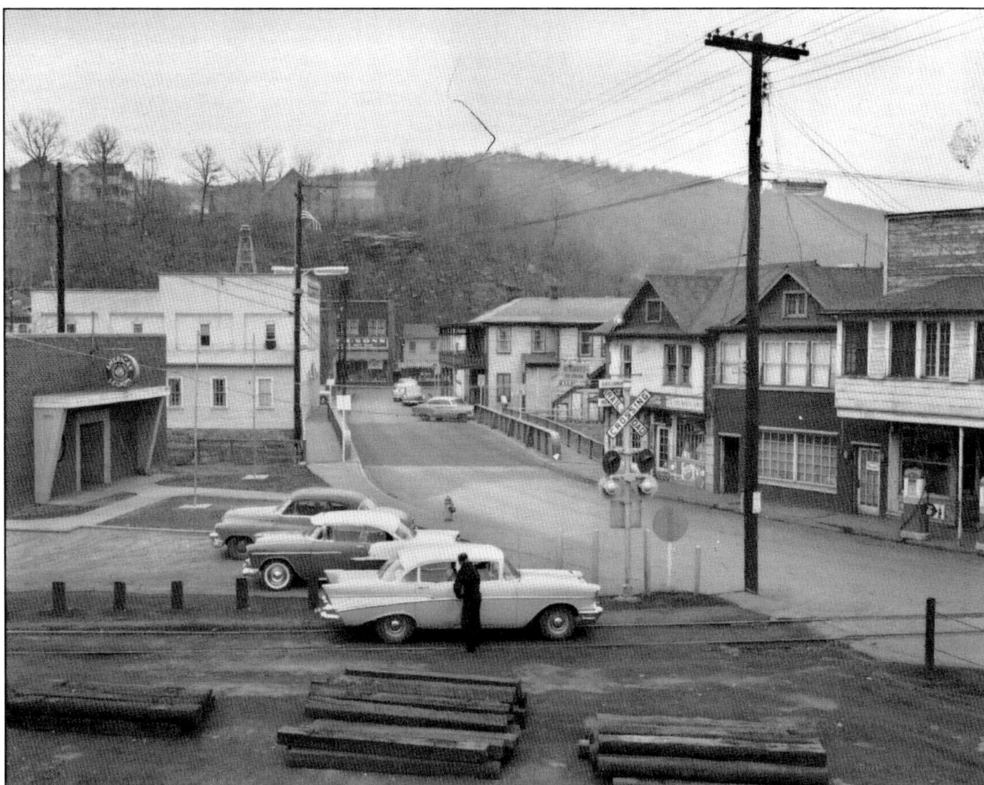

Pictured is the American Legion and downtown Westernport around 1960.

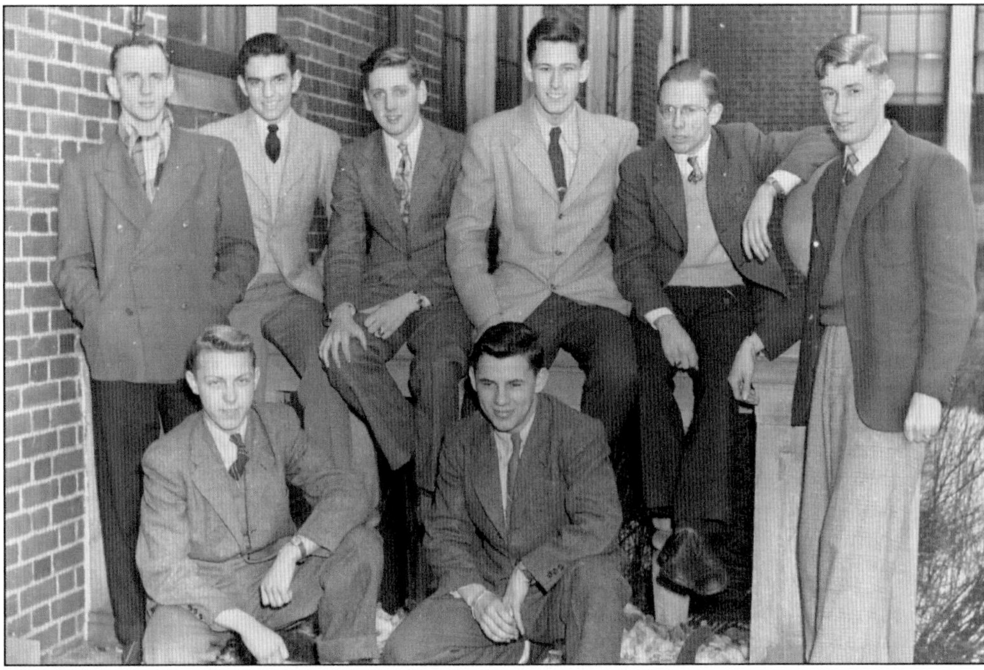

Early graduations were held in Allegany County Public Schools during World War II for senior male students entering the armed forces. Students graduated at the conclusion of the first semester. The Allegany High School class of 1945 early graduates are, from left to right, (first row) Bill Swain and James McHenry; (second row) Bill Smith, John Cox, unidentified, John Millar, Owen Morris, and unidentified.

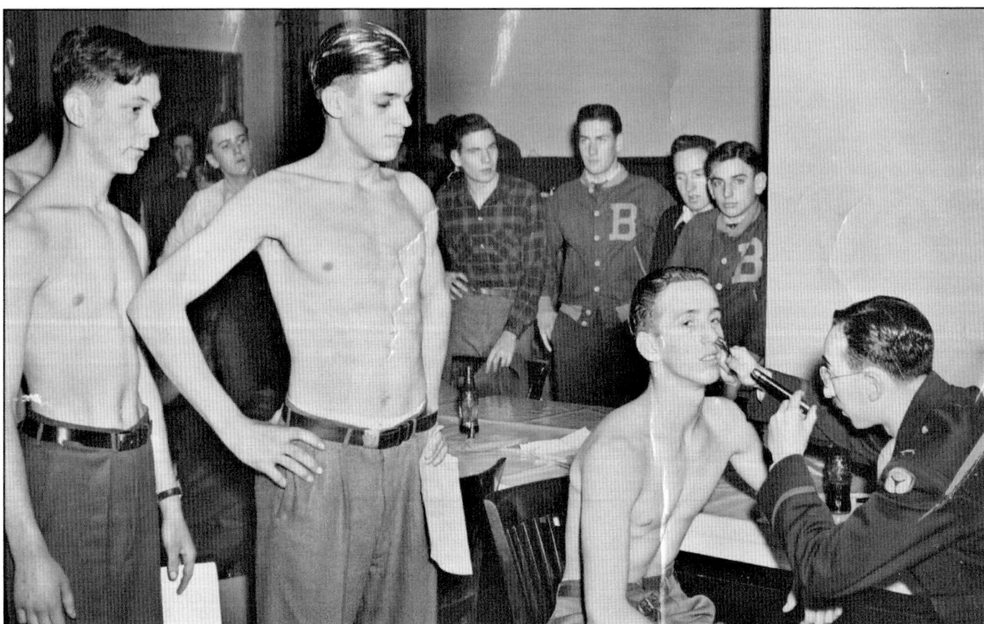

Young men were required to pass physical examinations prior to induction into the armed forces. Frostburg resident Glenn "Speed" Hanna, in the Beall High School jacket at left, graduated in January 1944.

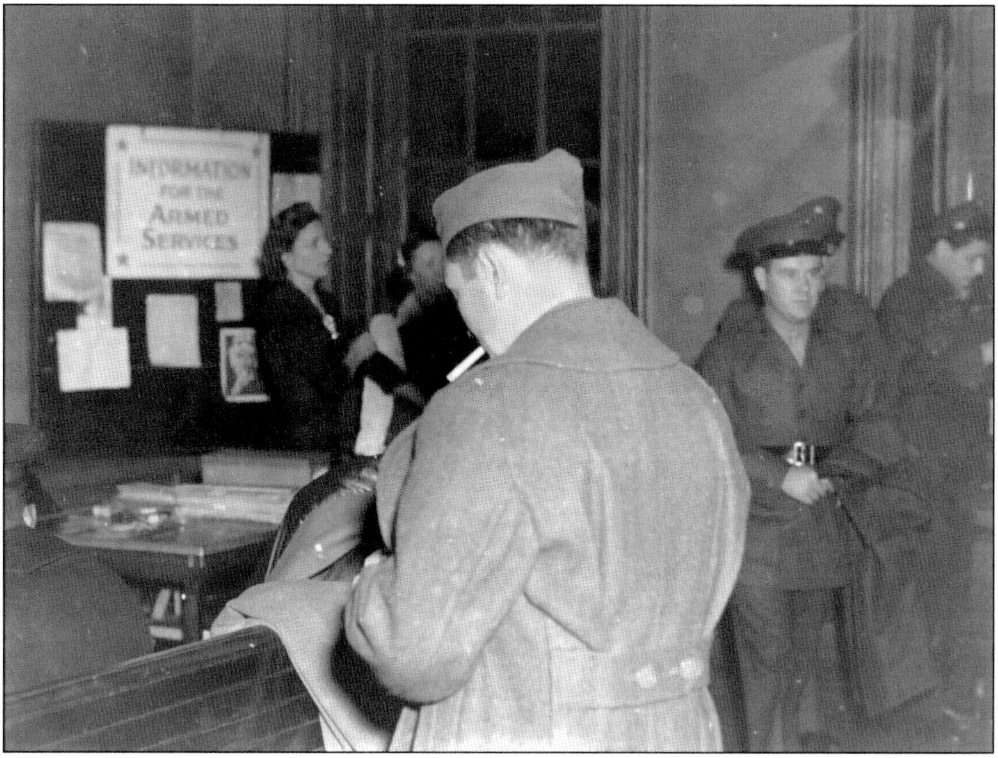

Troop trains, referred to as "mains" by the railroads, kept the Queen City Station busy during World War II. This interior view of the station shows an informational booth intended for military personnel.

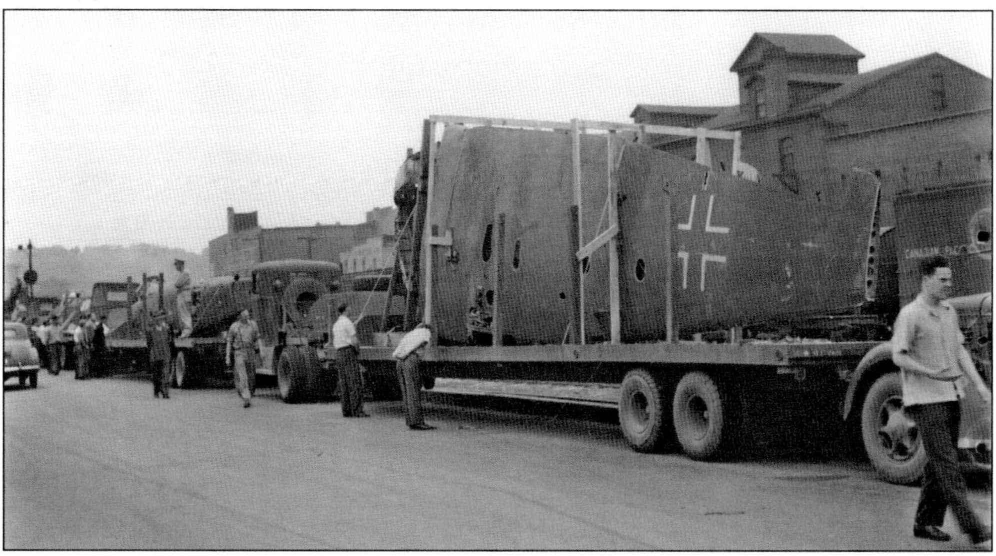

A German Messerschmitt BF 110 shot down during the Italian campaign of World War II was the main attraction of a February 1944 war bond drive. The plane was transported from Westernport to towns along George's Creek and Frostburg. The main event of the rally was held in Cumberland where bondholders were provided free tickets to the Strand Theatre. This photograph was taken along Henderson Boulevard in Cumberland.

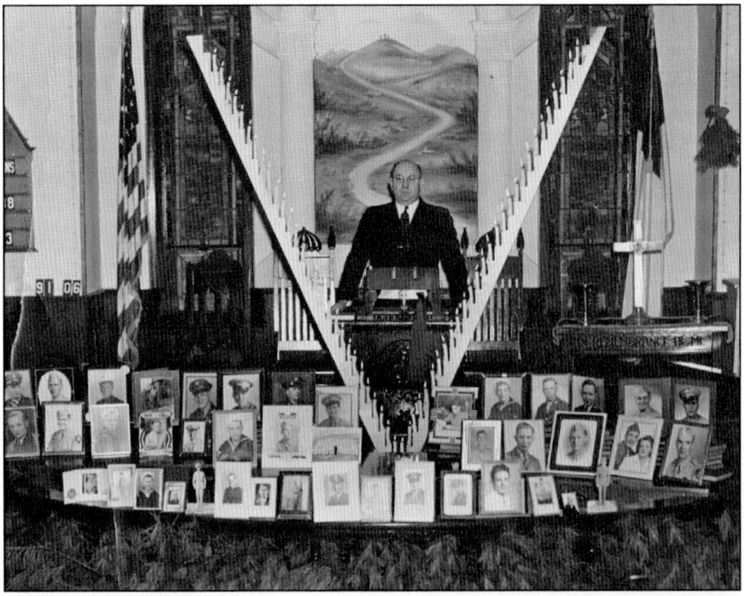

The First Presbyterian Church congregation and pastor Eisenberger recognized service personnel during World War II. The church is located on Washington Street in Cumberland.

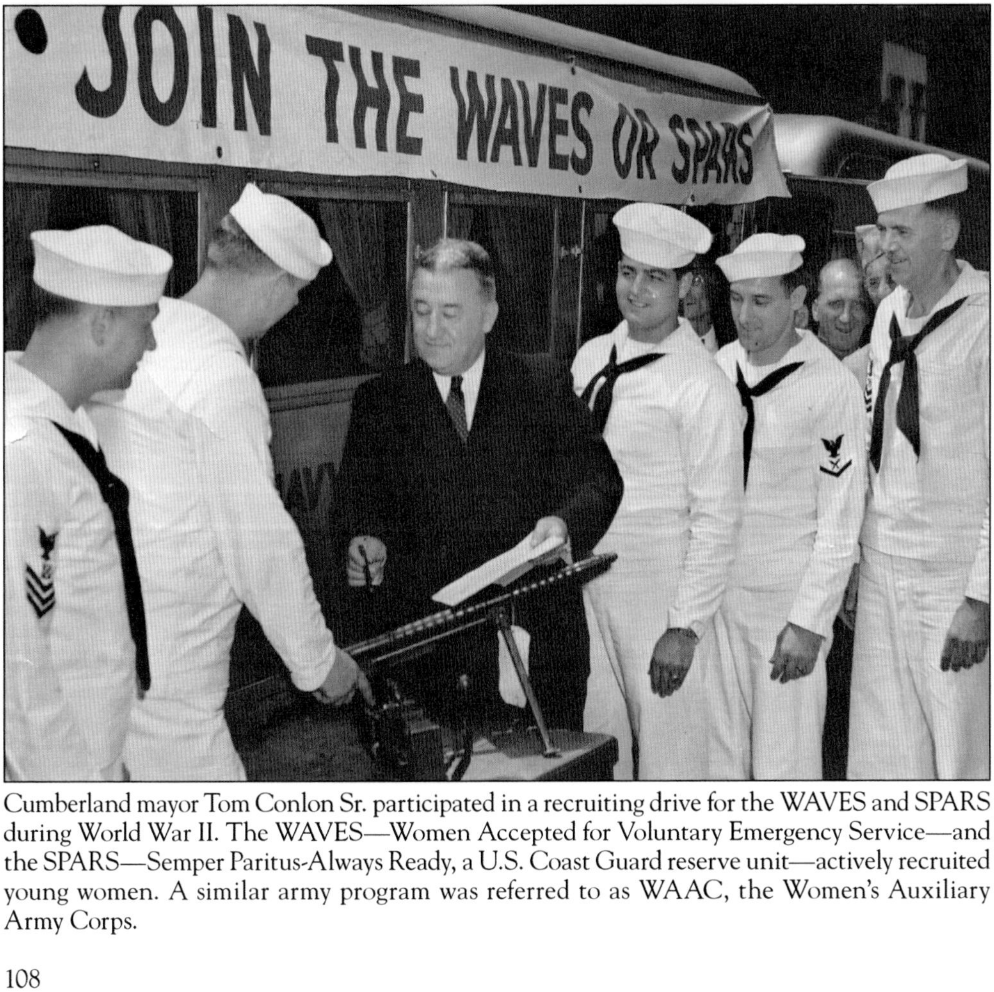

Cumberland mayor Tom Conlon Sr. participated in a recruiting drive for the WAVES and SPARS during World War II. The WAVES—Women Accepted for Voluntary Emergency Service—and the SPARS—Semper Paritus-Always Ready, a U.S. Coast Guard reserve unit—actively recruited young women. A similar army program was referred to as WAAC, the Women's Auxiliary Army Corps.

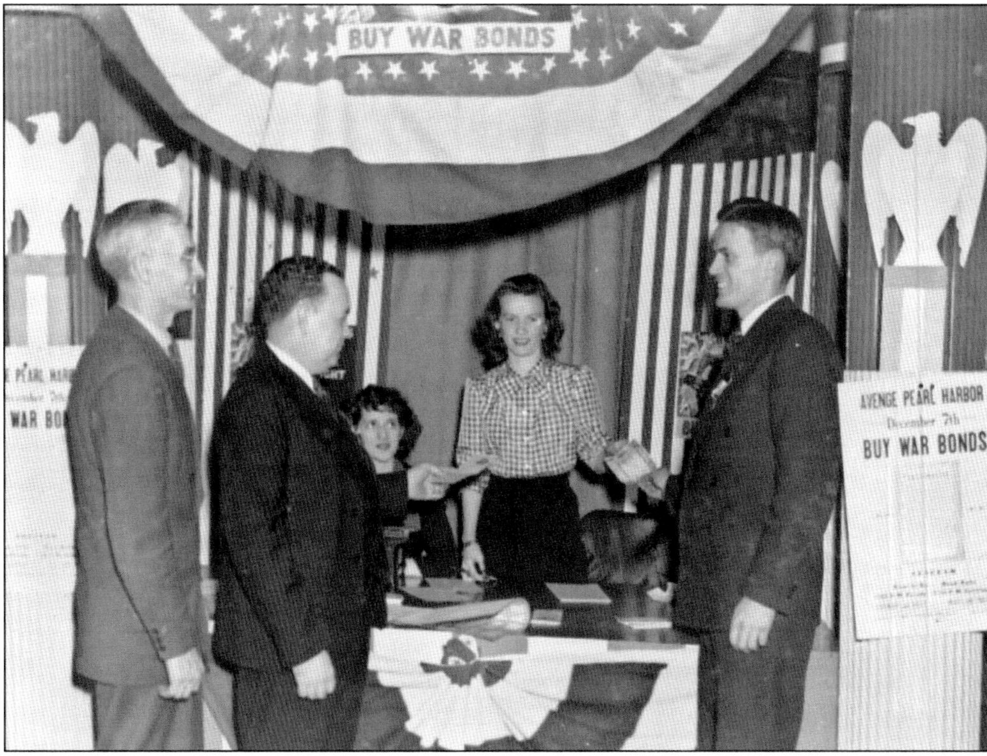

Cumberland residents were urged to purchase war bonds on December 7, 1942, known as Avengement Day. Advertisements appeared in the Cumberland newspapers to mark the day of Japan's attack on Pearl Harbor one year earlier.

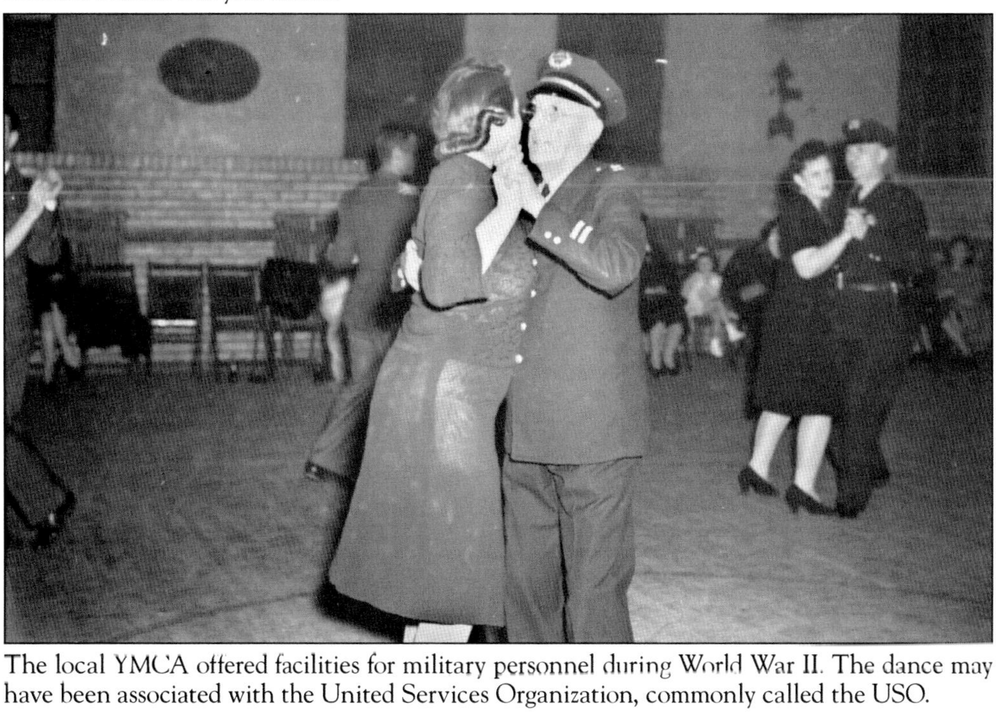
The local YMCA offered facilities for military personnel during World War II. The dance may have been associated with the United Services Organization, commonly called the USO.

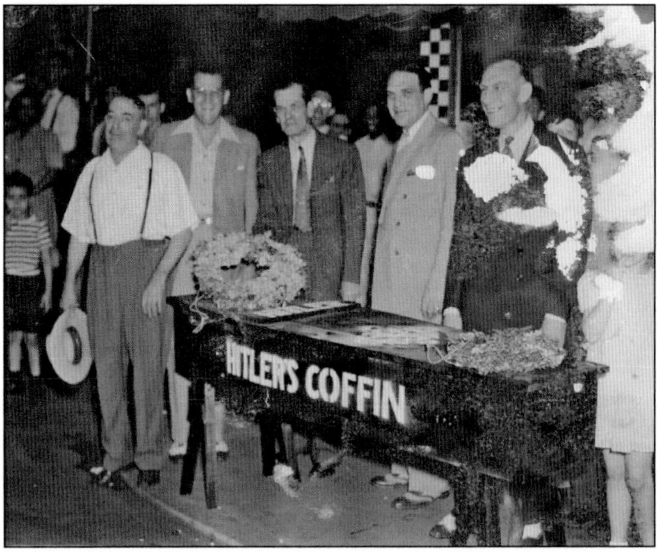

The Mercantile Bureau of the Allegany County Chamber of Commerce provided for the construction of Hitler's coffin during World War II, for the purpose of promoting war bond sales. Residents were reminded that every dollar donated was a nail in the Nazi fuehrer's coffin. The "funerals" started at North George and Baltimore Streets and ended at the Western Maryland Railway crossing. Businessman Mort Peskin Sr. is wearing the light coat behind the word "coffin."

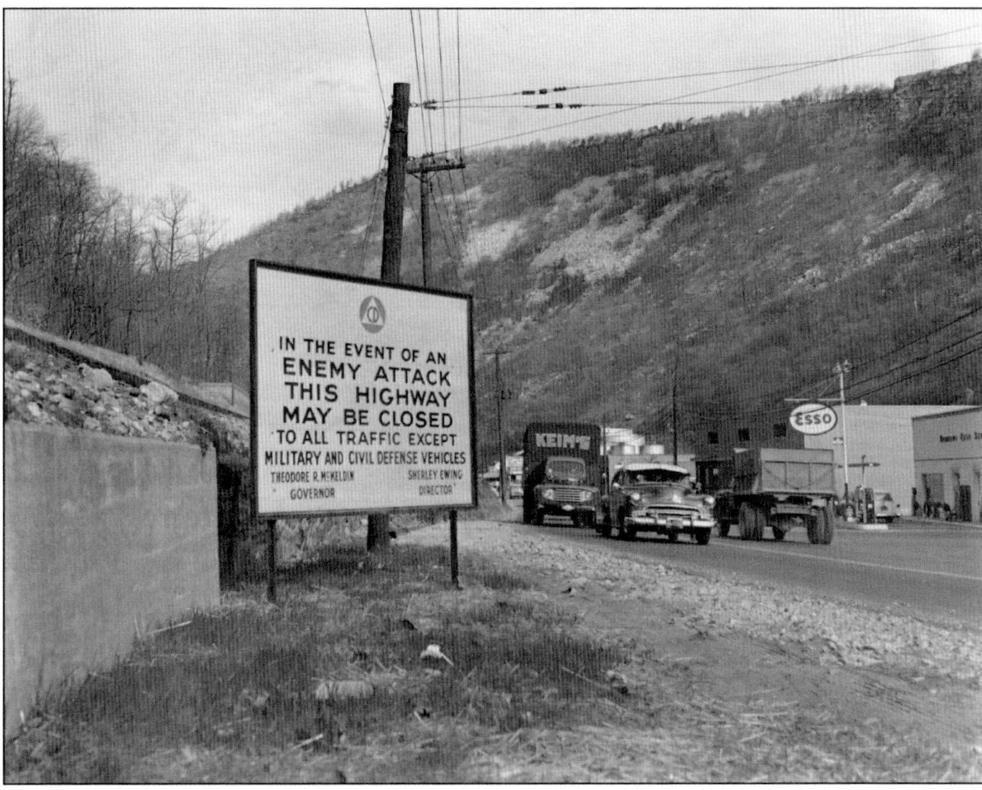

Following World War II, the United States and Soviet Union locked into the cold war. Allegany County residents participated regularly in civil defense drills that were organized by federal, state, and county governments. A daily reminder of the tense situation was posted in the Cumberland Narrows. The reference to Gov. Theodore McKeldin places this photograph between 1951 and 1959.

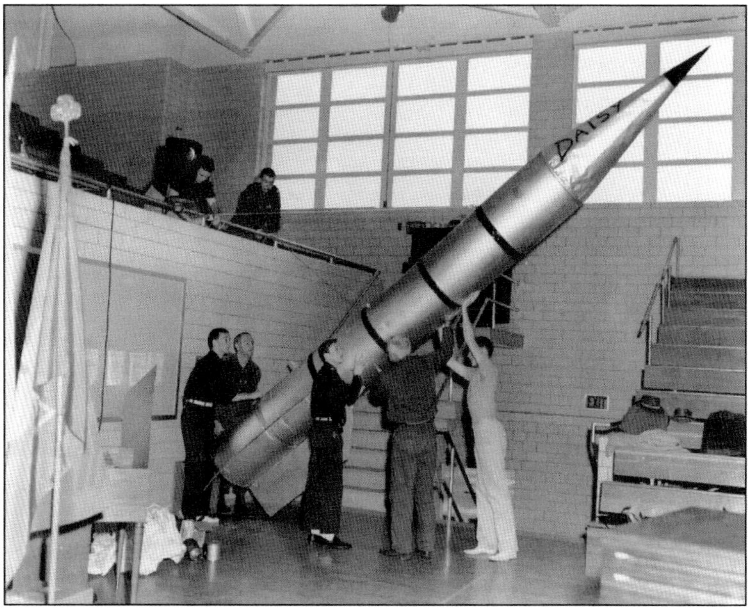

High school students were reminded of the cold war by participating in drills and viewing displays of weapons. This rocket, labeled "Daisy," was set up in the Allegany High School gymnasium around 1965.

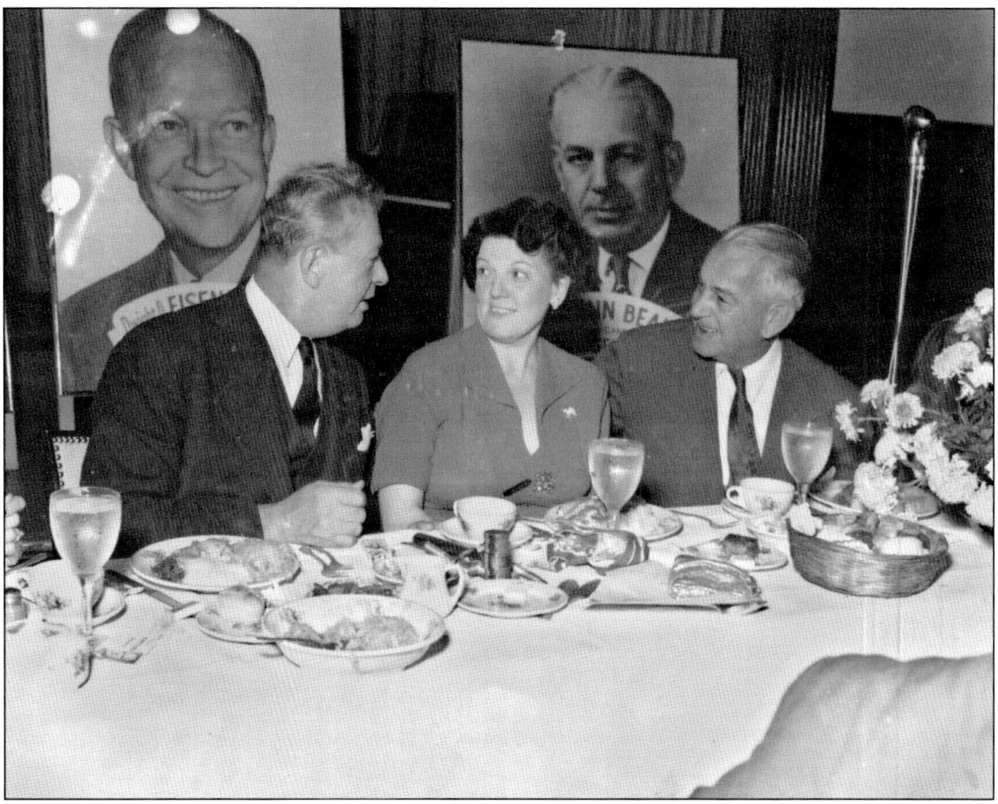

Frostburg resident and U.S. senator J. Glenn Beall Sr., right, served from 1953 to 1965. The campaign photographs in the background suggested that Illinois Republican senator Everett Dirksen, left, was campaigning on behalf of Beall in the 1952 election.

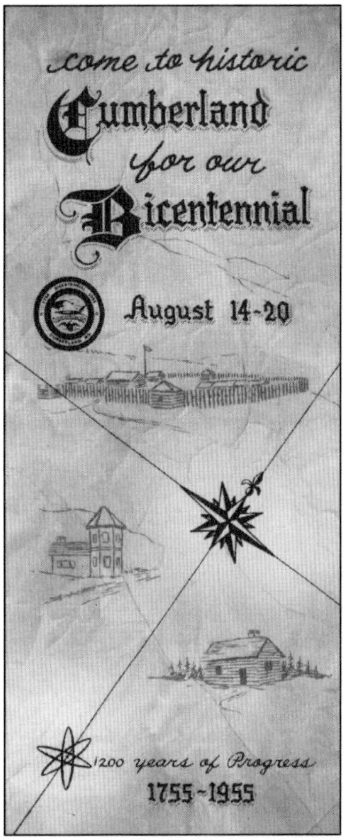

Allegany County celebrated the bicentennial of Fort Cumberland in August 1955. An original play, parades, fireworks, and a variety of other events occurred during the week-long event.

The Allegany County Public Library stands on Washington Street at Prospect Square. The structure was erected in 1849–1850 as a school. In 1934, the Cumberland Free Library obtained a lease from the county to use the building. Works Progress Administration funding during the late 1930s provided needed repairs and renovations. The building barely visible to the west was torn down in 1965 to make way for a new library addition.

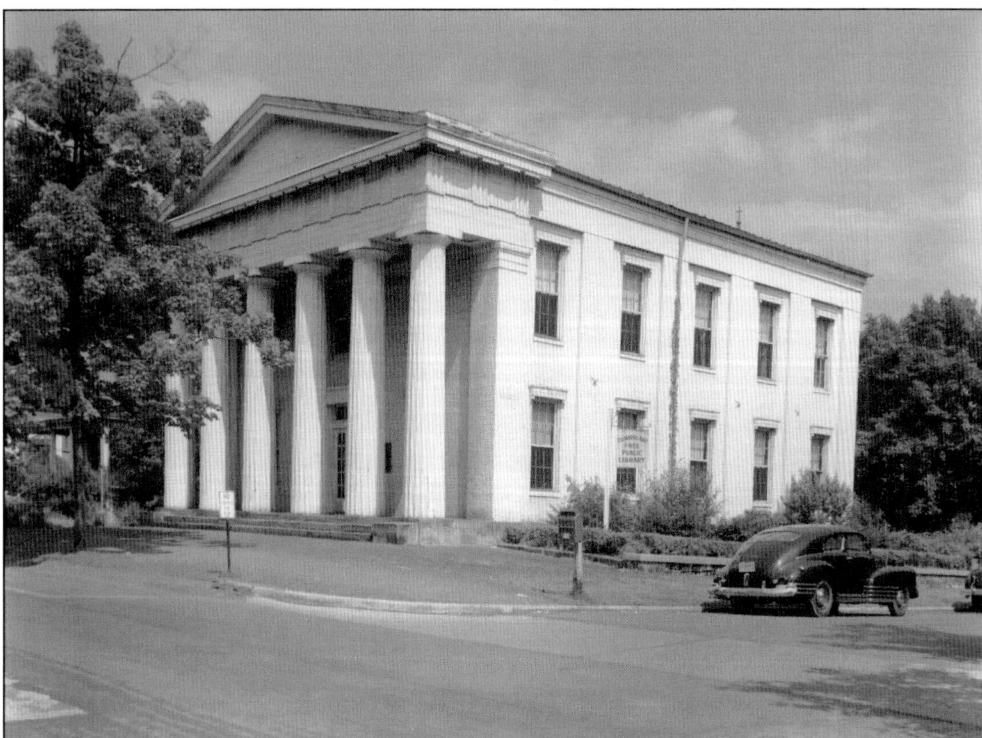

The Allegany versus Fort Hill Turkey Day football game was a major community event. The high school rivalry game began in 1936 and was held on Thanksgiving with the Allegany High School Campers winning the inaugural game 19-12. The Turkey Day game tradition ended when the homecoming game began in 1974. Shown in this photograph is Allegany High School cheerleader Rita Schoenadel, back row, far left, who would later become a teacher and cheerleading advisor at the school.

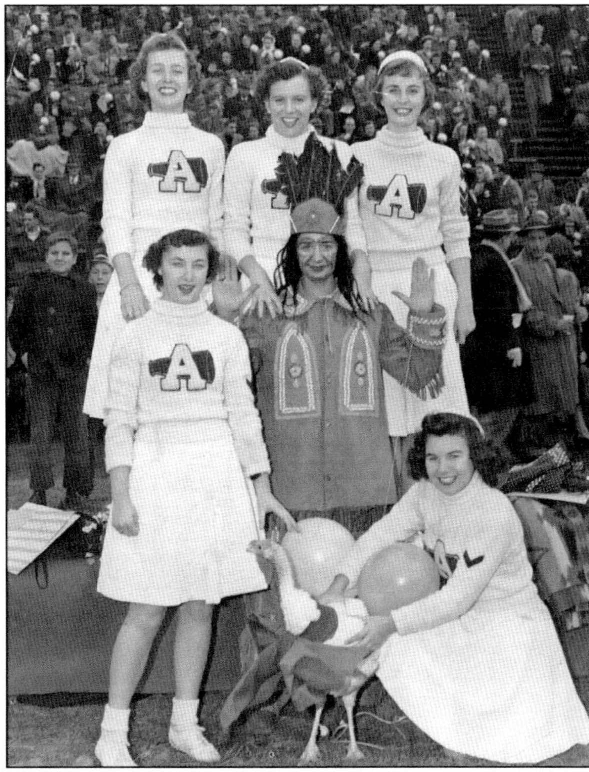

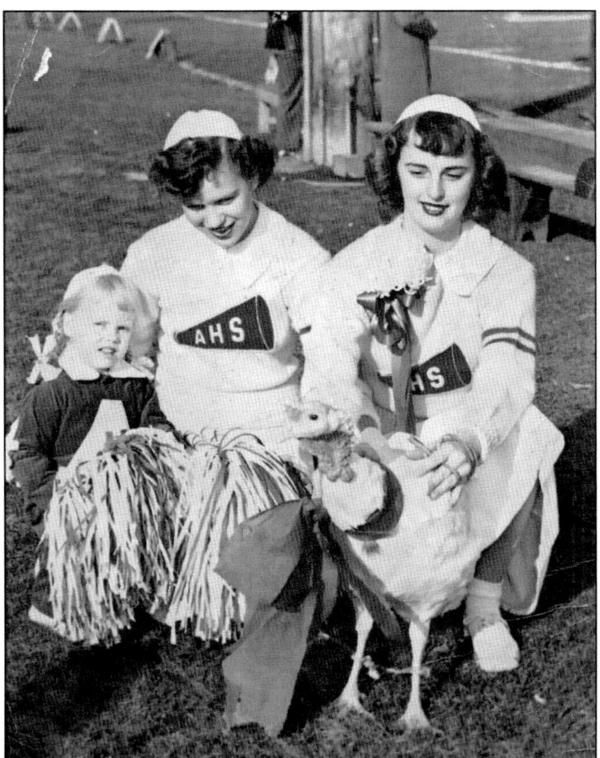

Allegany cheerleaders Sharon Cunningham and Barbara Fulton prepare for the Turkey Day game.

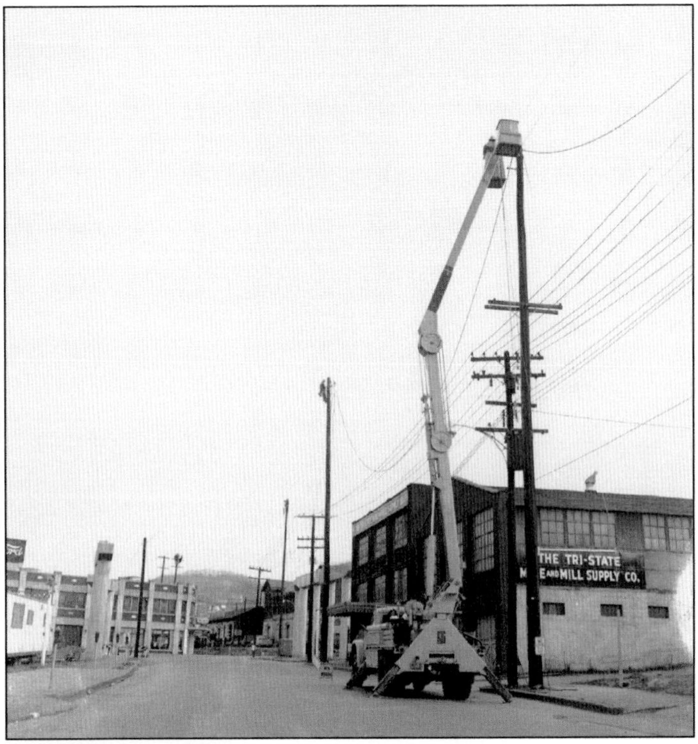

This view of South George and Commerce Streets shows the Tri State Mine and Mill Company and the building of the crosstown bridge.

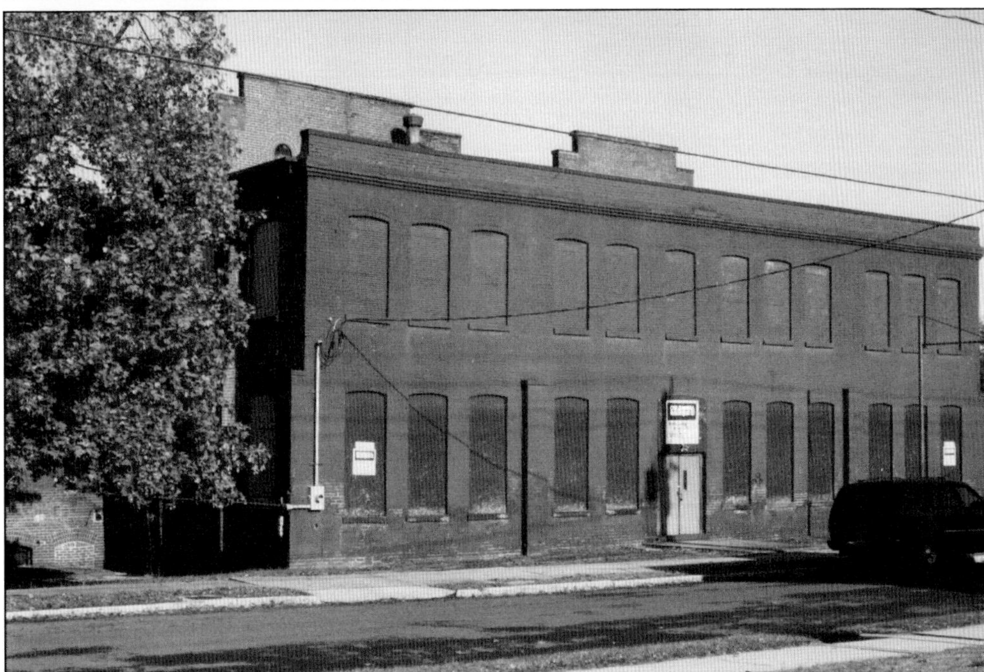

The Klotz Throwing Company, located at 97 Gay Street, broke ground for its factory on November 13, 1902. The location was chosen because of its proximity to the Baltimore and Ohio Railroad's mainline track. The mill processed raw silk until 1929 when it closed. In 2010, the former mill was converted to an apartment complex. This photograph was taken in 2006.

In 1848, John Neumann (1811–1860), superior of the Redemptorists in the United States, chose the site of Saints Peter and Paul's Church and Monastery. The Redemptorists began building a six-story monastery overlooking the city of Cumberland a few years later. The crucifix depicted in this photograph was located inside the monastery. The religious facility became vacant in the mid-1980s and was later torn down.

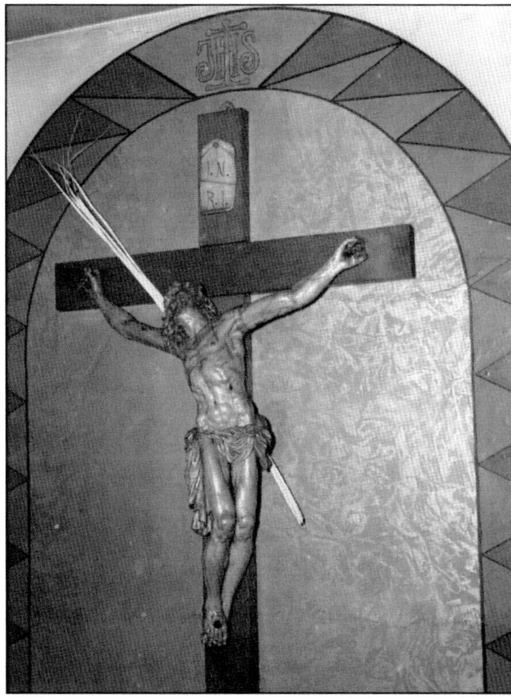

Emmanuel Episcopal Church dominates the western Cumberland skyline from its Washington Street location. The cornerstone for the church was laid in 1849, and the dedication occurred in 1851. The church location holds additional historical significance because it was the site of Fort Cumberland. Christmas displays, as shown in this 2002 photograph, have become a local holiday tradition.

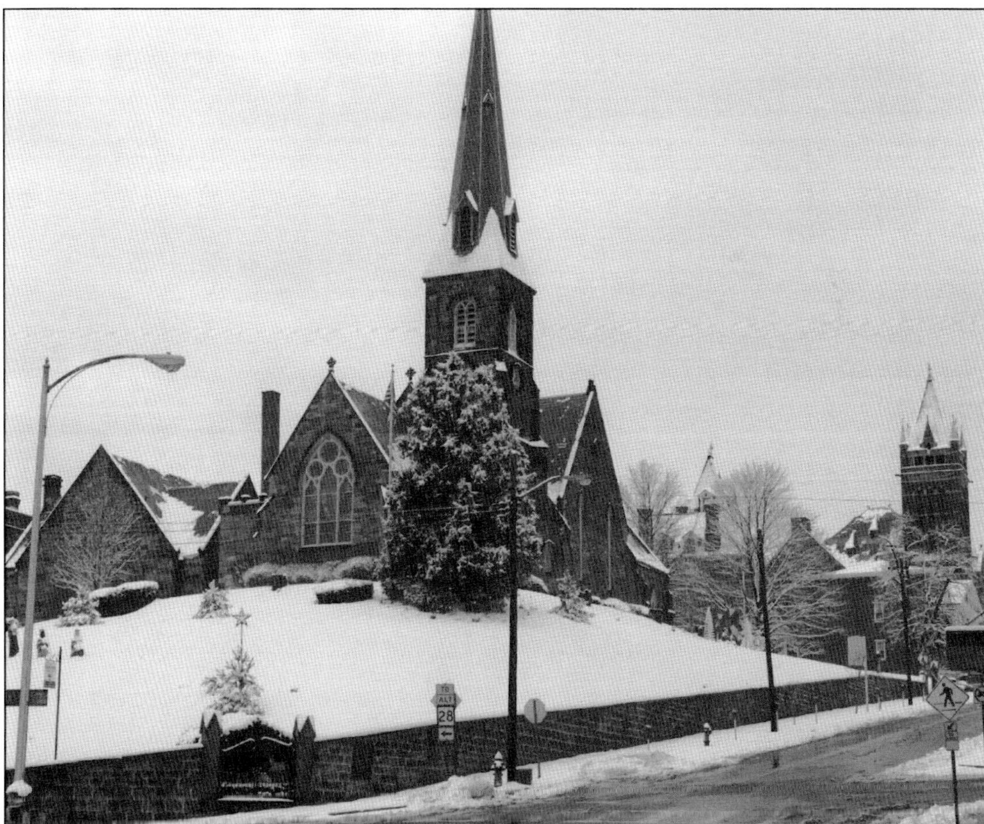

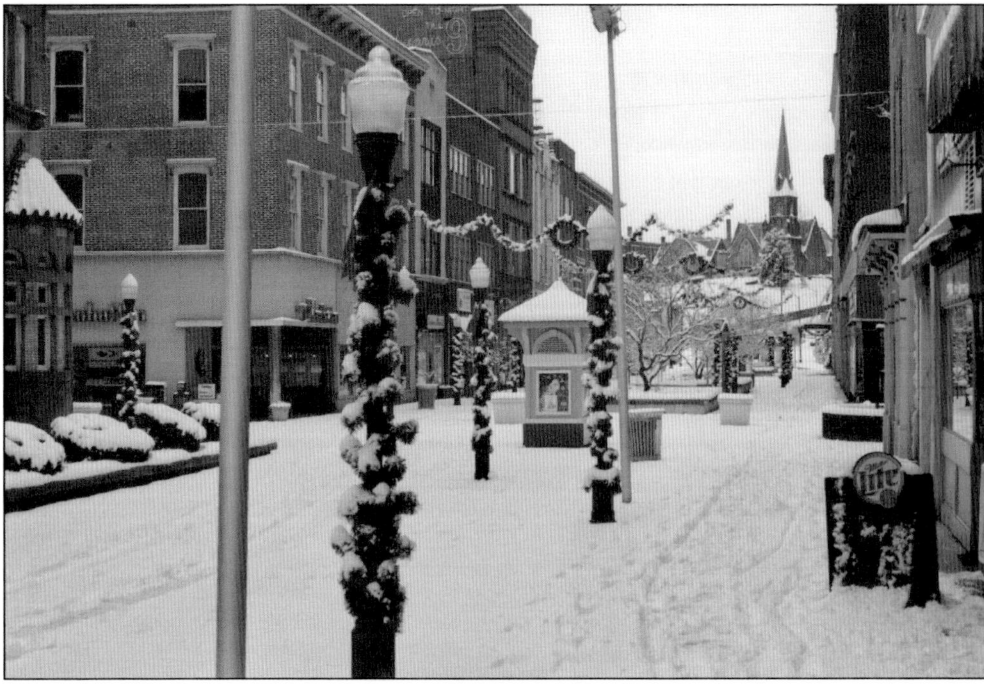

The downtown Cumberland pedestrian mall was covered with a blanket of snow on Christmas Day 2002. This view looks west.

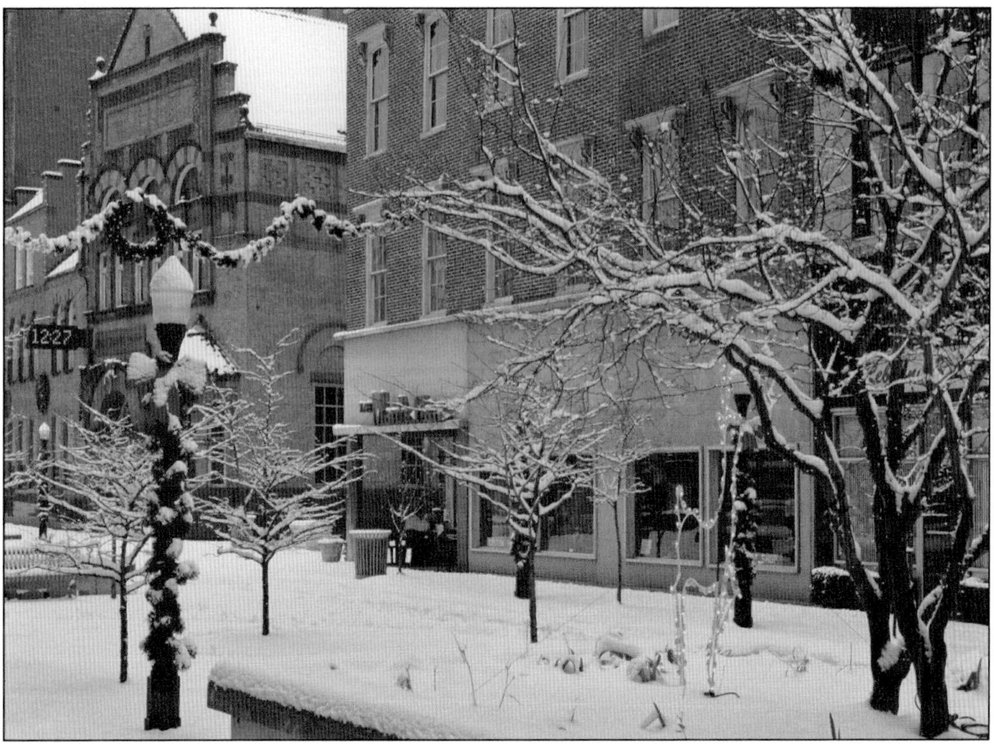

This photograph gives a view of downtown Cumberland looking east at South Liberty Street on Christmas Day 2002.

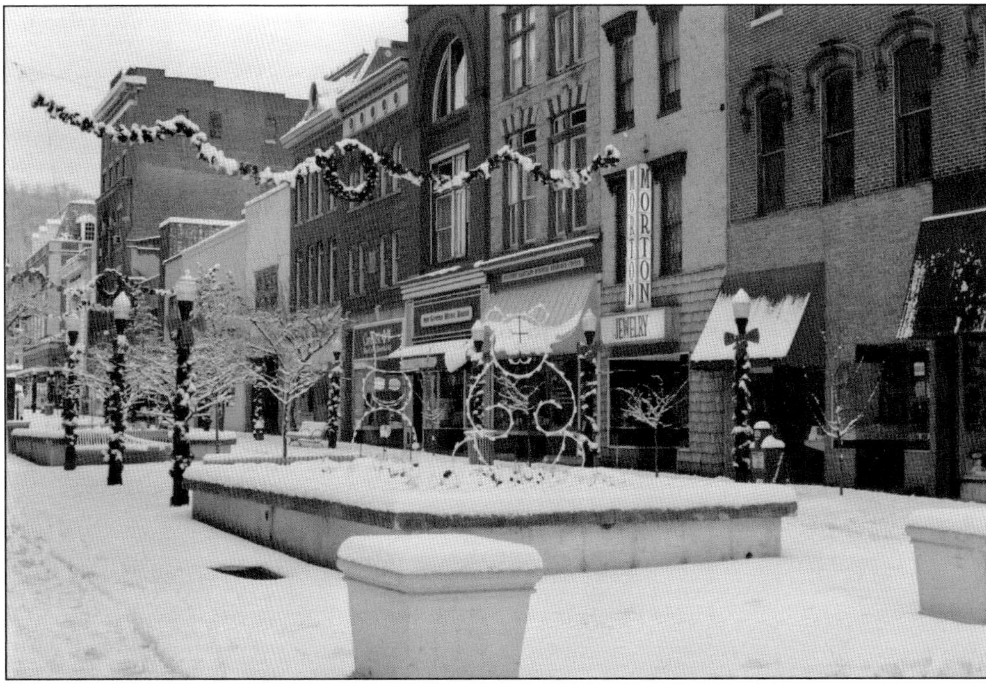

This view of downtown Cumberland looks east from Centre Street.

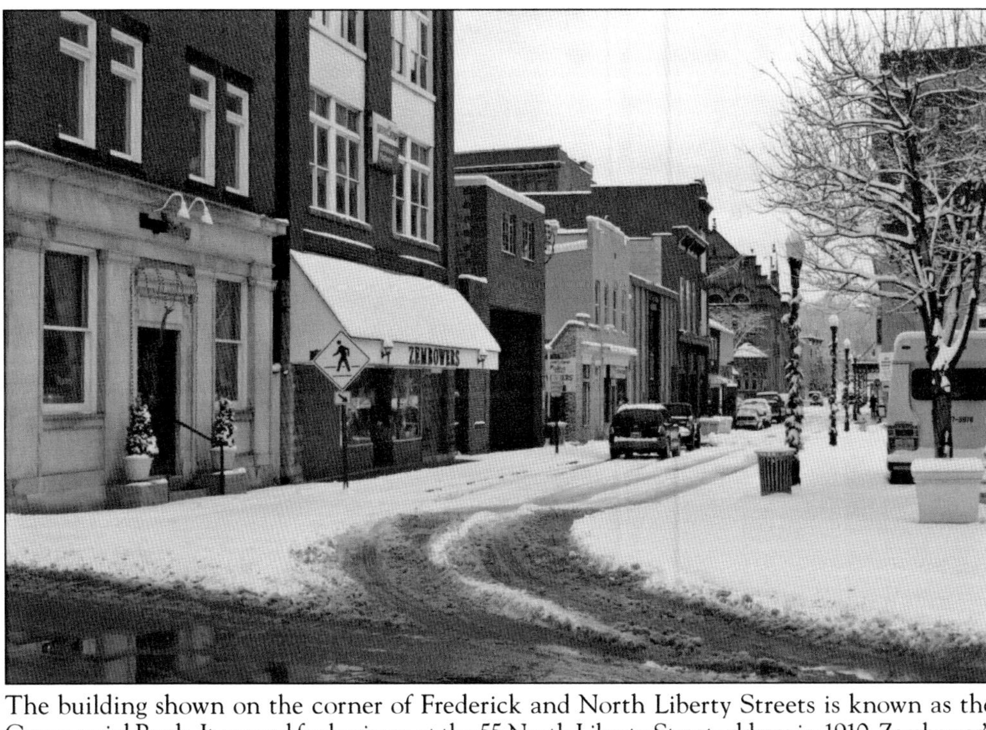

The building shown on the corner of Frederick and North Liberty Streets is known as the Commercial Bank. It opened for business at the 55 North Liberty Street address in 1910. Zembower's Hardware, formerly Liberty Hardware, occupied the adjacent building though it has since moved to North Mechanic Street. This photograph is from 2002.

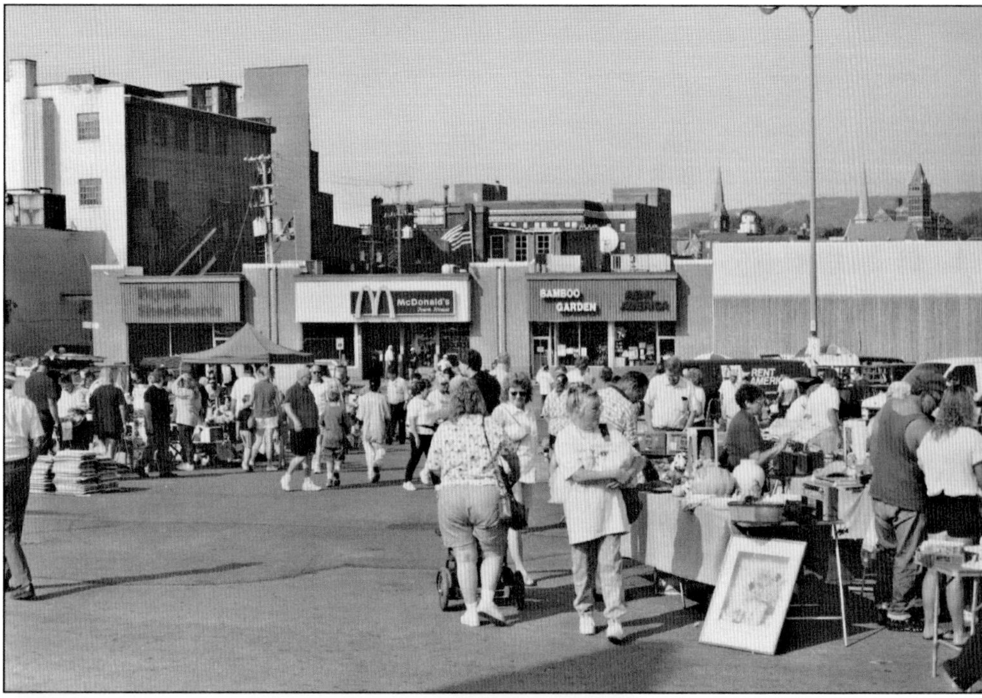

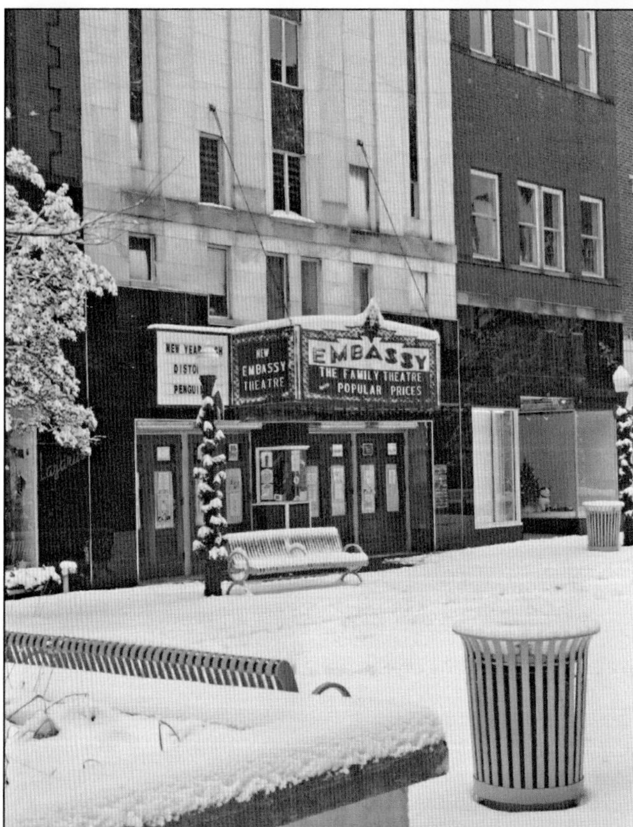

A popular event during the late 1990s was the flea market held on the Value City parking lot in downtown Cumberland. The McDonald's restaurant, shown in the background, later opened a new freestanding store in the parking lot, thus ending the Sunday flea market sales at that location.

The original Embassy Theatre held its grand opening on November 18, 1931, at 49 Baltimore Street. More than 2,000 citizens assembled for the festivities. Grace Fisher owned the business but leased the building from the Kaufman family. It closed in 1957, and the building was later part of Cumberland Cloak and Suit store. The New Embassy Theatre opened in recent years under the direction of Mark Baker and offers original plays and other events.

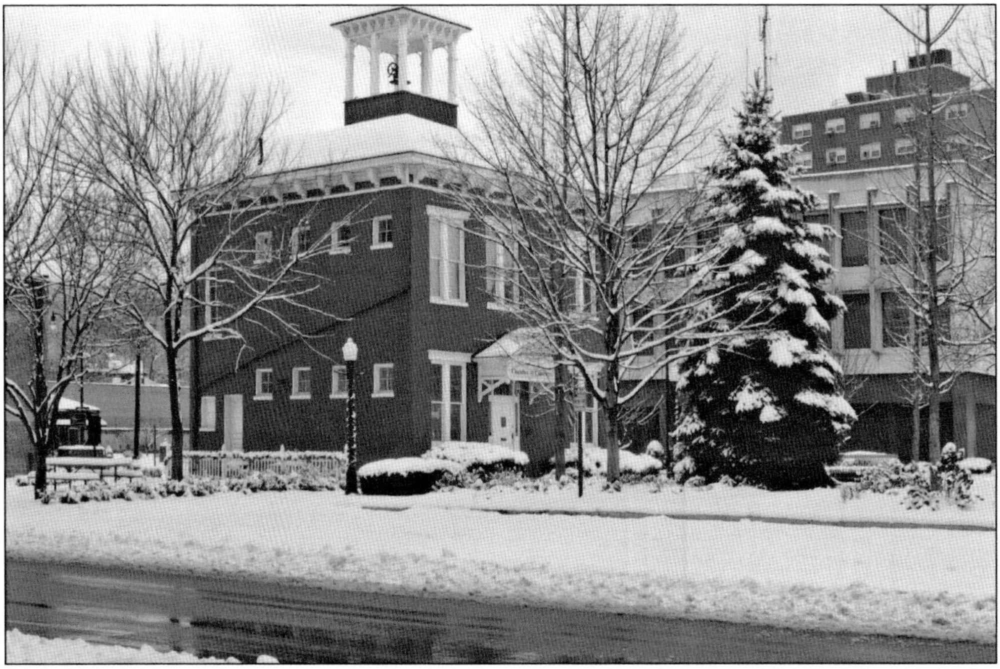

At one time, the Allegany County Chamber of Commerce building served as a jailhouse for the city of Cumberland. Because of the cupola, the structure was known as the Bell Tower building, although a bell was not present until recent times. This photograph was taken in 2002.

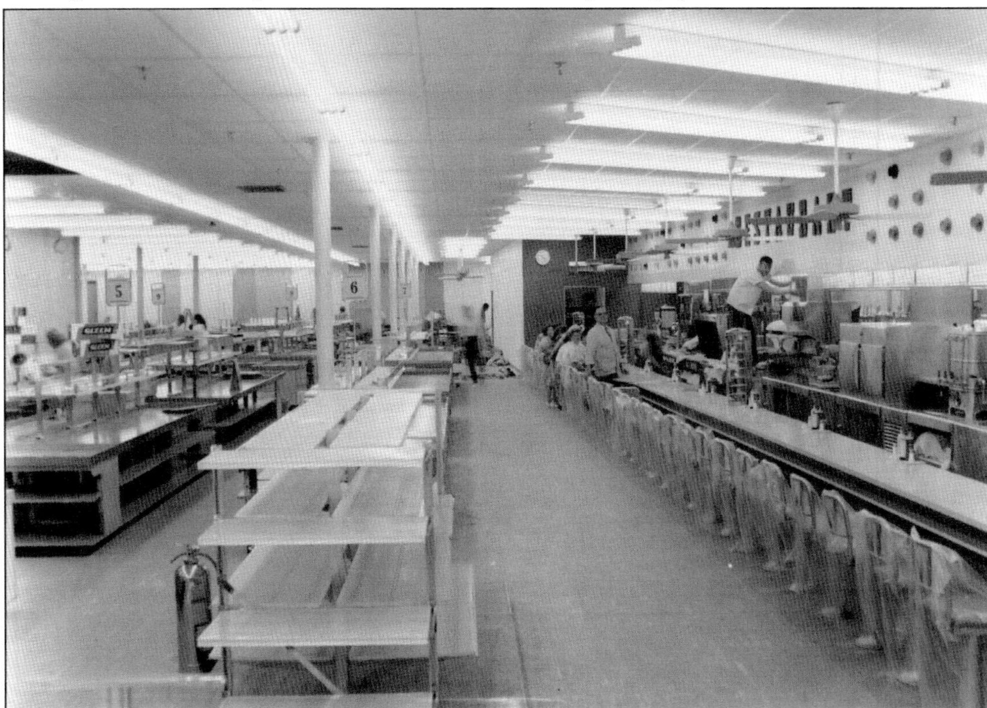

The remodeling of G. C. Murphy's in 1958 resulted in a new dining area. Murphy's was located on the corner of Baltimore and North George Streets.

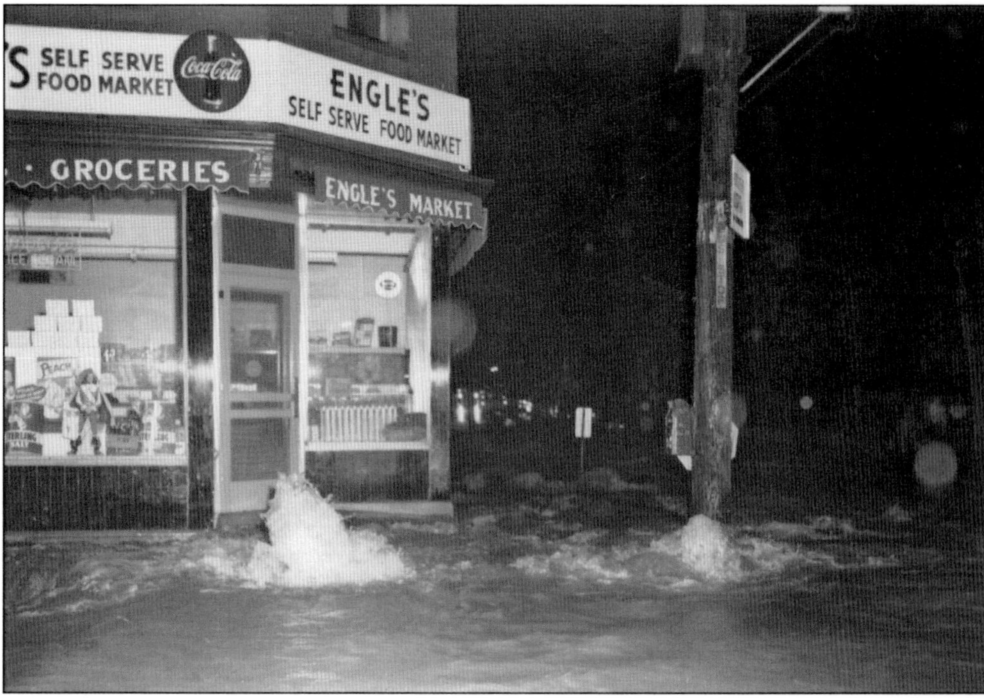

Engle's Self Serve Food Market, a well-known business located on the corner of Baltimore Avenue and Decatur Street, suffered water damage caused by waterline failure.

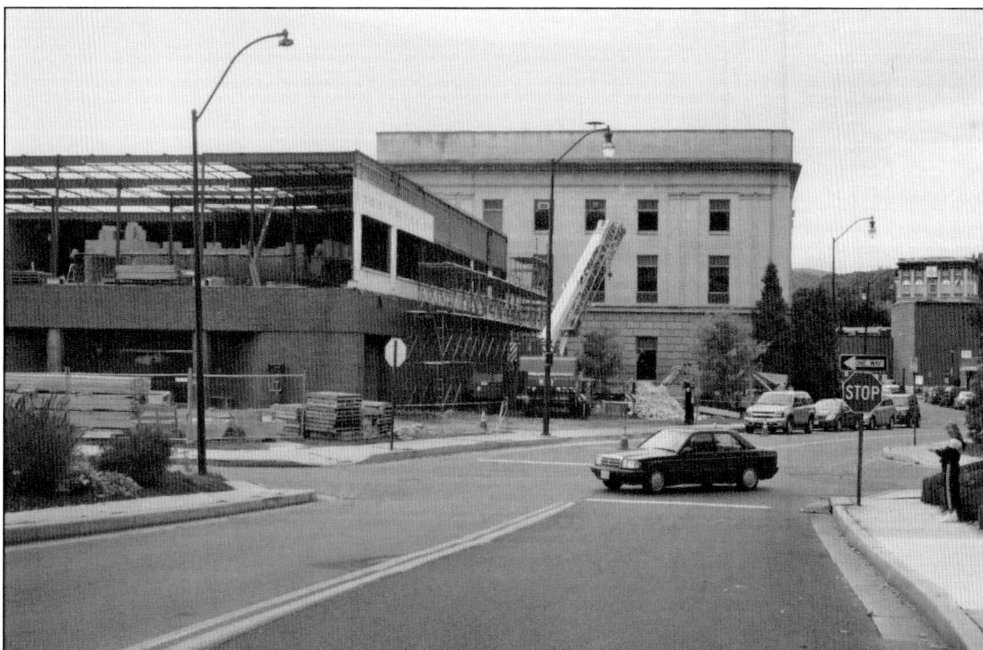

The Maryland District Court House moved from the William Donald Schaefer building in 2009. The new location was once the site of the Strand Theatre and later the Chesapeake and Potomac Telephone building. The courthouse work, seen in this photograph, involved adding a second story to the existing telephone building that was last occupied by Verizon.

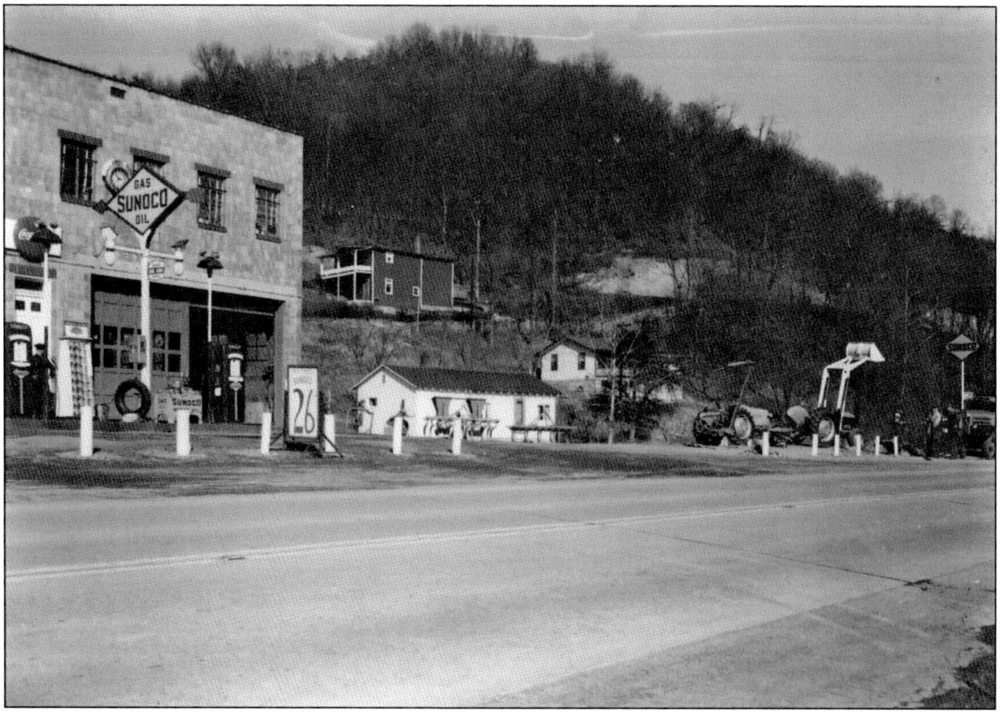

The Sunoco Service Station located east of Cumberland along U.S. Route 40, also called Baltimore Pike, sold gasoline for 26¢ per gallon during the 1950s.

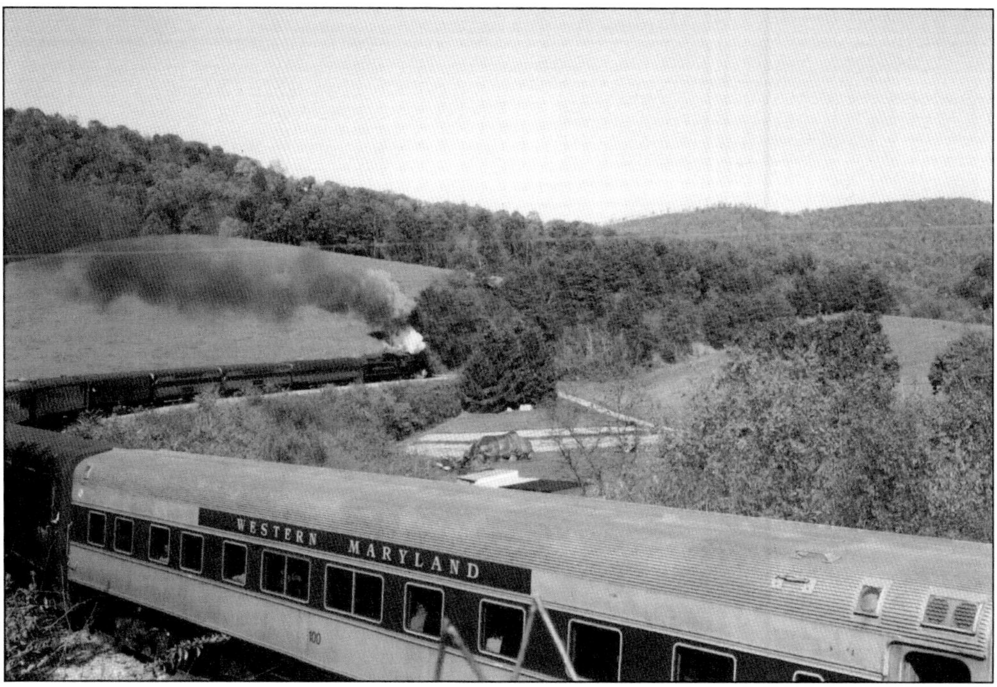

The Western Maryland Scenic Railroad attracts thousands of visitors annually. One of the most scenic views on the Cumberland-to-Frostburg excursion is found at Helmstetter's Curve, located near Corriganville. The railroad features a 1916 Baldwin steam locomotive.

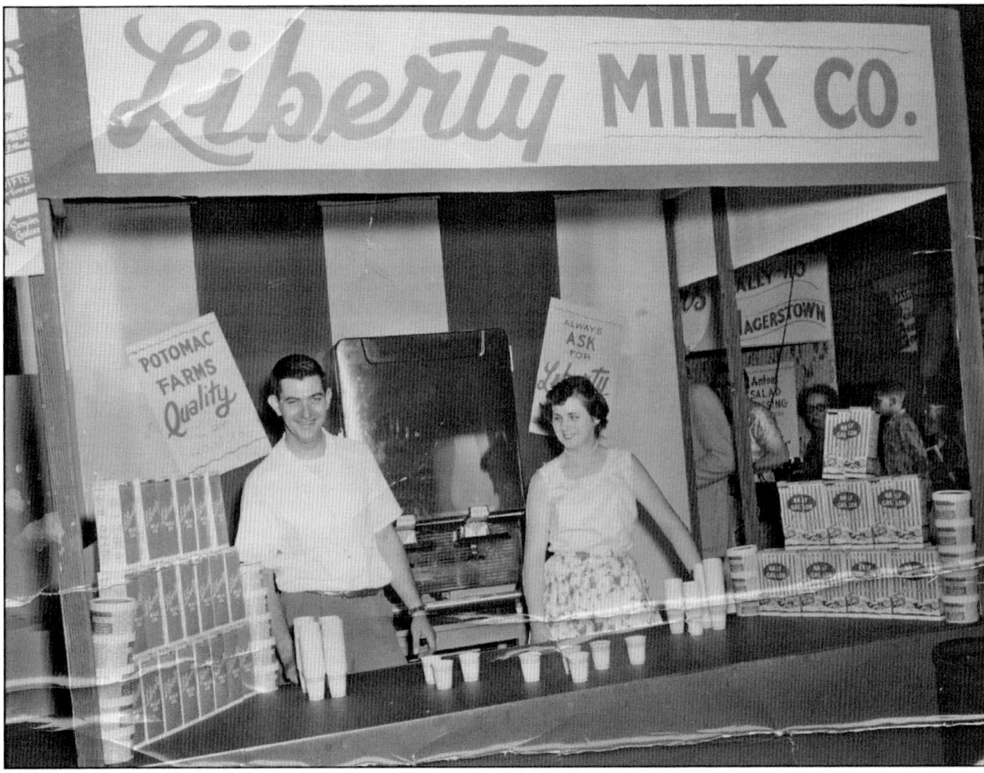

Liberty Milk Company operated at Fifth Street in South Cumberland. This photograph was likely taken at a business exposition that occurred at the National Guard Armory on South Centre Street.

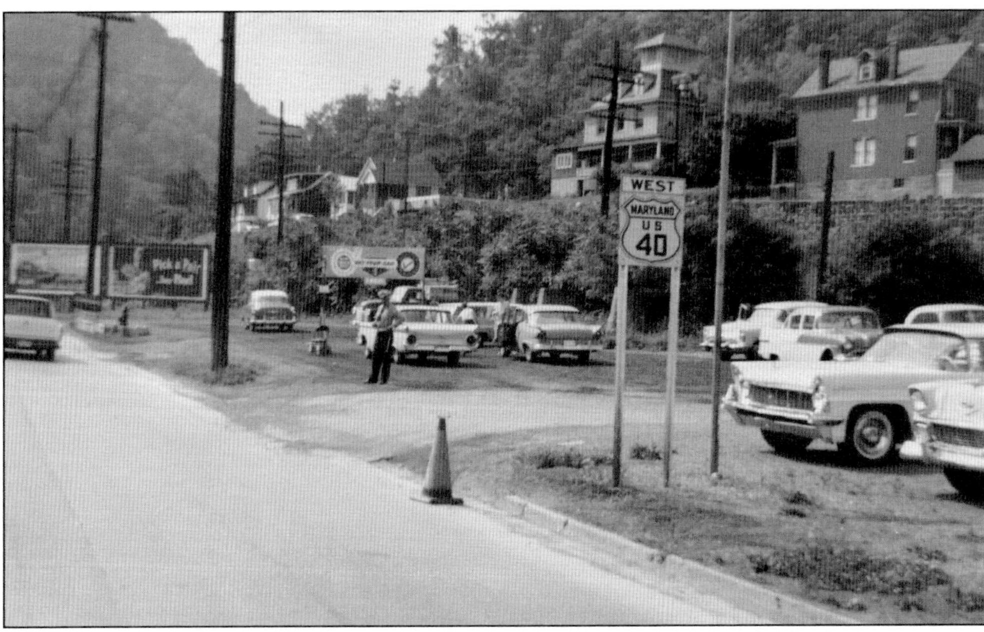

Spoerl's Used Car Lot once operated along U.S. Route 40, near the Cumberland Narrows, until a gasoline service station later built on that location. This photograph is dated 1960–1961.

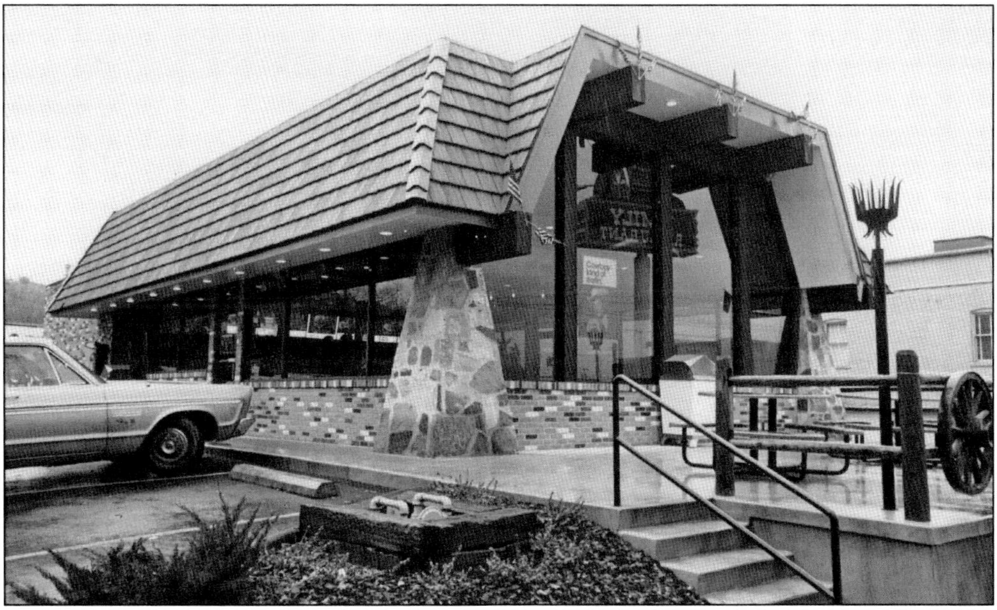

Roy Roger's Restaurant became part of the Cumberland Urban Renewal Agency, Center City II Plan during 1972–1973. The restaurant is located along Queen City Drive on property cleared under the direction of urban planners. A later renovation to it enclosed the outdoor seating area.

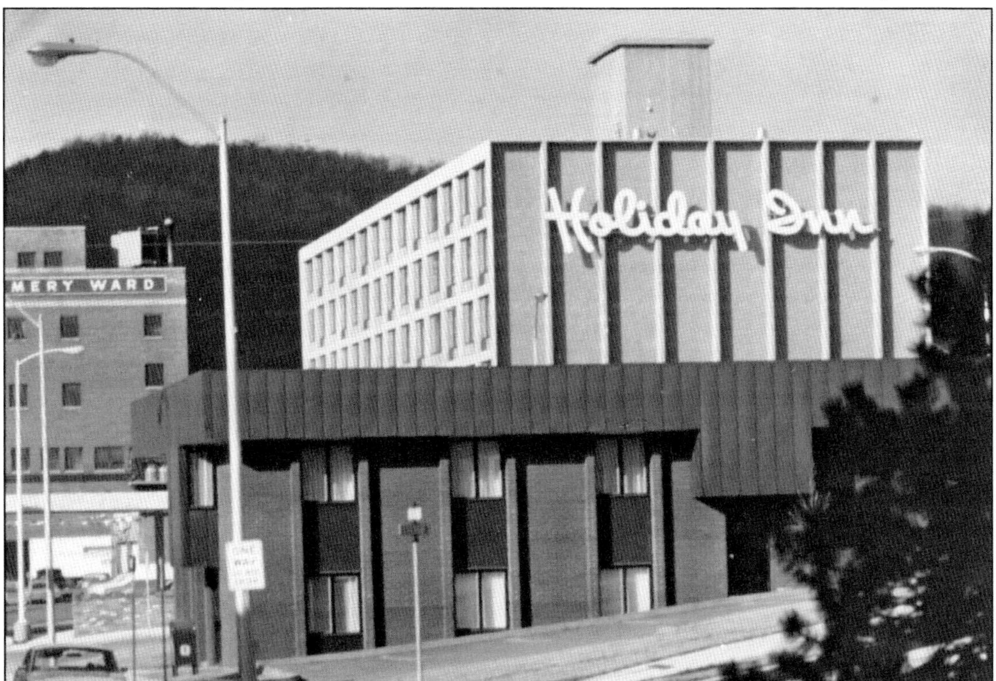

The Holiday Inn was the first new hotel built in Cumberland since the Algonquin in 1926. Announcement of the project was made in February 1968. The hotel was a key part of the Cumberland Urban Renewal Agency's plans to revitalize the downtown area. The brick building in front of the Holiday Inn was occupied by Beall, Garner, Screen, and Geare, Inc., an insurance agency.

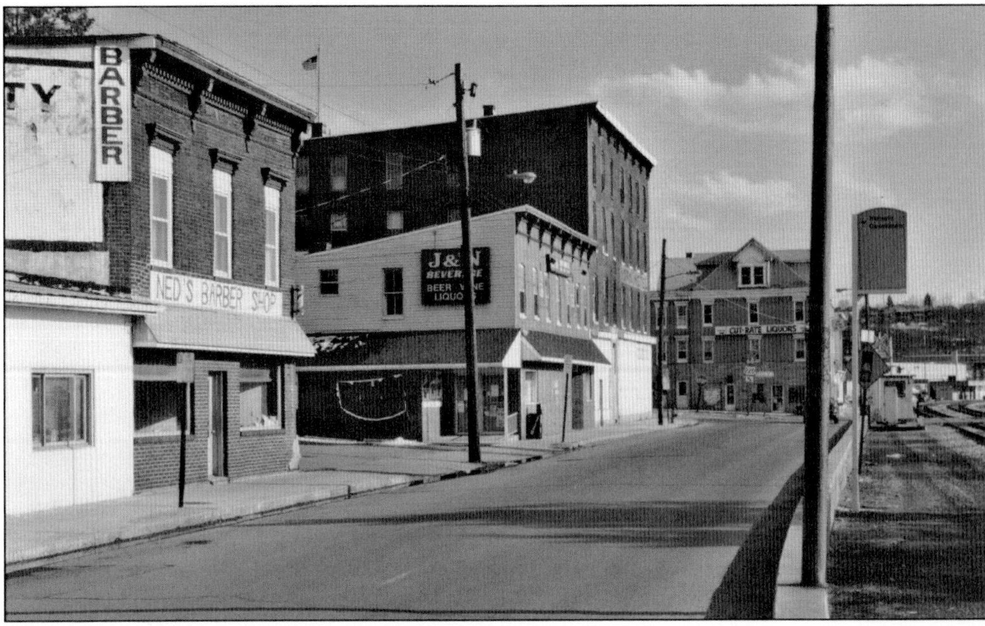

This 2003 view looking south along Henderson Boulevard has changed in recent times. The York Hotel, the last building on the left, was demolished in 2005 and the adjacent structure with "J & N" signs was torn down at a later date.

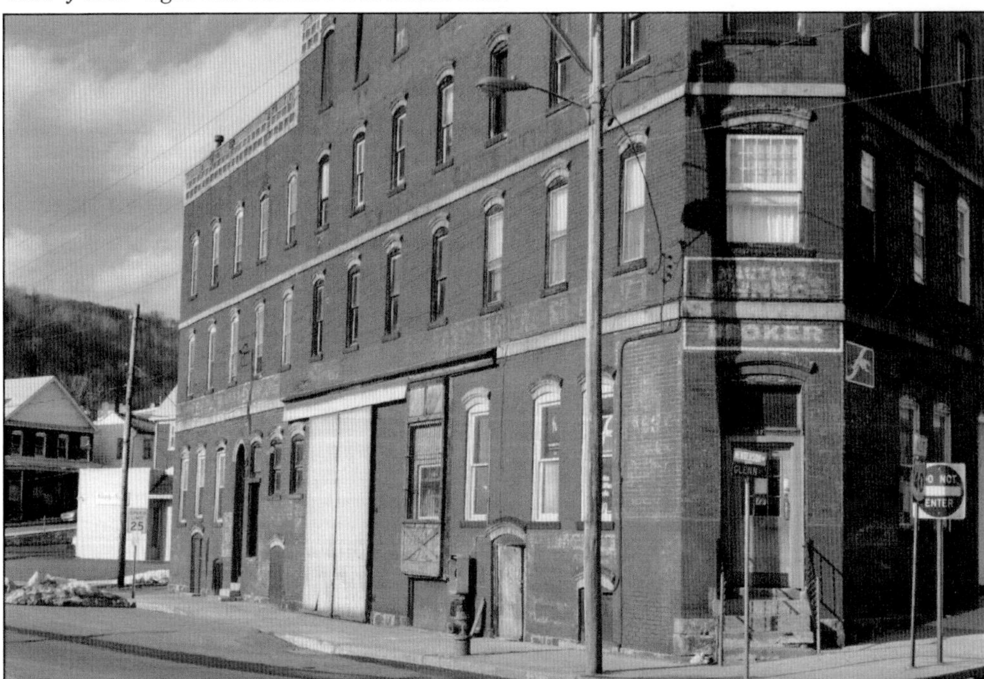

The Deal Building, located on Henderson Boulevard at Glenn Street, was the second facility constructed by the Deal family, which operated flour mills on the site. In this 2003 photograph, a subsequent business owner's name is still visible—Martin Johnson. The Johnsons were food brokers. In recent years, the building has been converted to office use.

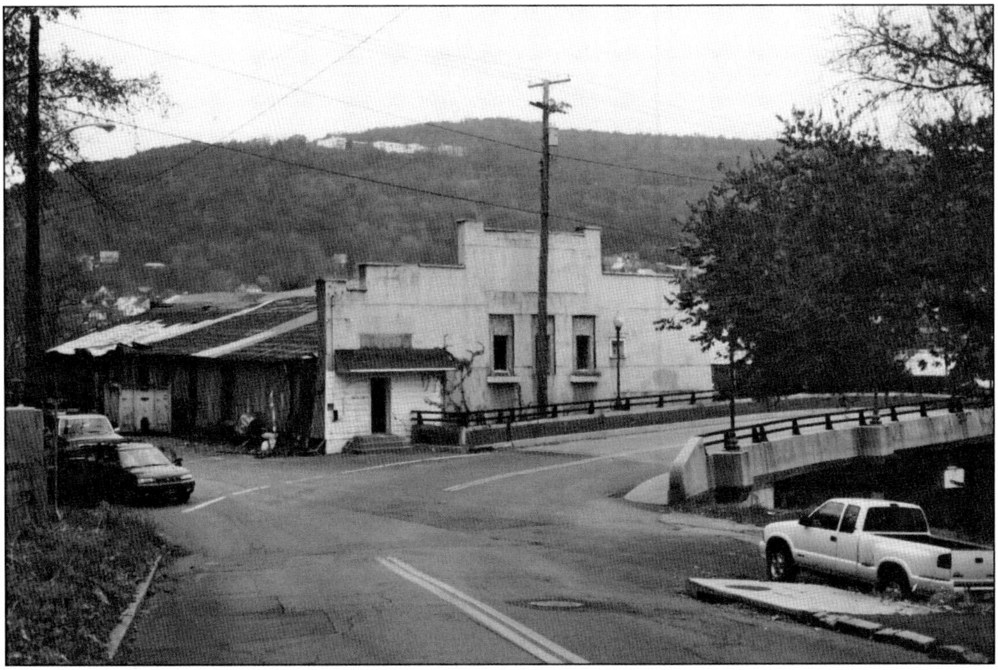

The city of Cumberland's warehouse, located at the west end of the Valley Street Bridge, underwent demolition in 2007. Today the Great Allegheny Passage runs through the site.

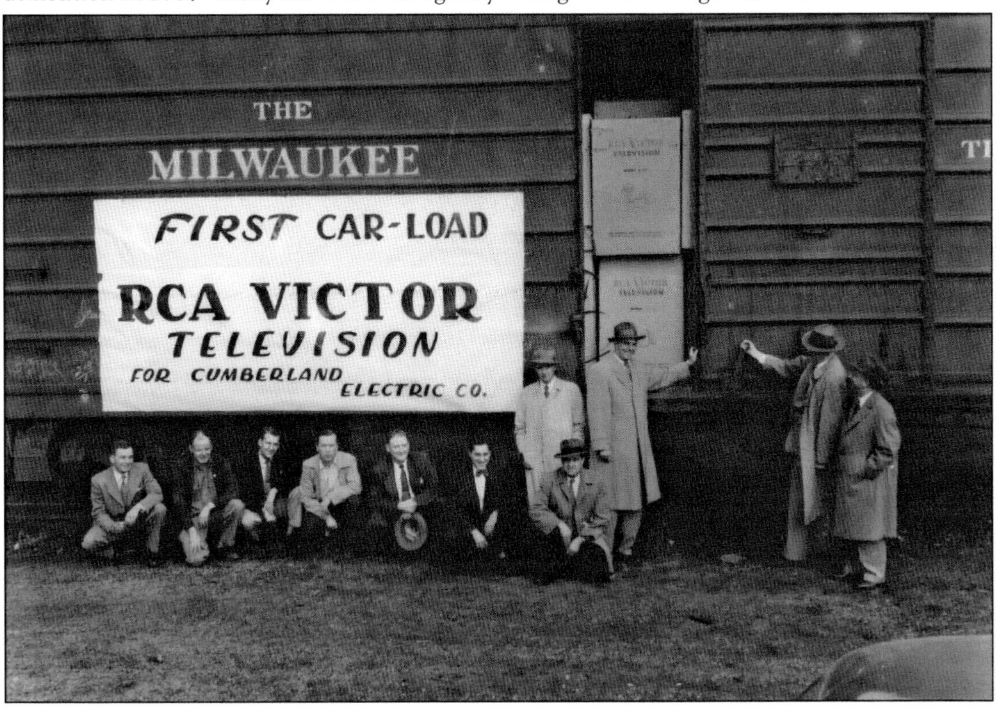

The arrival of new RCA televisions created a newsworthy moment. The sets were sold at the Cumberland Electric Company, a locally owned and operated business. The exact date of this photograph cannot be determined, but RCA televisions began to appear in local advertisements in 1951.

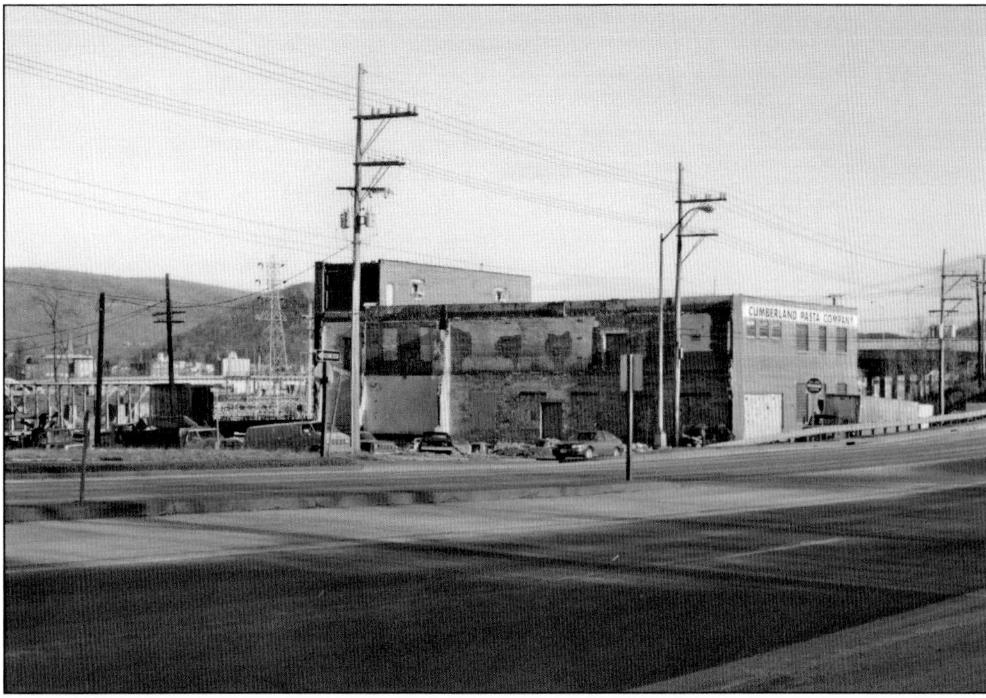

The Cumberland Macaroni Company opened for business in 1915 at 31–39 Thomas Street. The business marketed pasta under the brand name "Cumberland's Alpine Brand." After changing owners, production ended in 2000 and the building was purchased by the Cumberland Outdoor Club in 2001.

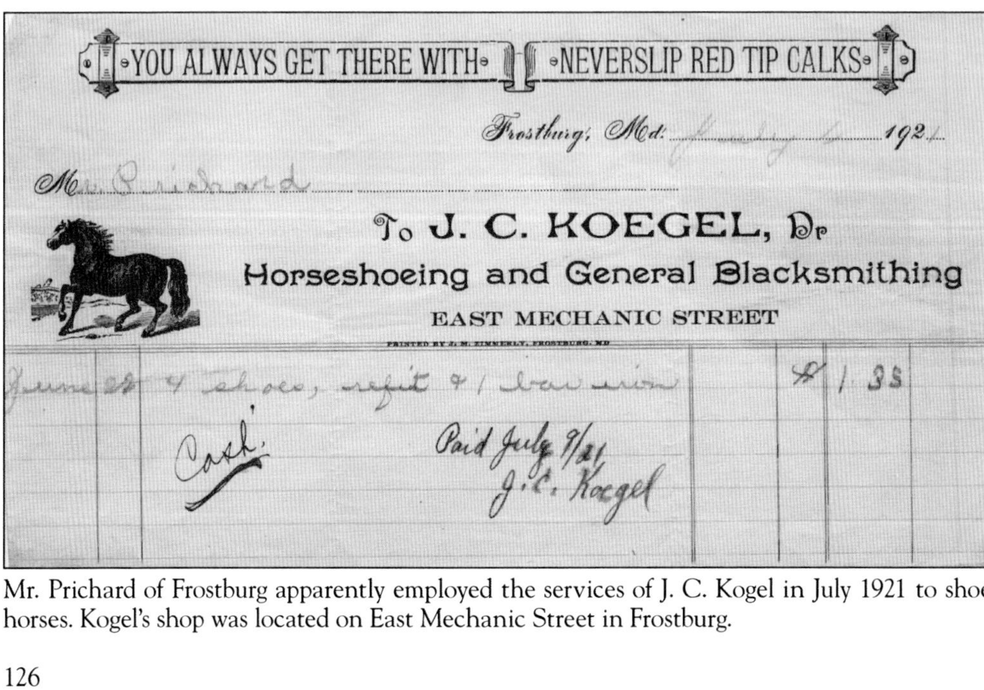

YOU ALWAYS GET THERE WITH NEVERSLIP RED TIP CALKS

Frostburg, Md: 192

Mr. Prichard

To J. C. KOEGEL, Dr.

Horseshoeing and General Blacksmithing

EAST MECHANIC STREET

June 28 4 shoes, refit & 1 bar iron $1.35

Cash.

Paid July 9/21 J.C. Koegel

Mr. Prichard of Frostburg apparently employed the services of J. C. Kogel in July 1921 to shoe horses. Kogel's shop was located on East Mechanic Street in Frostburg.

Bibliography

Annual Reports. Maryland State Department of Education.
The *Cumberland Evening Times*.
The *Cumberland Times-News*.
Feldstein, Albert. *Cumberland*. Charleston, SC: Arcadia Publishing, 2006.
The Lonaconing Silk Mill, 1907-1957. Cumberland, MD: Allegany High School, 2000.
Maryland Inventory of Historic Places, Maryland Historical Trust.
Minutes, Board of Education of Allegany County. Cumberland, MD.
Reflections of the Silver Screen. Cumberland, MD: Allegany High School, 2001.
Scharf, J. Thomas. *History of Western Maryland, Vol. II*, 1882. Reprinted Westminster, MD: Clearfield Company and Family Line Publications, 1995.
Schwartz, Lee, Albert Feldstein, and Joan Baldwin. *A Pictorial History of Allegany County*. Donning, Virginia Beach/Norfolk, 1980.
Stegmaier, Harry, David Dean, Gordon Kershaw, and John Wiseman. *Allegany County, A History*. Parson WV: McClain Printing Company, 1976.
Thomas, James, and T. J. C. Williams. *History of Allegany County, Maryland*. L. R. Titsworth and Company, 1923.
Whetzel, Dan. *A Photographic History of Downtown Cumberland, Maryland*, 2005.
———*A Photographic History of Cumberland, Maryland Featuring South Cumberland*, 2007.
——— and Mike Lewis. *The Coal Heritage Trail, A Cultural Survey*. Maryland Historic Trust, 2001–2002.